AF771241

A Brief Guide to AutoCAD® Release 14

Scott E. Davis
Montana State University

Prentice Hall
Upper Saddle River, New Jersey *Columbus, Ohio*

Library of Congress Cataloging-in-Publication Data

Davis, Scott E.

A brief guide to AutoCAD release 14 / Scott E. Davis.

p. cm.

Includes index.

ISBN 0-13-763013-1

1. Computer graphics. 2. AutoCAD (Computer file) I. Title.

T385.D397 1999

604.2′0285′5369--dc21 98-4144

CIP

Cover art: Scott E. Davis
Editor: Stephen Helba
Developmental Editor: Katie E. Bradford
Production Coordinator: Lisa Garboski, bookworks
Design Coordinator: Karrie M. Converse
Text Designer: STELLARViSIONs
Cover Designer: Brian Deep
Production Manager: Deidra M. Schwartz
Marketing Manager: Frank Mortimer, Jr.

This book was set in Palatino by STELLARViSIONs and was printed and bound by Banta Company. The cover was printed by Phoenix Color Corp.

Simon & Schuster / A Viacom Company
Upper Saddle River, New Jersey 07458

Printed in the United States of America

10 9 8 7 6 5 4 3 2 1

ISBN: 0-13-763013-1

Prentice-Hall International (UK) Limited, *London*
Prentice-Hall of Australia Pty. Limited, *Sydney*
Prentice-Hall of Canada, Inc., *Toronto*
Prentice-Hall of Hispanoamericana, S. A., *Mexico*
Prentice-Hall of India Private Limited, *New Delhi*
Prentice-Hall of Japan, Inc., *Tokyo*
Simon & Schuster Asia Pte. Ltd., *Singapore*
Editora Prentice-Hall do Brasil, Ltda., *Rio de Janeiro*

Preface

A Brief Guide to AutoCAD Release 14 is a beginner's guide for learning AutoCAD Release 14 software to create 2D and 3D computer-aided drawings. This text provides a method that enables the reader to learn to use the software in the easiest possible manner. The information is based on a generic systems approach. Moreover, the approach taken in writing the text was to define and explain the terms most commonly used in creating, editing, displaying, plotting, and printing drawings. In this manner, readers can understand the basics for using the software and then apply these to their own areas of expertise.

This text should appeal to students and teachers at the secondary and collegiate level, including those who are involved in Technology Education and Industrial Technology programs. *A Brief Guide to AutoCAD Release 14* is not meant to be all-inclusive. CAD users will need to consult more detailed manuals to address specific questions and to learn to produce advanced drawings.

The following features in the text make it unique as a learning and teaching tool:

Key Concepts listed at the start of each chapter specify commands and new content reviewed in the chapter.

Margin definitions provide explanations of new terms introduced in the chapter and reinforce Key Concepts. Because some of the terminology may be new to the reader, margin definitions help the reader understand and review new terms when they are used in context.

"Try This" activities woven throughout every chapter are abbreviated lessons and drawing activities that give the reader a chance to practice a command or concept immediately after it has been introduced.

Drawing Activities located at the chapter end provide a more in-depth use of the commands and concepts covered in the chapter. Drawing activities cover creating both mechanical parts and architectural drawings.

In addition to these features, *A Brief Guide to AutoCAD Release 14* provides chapter content that is sequenced logically and arranged so that the content learned in one chapter is applied in later chapters. Chapters 1 through 5 focus on creating objects using AutoCAD R14 layout techniques and drawing tools. Readers will learn commands to:

- create a drawing sheet template;
- place geometric figures on the drawing sheet;
- use drawing aids that help improve the layout of a drawing;
- change how objects are displayed on the computer screen; and
- use object snaps, drawing tools that help in drawing more precisely.

As users draw, it is inevitable that they will make mistakes. AutoCAD R14's editing commands make correcting these mistakes easy and also help the user locate dimensions correctly. In addition, some common mistakes can be avoided with the use of template files that have predefined characteristics consistent from drawing to drawing. Chapters 6 through 8 cover commands that help the reader to:

- correct drawing errors;
- properly locate and use dimension variables; and
- use template files.

Once the drawing and editing stages have been completed, the next step is to plot and print the file. Chapters 9 and 10 provide a brief discussion of how to:

- plot and print drawings and
- set dimension variables so that they appear correctly on mechanical and architectural drawings.

Finally, because drawings can be complex in nature, users often find it necessary to identify object properties, such as layer, length, and distance. AutoCAD R14 has built-in commands that help the user determine object properties. Other commands help the user create objects that can be used from one drawing to the next. Chapter 11 discusses:

- commands for determining object properties and
- block commands for inserting objects into drawings.

Readers will find this text easy to use. The numerous illustrations throughout the text assist the reader in grasping the concepts discussed. In addition, the level and scope of the technical content covered in the text enable the reader to create drawings almost immediately—giving the reader that early sense of accomplishment so important to beginning users.

Acknowledgments

The author wishes to acknowledge the following individuals who reviewed the manuscript and offered suggestions on the content: Douglas C. Acheson, Purdue University at Indianapolis; Andrew Ellis, Holyoke Community College, Massachusetts; Kris Johnson, Montana State University–Bozeman; Alex Lepeska, Pierce College, Washington; Carol L. O'Loughlin, Purdue University at Indianapolis; Courtney Smith, Boise High School, Idaho; and Matthew Whiteacre, Texas A&M University.

All screen captures for the text were made using SuperClip™ screen capture software by AndroSoft™.

Contents

CHAPTER

1

Introduction to AutoCAD R14

AFTER READING THIS CHAPTER, YOU WILL BE ABLE TO:

- Open the AutoCAD R14 software in Windows 95/Windows NT.
- Identify drawing editor components.
- Recognize drawing editor menus.
- Understand how drawing files are saved.

KEY CONCEPTS:

Button
Command prompt
Drawing editor
Icon
Layer
Model space
Paper space
Pull-down menu
Screen menu
Toolbar
User coordinate system (UCS)

The information presented in this chapter provides a general overview of how AutoCAD R14 software operates. Understanding how the software enables you to create drawings is an important first step in being able to use AutoCAD R14 correctly.

WINDOWS 95 OPERATING PLATFORM

AutoCAD R14 software functions in a variety of operating systems; however, for the purposes of this book, AutoCAD R14 operation in Windows 95/Windows NT is the sole operating system reviewed. Software application is discussed as it relates to desktop PCs commonly used either at home or in an office setting.

The Windows desktop can take on a variety of appearances. Typically there are a number of programs that have been loaded on the PC (see Figure 1–1). In order to open AutoCAD R14, double click on the shortcut AutoCAD R14 icon or on the Start icon located in the lower left corner of the PC screen. Locate the Program icon at the top of the column and click on it. A listing of programs is displayed at this point. Locate the AutoCAD R14 icon and click on it once. A listing of AutoCAD R14 options is displayed in the dialog box. If you have any problems in opening the software, check your installation manual for troubleshooting help, or call your software dealer.

Icon—a graphical symbol representative of a command.

STARTUP SCREEN MENU OPTIONS

The startup screen menu (Figure 1–2) provides the option for using either metric or English standards. Other options included in the startup screen include Use a Wizard, Use a Template, Start from Scratch, or Open a Drawing.

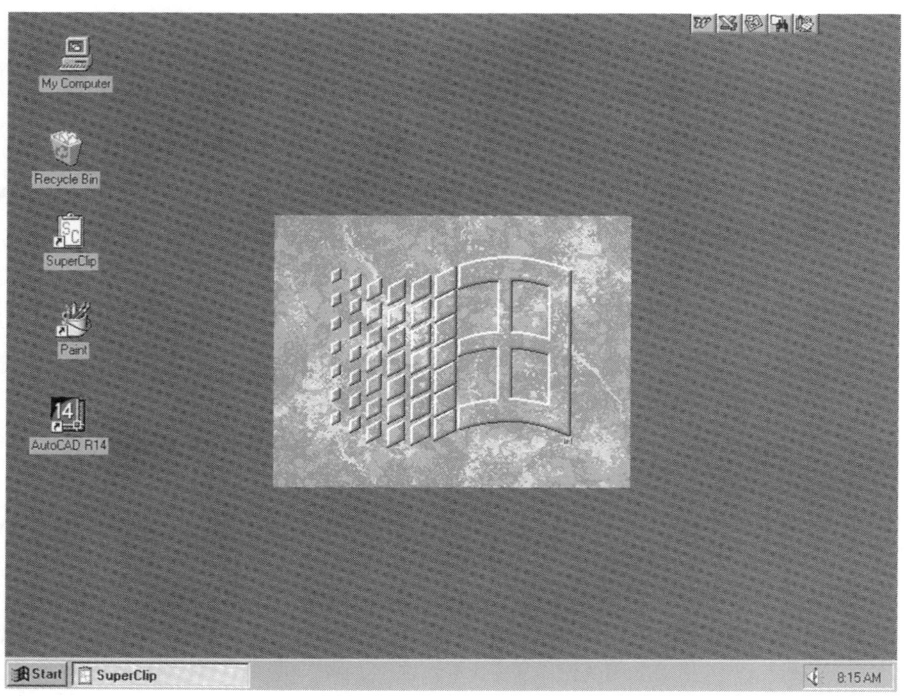

Figure 1–1
Windows 95 desktop.

Use a Wizard

There are two options, Quick Setup or Advanced Setup, if the Use a Wizard option is selected. The Quick Setup option allows you to set the Units (Decimal, Architectural, Fractional, Engineering, or Scientific) used in the drawing and paper size. Once the data for these two options have been entered, the screen defaults to the AutoCAD drawing editor so you can begin your drawing.

Paper space—an area that is used for creating a finished layout for printing or plotting, as opposed to doing drawing.

Model Space—that viewport where most or all of the drawing is created

The Advanced Setup (Figure 1–3) has seven choices for entering data: Units, Angle, Angle Measure, Angle Direction, Area, Title Block, and Layout. The Layout option in the Advanced Setup option allows for the setup of a drawing that uses paper space. **Paper space** is an area that is used for creating a finished layout for printing or plotting, as opposed to drawing objects. Paper space is used to arrange **viewports** (a bounded area that displays some portion of the **model space** of a drawing), and includes a title block and border.

TRY THIS

Open AutoCAD and use the Advanced Startup for a drawing that is to be drawn in inches with a precision level of two decimal places.

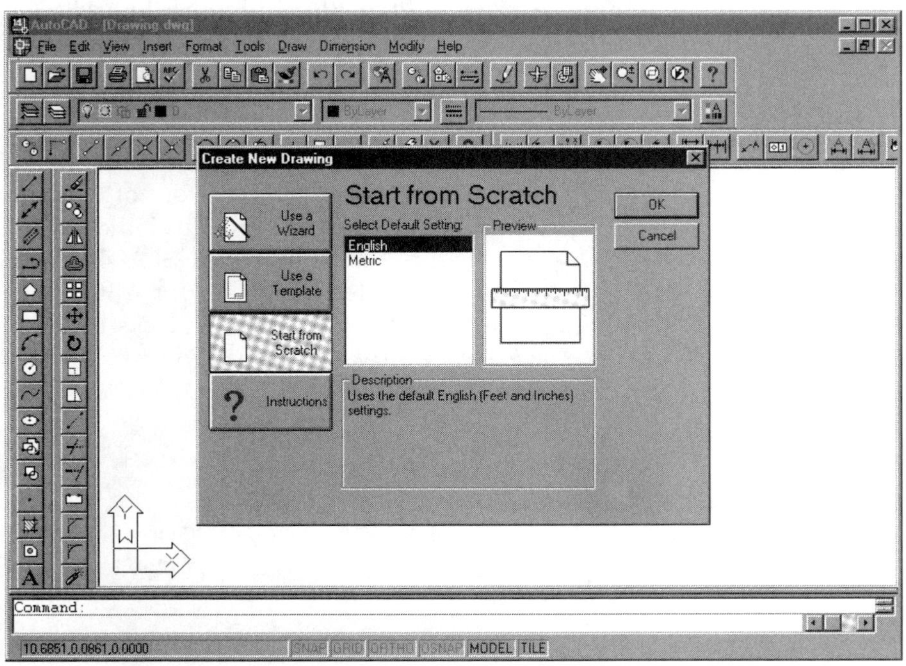

Figure 1–2
Startup screen menu options.

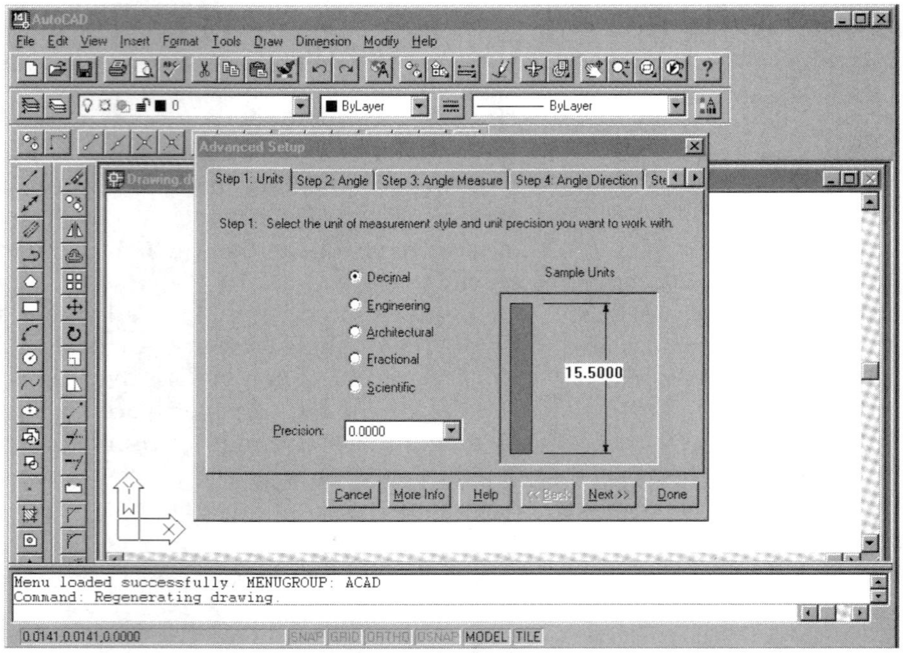

Figure 1–3
The Advanced Setup screen.

Use a Template

There are numerous template files that can be selected. These template files correspond to the different sizes of paper used to create plots. The template files also have different border styles based on the particular application (e.g., architectural, engineering, English, or German). Borders and title blocks are placed in paper space, while the actual drawing of the object occurs in model space.

If an AutoCAD template file is opened, the title block and border are set up in paper space. In order to edit any text or borderlines created in paper space, type ps at the command prompt, or double click on the MODEL button icon located at the bottom of the AutoCAD drawing editor. MODEL should change to PAPER, thus indicating that paper space is now active.

Figure 1–4 shows the ANSI A-size template file that is part of AutoCAD R14. All the template files for AutoCAD R14 have a .dwt file extension. There are 13 standard title blocks that can be inserted into a layout when using the Advanced Setup wizard.

TRY THIS

Open AutoCAD and select Use a Template. Load the template ANSI_A.dwt. Repeat the process and load the template ISO_A1.dwt.

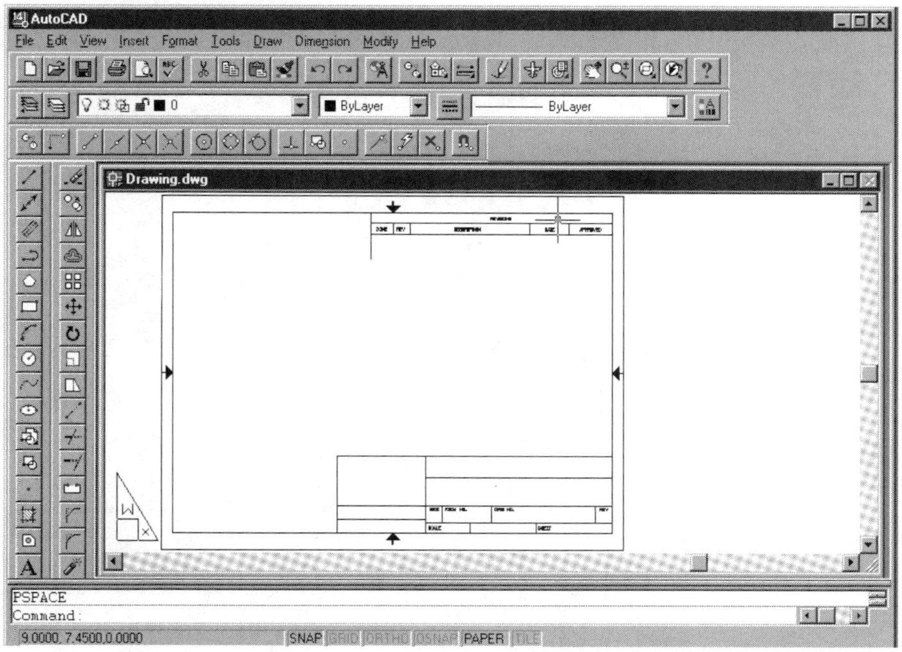

Figure 1–4
ANSI A-size template.

Start from Scratch

If you are beginning a new drawing and do not want the wizard to set any parameters or use a template, click on the Start from Scratch icon and you will automatically default into the drawing editor. When selecting this option you will have to set your parameters manually.

Open a Drawing

Another of the options in the Start Up dialog box is Open a Drawing. If you want to edit an existing drawing, use this method for opening it. You must know the directory path (for example, A:\ or c:\temp) to the drawing file in order to open it in the drawing editor.

COORDINATE TYPES

All drawings are superimposed on an invisible grid, or coordinate system, with a horizontal X axis and a vertical Y axis (Autodesk, Inc., 1997, p. 46). The Z axis is perpendicular to the X and Y axes. As you are looking at the initial drawing editor when you open AutoCAD, think of the Z axis as coming out of the computer screen. In Figure 1–5 the UCS icon in the lower left corner of the drawing editor depicts the position of the X, Y, and Z axes.

As you draw, you can enter coordinate values to locate a point, using one of three common coordinate systems. The absolute coordinate system

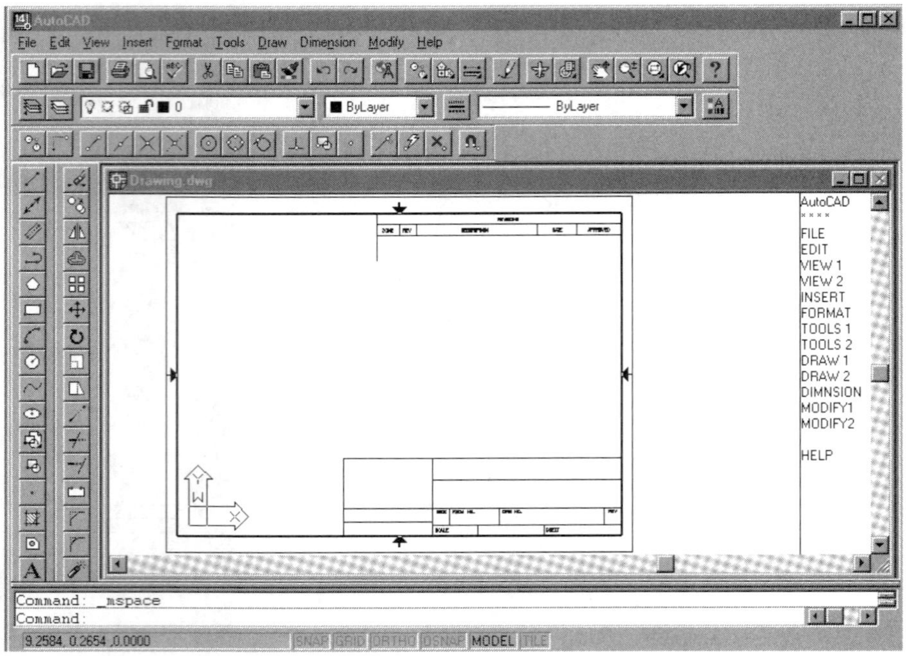

Figure 1–5
UCS icon depicting X, Y, and Z axes.

uses values based on the origin point 0,0. Relative coordinate values are based on the last point entered. The polar coordinate system uses a distance and angle.

Entering Absolute Coordinates

To draw a line from a beginning point that has an X value of 1.5 and a Y value of 2 and an ending point that has an X value of 5 and a Y value of 5, make the following entries on the command prompt line:

TRY THIS

Open AutoCAD and start a drawing from scratch.

1. At the command prompt, type l and press <Enter> or press the right mouse key. (This is the same as pressing the <Enter> key.)
2. At From Point:, type 1.5,2 and press <Enter>.
3. At To Point:, type 5,5 and press <Enter>.
4. At To Point:, press <Enter> to exit the command.

A diagonal line should appear on the drawing screen that starts at 1.5,2 and ends at 5,5.

Entering Relative Coordinates

Relative coordinate points are used when you know the position of a point in relation to a previous point. To locate a point relative to 1.5,2 use the @ symbol before the next coordinate.

TRY THIS

Open AutoCAD and start a drawing from scratch.

1. At the command prompt, type l and press <Enter> or press the right mouse key. (This is the same as pressing the <Enter> key.)
2. At From Point:, type 1.5,2 and press <Enter>.
3. At To Point:, type @3.5,3 and press <Enter>.
4. At To Point:, press <Enter> to exit the command.

A diagonal line should appear on the drawing screen that starts at 1.5,2 and ends at 5,5.

This sequence should draw the same line that appeared in the previous example.

Entering Polar Coordinates

Polar coordinates are entered as a distance and angle. The values are separated with the angle bracket (<) symbol. To draw a line with a starting point of 1.5,2 that is 3″ long at a 45° angle enter the following commands:

1. At the command prompt, type 1 and press <Enter> or press the right mouse key. (This is the same as pressing the <Enter> key.)
2. At From Point:, type 1.5,2 and press <Enter> .
3. At To Point:, type @3<45 and press <Enter> .
4. At To Point:, press <Enter> to exit the command.

A diagonal line should appear on the drawing screen that starts at 1.5,2 and ends at 5,5.

THE DRAWING EDITOR

If you choose to start from scratch, the computer screen should look similar to the one in Figure 1–6, which is an example of the **drawing editor** screen.

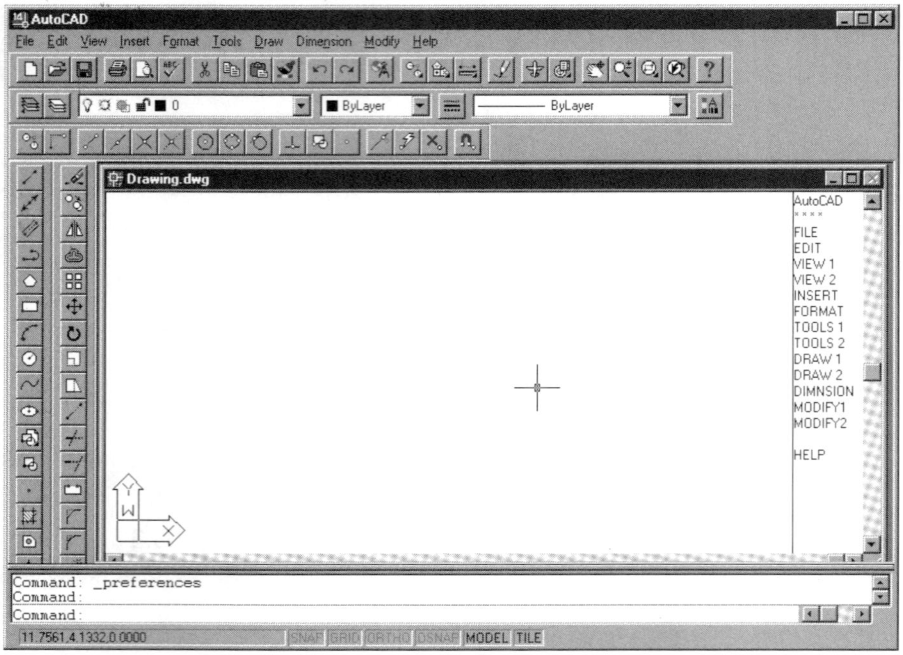

Figure 1–6
Drawing editor.

Figure 1–7
Pull-down menu bar.

The **pull-down menu bar** includes the following options: File, Edit, View, Insert, Format, Tools, Draw, Dimension, Modify, and Help.

Toolbars contain tools, represented by icons, that start commands.

Screen menu—command list typically located on the right side of the drawing editor screen.

The **UCS icon** (Figure 1–9) represents the orientation of the X, Y, and Z axes and the position of the current UCS origin.

Command prompt—that area in the drawing editor where text can be entered to start commands.

Commands in the drawing editor are initiated in a variety of ways, including using the pull-down menu bar, the screen menu, toolbars, or typing the command at the command prompt. Across the top of the drawing editor is the **pull-down menu bar** containing options such as File, Edit, View, Draw (Figure 1–7). Under each of these terms are submenus that make up the numerous commands that AutoCAD R14 uses to perform its operations.

Below the pull-down menu items are toolbars. The toolbars are composed of **icons** that represent individual commands or functions used in AutoCAD. AutoCAD has multiple toolbars that allow point-and-click operations. Figure 1–8 shows two rows of toolbars across the top of the drawing editor and two vertical columns with icons that activate commands.

The **screen menu** is the column of commands found on the right side of Figure 1–8. The default for the screen menu is to be off. If you want the screen editor to be on, you must go into the Preferences dialog box and select the box to display it. Submenus linked to each term, when selected, allow access to more commands.

Along the bottom of the drawing editor screen is a row of **button** icons (see Figure 1–8). These buttons control coordinate display read out, snap, grid, ortho, osnap, model/paper space, and tilemode. Clicking on a button activates the command associated with it.

In the lower left-hand corner of the drawing editor is the user coordinate system (UCS) icon. It represents the orientation of the X, Y, and Z axes.

Located near the bottom of the drawing editor screen and below the UCS icon are two dialog boxes. The uppermost dialog box displays the last command(s) used. By clicking on the up or down arrow in the dialog box, it is possible to review all the commands executed since starting the drawing. The **command prompt** is displayed in the lower dialog box. Text commands are typed at the command prompt.

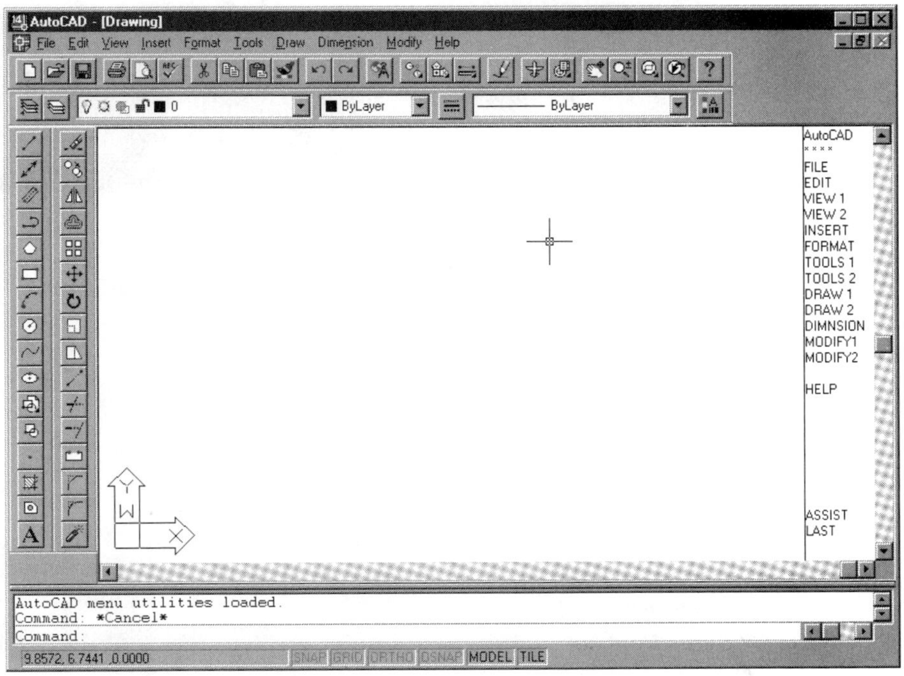

Figure 1–8
Screen menu.

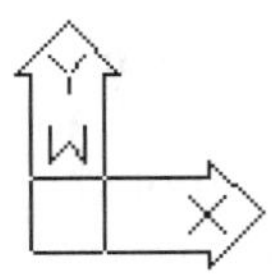

Figure 1–9
UCS icon.

SETTING DRAWING PARAMETERS

In order to create a drawing that correctly represents the image you want to relate to the viewer, you must set certain parameters. Most of these parameters are located in the Format pull-down menu. Parameters that need to be set include color, limits, layers, linetypes, and units (see Figure 1–10).

Each option listed in the pull-down menu is a submenu. Some of the parameters are also located in the screen menu, and the English word equivalent can be typed at the command prompt.

Color, Layers, and Linetypes

Layers are similar to multiple sheets of paper on which certain characteristics of a drawing are assigned. Entities are drawn on certain layers. Each layer is assigned a name and has specific attributes such as color and linetype assigned to it. Clicking on Layer in the Format pull-down menu opens the Layer dialog box. Figure 1–11 depicts the Layer & Linetype Properties dialog box.

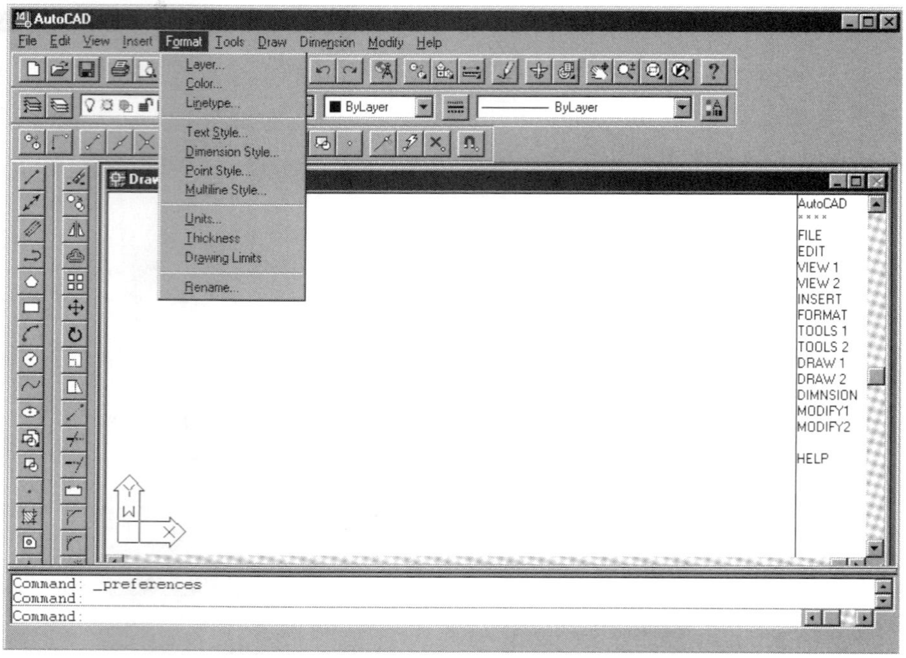

Figure 1–10
Drawing format options.

In order to create a new layer in the dialog box, click on the New button. The new layer name should appear in the layer window. Specific naming conventions are used for naming layers. Layers can be turned off, which means the entities on that layer do not show on the drawing screen. Layers can also be frozen. No editing can take place on a frozen layer.

Now let's see how to save a drawing once you have made one.

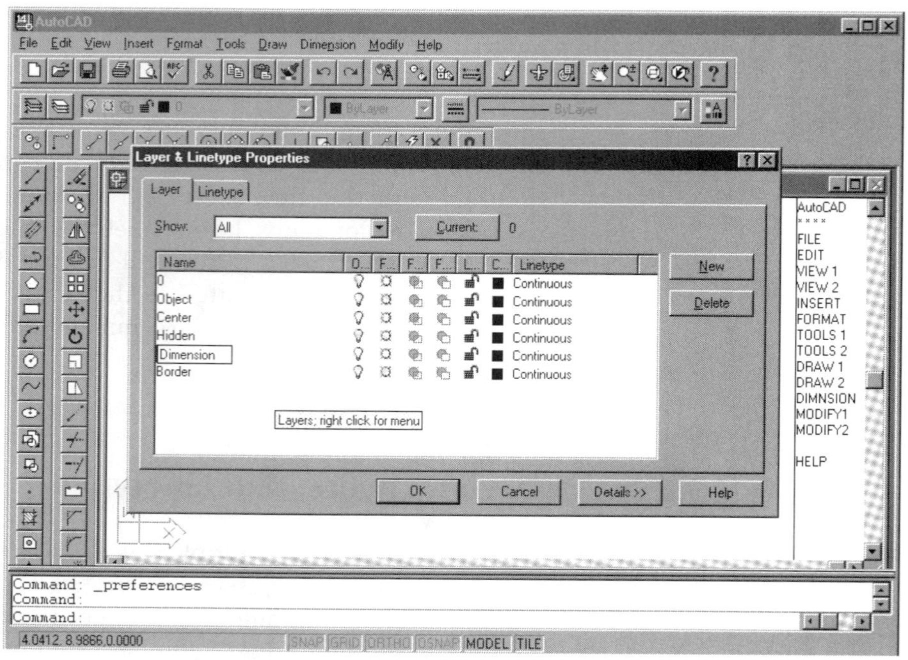

Figure 1–11
Layer & Linetype Properties dialog box.

SAVING DRAWING FILES

This section provides information on those options associated with creating an archival drawing file. There are three commands that are associated with creating an archival drawing file: **quit, save,** and **saveas.** Archival files will have a file extension of .dwg.

Two of the options, Save and Saveas, are found in the File pull-down menu or by clicking the save icon. The screen that appears at the saveas command is displayed in Figure 1–12. When Saveas is selected, the format and name of the drawing file can be selected.

The save command can also be typed at the command prompt.

At the command prompt, type save

If the drawing is named, AutoCAD displays the Save Drawing As dialog box.

If a different file name is entered, AutoCAD saves a copy of the drawing under the specified name.

If the drawing is unnamed, AutoCAD displays the Save Drawing dialog box.

If the current drawing has not been named, AutoCAD displays a dialog box in which you name the drawing before exiting.

The quit command exits AutoCAD if there have been no changes since the drawing was last saved. If the drawing has been modified, AutoCAD displays the Drawing Modification dialog box to prompt you to save or discard the changes before quitting.

If a template drawing is used, and you choose to save the drawing, the Save Drawing As dialog box will appear when the Save command is selected.

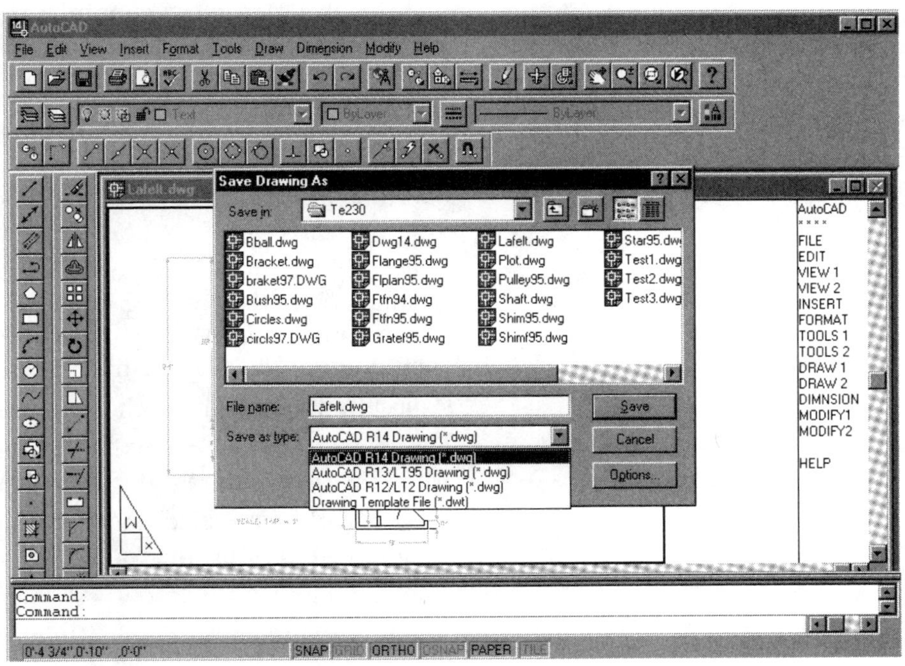

Figure 1–12
Save Drawing As dialog box.

Chapter 1 ■ Activities

Activity 1–1

Become Familiar with Options Associated with the Startup Screen

ACTIVITY STEPS:

1. Select Use a Wizard from the startup screen to create a format for the drawing sheet.
   - Use the Quick Setup to format a drawing sheet for A-size paper.

     Set the Units of the drawing to Decimal.

     Set the size of the paper to 10 × 7.7.
   - Use the Advanced Setup to format a drawing sheet for both A-size and B-size paper. In the Advanced Setup dialog box:

At Step 1 (Units):	Set the Units to Decimal and the Precision to 0.
At Step 2 (Angle):	Set the Angle to Decimal Degrees and the Precision to 0.
At Step 3 (Angle Measure):	Set Angle Measure to East.
At Step 4 (Angle Direction):	Set Angle Direction to Counter-clockwise.
At Step 5 (Area):	Enter 10 as the width (X axis) and 7.7 as the length (Y axis).
At Step 6 (Title Block):	Set the Title Block to ANSI_A.
At Step 7 (Layout):	Select Yes and View the Layout while working on the drawing.

   Click on New and when prompted, answer Yes to save the drawing changes. Save the drawing as Borda. Repeat the previous steps, this time changing the Area in Step 5 to 15.5 × 10. Change the Title Block in Step 6 to ANSI_B. Save the drawing as Bordb.

2. Select Use a Template to choose a predefined title and border.

   There are 29 different template files. Open six different template drawings to explore the differences among them.

3. Select Start from Scratch and at the next menu select English, which allows you to define the parameters that you want.

At the command prompt:	Enter limits.
Lower left corner:	Enter 0,0.

Upper right corner:	Enter 15.5, 10.
At the command prompt:	Enter z (zoom)
	Enter a (all)

The drawing editor screen has been set to have a width of 15.5 units and a length of 10 units.

ACTIVITY 1–2

Identify the Components of the Drawing Editor

At the startup screen, select Start from Scratch. Upon entering the drawing editor, go to the Help pull-down menu and select Quick Tour.

Two options will be listed: Introducing AutoCAD Release 14 and Drawing with AutoCAD. Select Introducing AutoCAD Release 14.

ACTIVITY 1–3

View the Tutorial on Drawing with AutoCAD

At the startup screen, select Start from Scratch. Upon entering the drawing editor, go to the Help pull-down menu and select Quick Tour.

Two options will be listed: Introducing AutoCAD Release 14 and Drawing with AutoCAD. Select Drawing with AutoCAD.

ACTIVITY 1–4

Add Layer Names to a Drawing

At the startup screen, select Start from Scratch. Upon entering the drawing editor, go to the File pull-down menu and select Open. Locate your previously saved Borda drawing and select it to open. After you have opened the drawing file, go to the Format pull-down menu and select Layer. After the new layer dialog box appears, select New in order to create new layers. Add five new layers, assigning a different color to each layer. Save the file and repeat the procedure for Bordb.

CHAPTER

2

2D Object Creation

AFTER READING THIS CHAPTER, YOU WILL BE ABLE TO:

- Use a limited number of commands for object creation.

KEY CONCEPTS:

- Arc (a)
- Circle (c)
- Donut
- Ellipse (el)
- Hatch
- Line (l)
- Mline (ml)
- Polygon
- Polyline (pl)
- Rectangle
- Solid
- Text

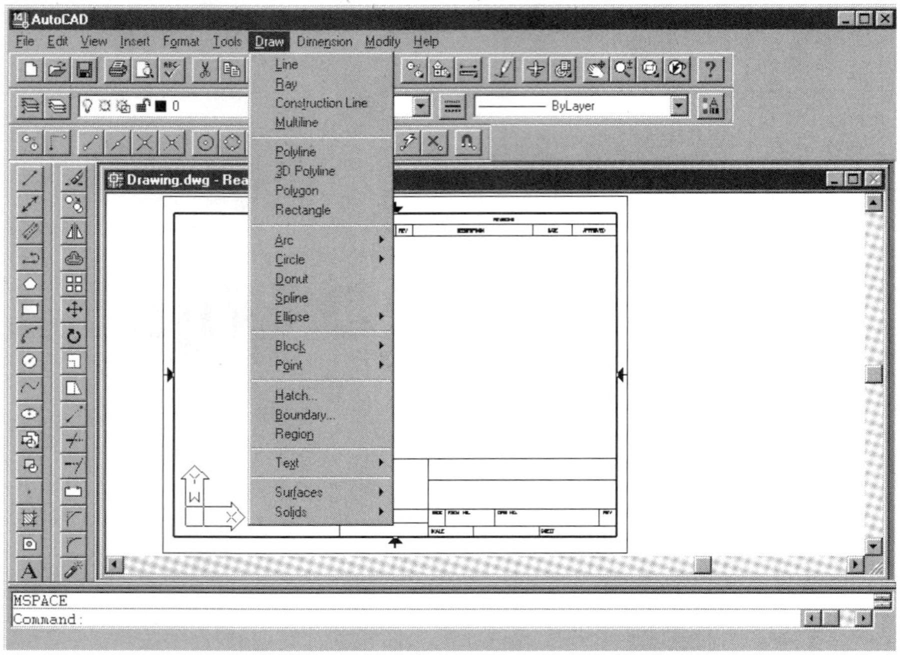

Figure 2–1
Draw pull-down menu.

Objects are created in numerous ways. Common commands for creating objects are either selected from pull-down menus or screen menus, or the English word equivalent is typed at the command prompt.

The pull-down menu in Figure 2–1 was activated by clicking once on Draw in the menu bar. Figure 2–1 displays the Draw menu commands available for creating objects. The more common commands include Arc (a), mline (ml), line (l), ellipse (el), circle (C), donut, hatch, polyline (pl), polygon, rectangle, solid and text. Some commands have what are known as **hot keys**. Hot keys are single or multiple letters that represent the command associated with it. For example, typing l at the command prompt would activate the line command. Typing c at the command prompt would activate the circle command.

The side bar menu also has two draw menus. Commands can be selected from either the Draw 1 or the Draw 2 menu. The method for selecting commands for creating objects again will vary depending on the users.

Text for general notes as well as for title blocks is created with the text command. Text is also used in creating dimensions. Dimensions (DIM) commands for describing objects and displaying the size of objects are also located in the dimension pull-down menu file structure.

CREATING OBJECTS

Lines, Polylines, and Multilines

Common commands used to create lines include **line (l)** and **polyline (pl)**. A **line** is one segment or a series of connected segments; however, each segment is an individual object. A **polyline** is a connected sequence of line or arc segments and is treated as a single object (Autodesk, Inc., 1997). When you create a line, AutoCAD requests the starting point and the ending point. Starting and ending points can be determined in a variety of ways.

To draw a line:

1. From the Draw menu, select Line.
2. Specify the start point.
3. Specify the endpoint.
4. Specify the endpoints of any other line segments.
5. Press <Enter> to complete the line.

TRY THIS

Draw a box by typing in or selecting the following coordinates:

1. From the Draw pull-down menu or the toolbar menu, select the Line command.
2. For starting point, enter or select the coordinates 2,2.
3. Next point: 4,2.
4. Next point: 4,4.
5. Next point: 2,4.
6. Next point: 2,2.
7. Press <Enter> to exit the line command.

A rectangular box should now be showing on the screen.

Note: Repeat the preceding example but instead of entering the last point (2,2), type **c** (for close).

Lines can also be created by typing in the relative or polar coordinates. For example (Figure 2–2), to draw a 2″ long horizontal line from the point 1,1 (absolute coordinates), the command would be @2<0 (polar coordinates). Recall that the @ symbol indicates a distance relative to the initial point.

TRY THIS

Enter the following distances and angles to draw a rectangle that measures 3″ × 2″.

1. From the Draw menu, select Line.
2. Type 1,1 as the starting point.
3. Type @3<0 and press <Enter>. (A horizontal line 3 units long should appear.)
4. Type @2<90 and press <Enter>. (A vertical line 2 units long should be drawn from the endpoint of the previous line.)
5. Type @3<180 and press <Enter>. (A horizontal line 3 units long should be drawn from the endpoint of the previous line.)

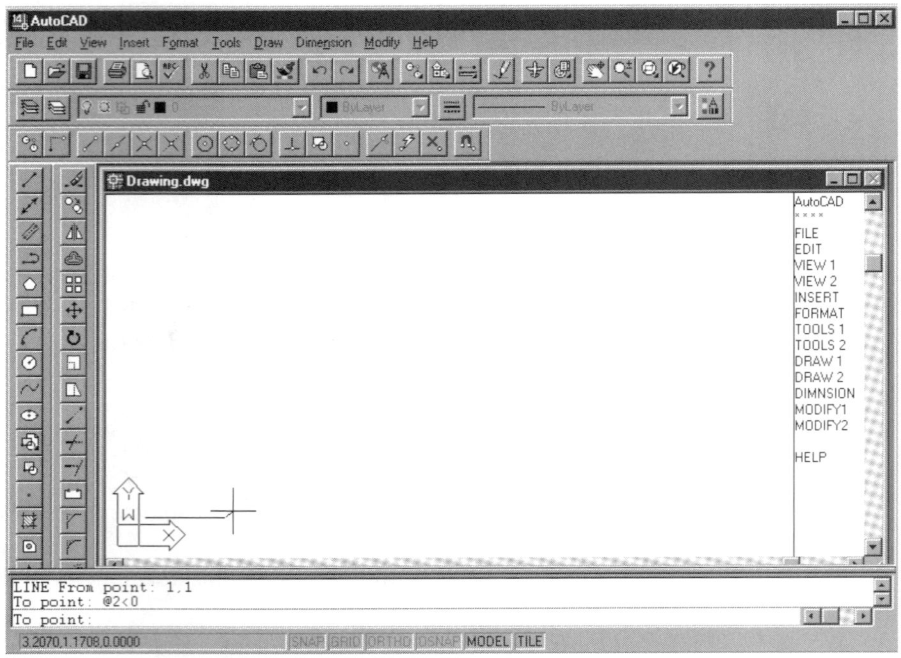

Figure 2–2
Using the polar coordinate system for entering data.

6. Type c (close) to draw a line from the endpoint of the previous line to the original starting point.
7. Press <Enter>.

Lines may also be drawn by manually selecting two points using the mouse. It is recommended that if you use this method, you turn the grid on and set the snap distance to the smallest increment. A **grid** is a visual representation of the drawing area. Grid points can be set to different values. A **snap** setting restricts the movement of the crosshairs by a distance you define. The relationship between the grid and snap is determined by the spacing of the visual reference points of the grid and the smallest increment the crosshairs move as determined by the snap setting (see Chapter 3).

Pline is an acronym for polyline. The pline (pl) command allows you to create multisegmented lines that are connected at the endpoints of each segment. Even though there may be many different segments, a polyline is treated as a single object. Plines are also different from lines in that plines can be assigned width. The pline in Figure 2–3 has a width of .03″. Plines are edited through the **pedit** command.

TRY THIS

Create a horizontal pline that is 4 units long and .03″ wide. The starting point of the pline is at .5,.5.

1. From the Draw pull-down menu, select Polyline.
2. Starting point is .5,.5.

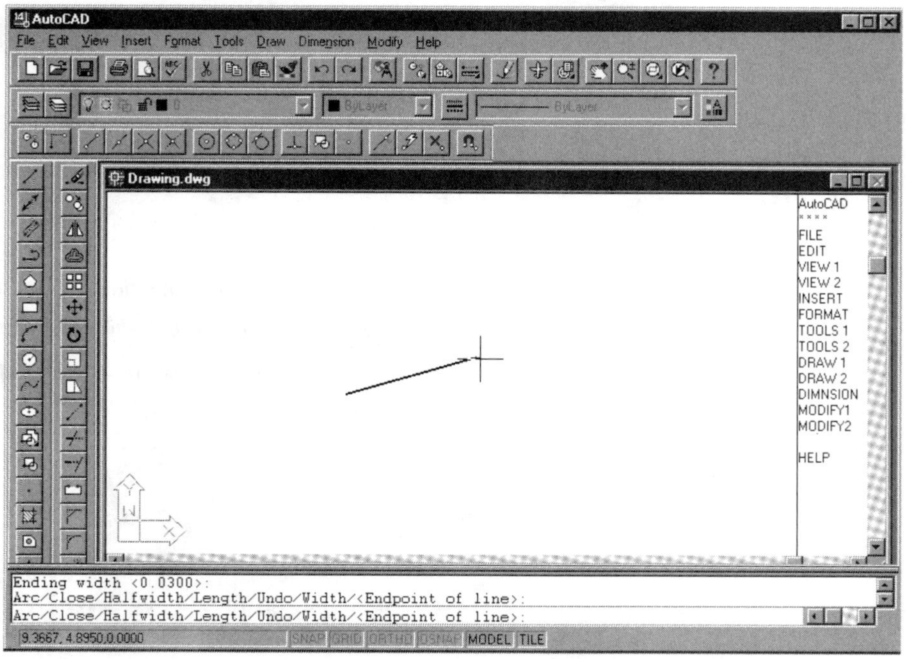

Figure 2–3
Creating a polyline.

3. Type W for entering the width of the line. Type .03″ for width value, both starting and ending.
4. Enter the polar coordinate @4<0 for the next point.
5. Select <Enter> to exit the polyline command.

The pline command is also used to create arcs that have pline characteristics.

TRY THIS

1. From the Draw menu, select Polyline.
2. Specify a starting point: 1,1.
3. Specify an endpoint: 1,2.
4. Enter a to switch to Arc mode.
5. Specify the endpoint of the arc (select a point).
6. Enter l to return to the line mode.
7. Press <Enter> to end the command, or type in the endpoint coordinates.

Other draw commands that use the pline characteristic for creating objects include the **polygon** and **rectangle** commands. A polygon is a multisided object that has between 3 and 1024 equal-length sides. A polygon is drawn by inscribing it in, or circumscribing it about, an imaginary circle. Polygons can also be drawn by specifying the endpoints of one of the edges of the polygon.

Inscribed polygons are used when you want to specify the distance between the center of the polygon and each vertex (Autodesk, Inc., 1997).

TRY THIS

Draw an inscribed square.

1. From the Draw menu, select Polygon.
2. Enter 4 to specify the number of sides for the polygon.
3. Enter 4,4 as the center point of the polygon.
4. Enter I (inscribed in circle).
5. Specify the radius as 3.

Circumscribed polygons are used when you want to specify the distance between the center of the polygon and midpoint of each side.

TRY THIS

Draw a circumscribed octagon.

1. From the Draw menu, select Polygon.
2. Enter 8 to specify the number of sides for the polygon.
3. Enter 3,4 to specify the center of the polygon.
4. Enter c (circumscribed about a circle).
5. Specify the radius length as 2.

Figure 2–4 depicts a five-sided polygon that was inscribed.

Multilines (ml) consist of between 1 and 16 parallel lines. The lines, called *elements,* are positioned by specifying the desired offset of each element from the origin of the multiline. You can create and save multiline styles. From the Format pull-down menu, select **Multiline Style**. A dialog box will appear with style options. The color and linetype of each element can be set and saved as a particular style.

TRY THIS

Create a series of lines using the Multiline command.

1. From the Draw menu, select Multiline.
2. At the command prompt, type st to select a style.
3. To list the available styles, type the style name or enter ?.

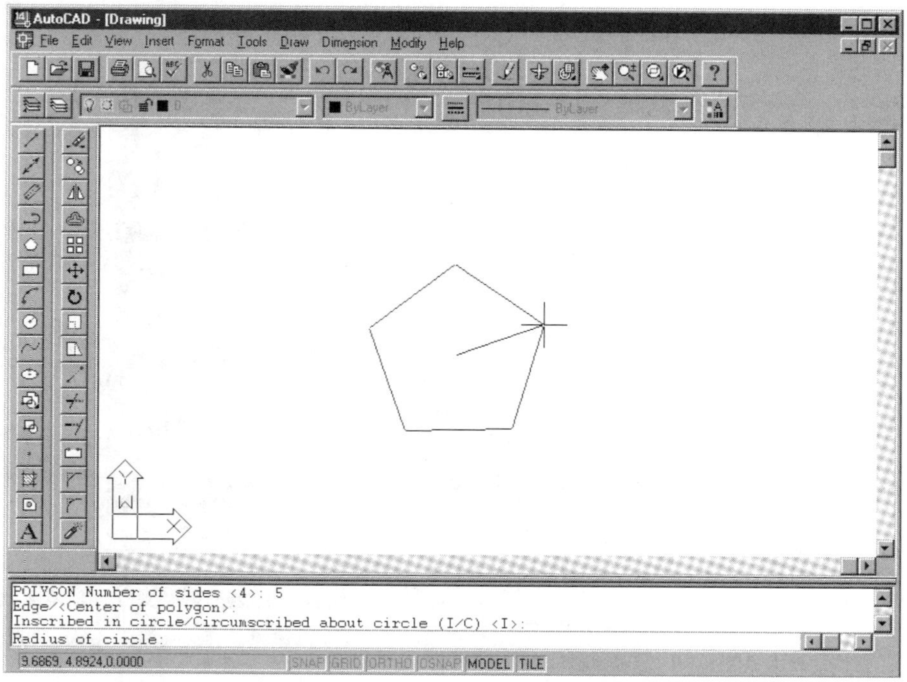

Figure 2–4
Five-sided polygon.

4. To justify the multiline, enter j and select from top, zero, or bottom.
5. To change the scale of the multiline, enter s and enter a new scale. The scale affects the distance between the lines. A scale of 0 would create a single line, since the distance between the lines would be 0.
6. Draw the multiline.
7. Specify a starting point.
8. Specify a second point.
9. Specify a third point.
10. Specify a fourth point, or enter c to close the multiline, or press <Enter>.

Arc

The Arc command is used to create a curved edge. There are several submenus for creating arcs (see Figure 2–5). The submenu options are represented by various letters such as (S) start, (C) center, (D) distance, (E) end, or (R) radius. These options are used in a variety of combinations to create an arc. For instance, the SER prompt would enable you to create an arc through the following process:

1. Select a start point (S).
2. Select an end point (E).
3. Determine the radius (R) of the arc by either typing in a value or moving the crosshairs to the selected point.

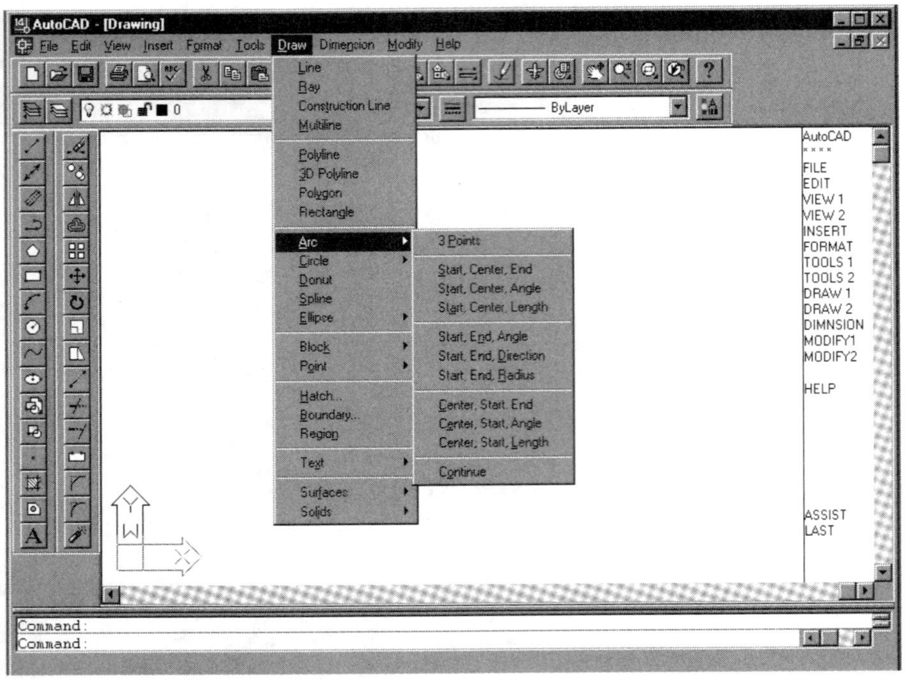

Figure 2–5
Arc command options.

Try This

Create an arc.

1. From the Draw menu, select Arc.
2. Select the SER option for creating this arc.
3. Pick a start point.
4. Pick an endpoint.
5. Enter a radius value for the arc.

Circle

Circles are created by picking a center point and then inputting a radius or diameter value. The center point of a circle can be selected by moving the cursor crosshair to a point for the circle center or by typing in the coordinates of the circle's center. The second prompt of the circle command determines the circle size based on the radius or diameter. In Figure 2–6 the circle command was selected from the pull-down menu.

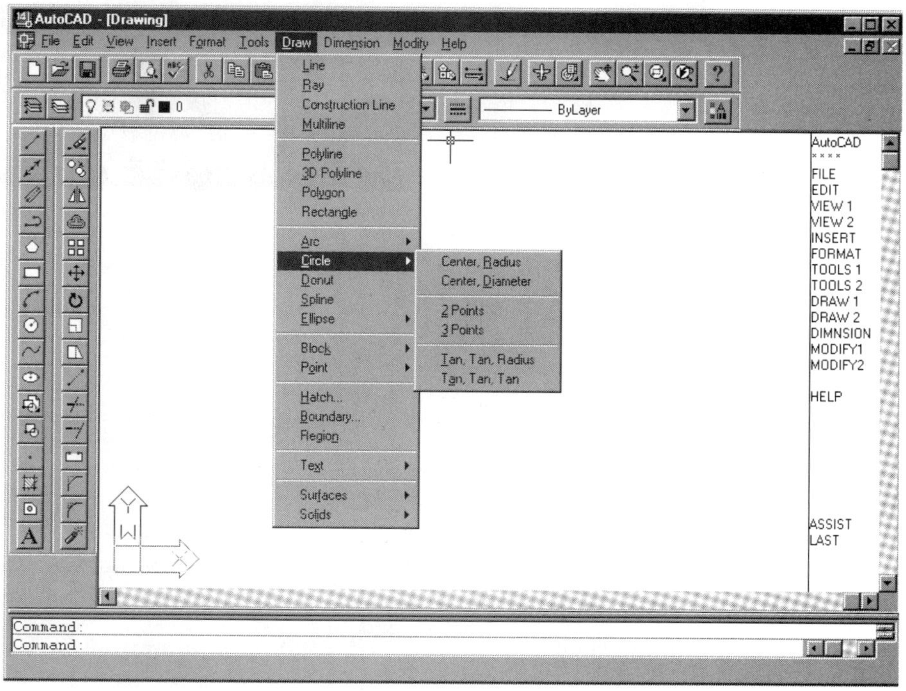

Figure 2–6
Using the pull-down menu to create a circle.

TRY THIS

Draw a circle by specifying the center point and radius.

1. From the Draw pull-down menu, select Circle.
2. Select Center, Radius.
3. Specify the center point at 3,3; press <Enter>.
4. Specify a radius of 2; press <Enter>.

Ellipse

There are two methods for creating an ellipse. The first method involves selecting the center of the ellipse, then clicking the mouse to pick axis endpoints or typing in values at the command prompt (see Figure 2–7). The second method defines the size of the major and minor axes.

TRY THIS

Draw an ellipse using endpoints and a distance.

1. From the Draw menu, select Ellipse.
2. Select option <Axis Endpoint 1>.

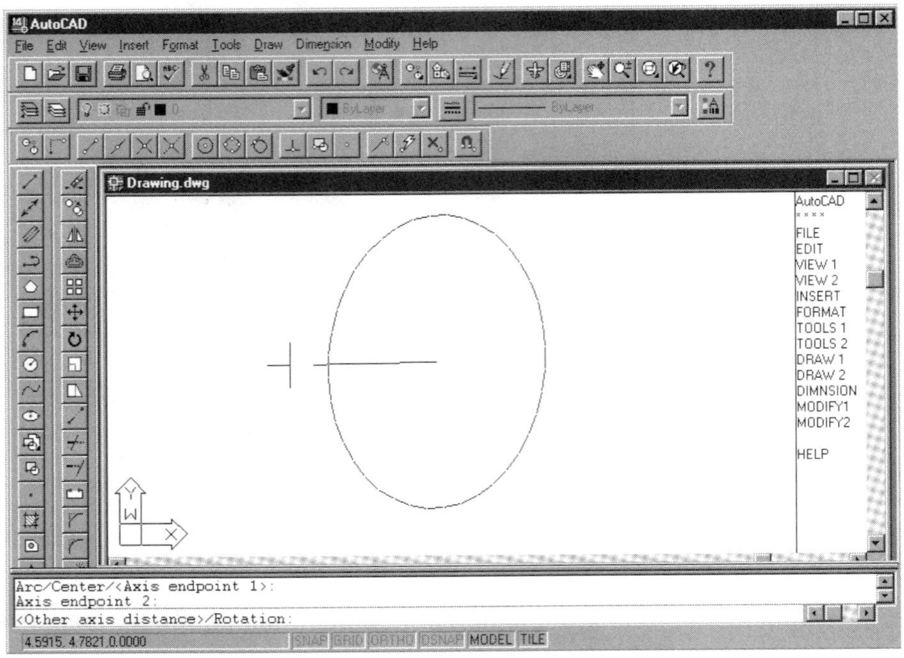

Figure 2–7
Creating an ellipse.

3. Specify the first endpoint of the first axis.
4. Specify the second endpoint of the first axis.
5. Move the pointing device from the midpoint of the first axis and click to specify a distance.

Hatch

Hatch fills an area with a pattern. AutoCAD has numerous predefined hatch patterns in the program. A hatch is applied by picking a point within an enclosed area or by picking an object that has closed endpoints. Hatch patterns are visual representations of materials. When the Hatch command is chosen from the Draw pull-down menu, a series of dialog boxes with options that pertain to hatch parameters appears (see Figure 2–8). Hatch properties include the pattern, scale, and angle. After selecting the pattern and setting the scale and angle, the next step would be to select either a point inside a closed boundary or the boundary itself.

If you choose the Pick Points< option, a dialog box appears that asks you to select an internal point. This prompt appears at the command prompt. After an internal point has been selected, the screen will display the original hatch dialog box.

The advanced options of the hatch command allow you to define the objects that determine the boundary. The boundary style of the hatch can also be set in the Advanced Options dialog box (see Figure 2–9). This determines the hatch style for the selection of objects.

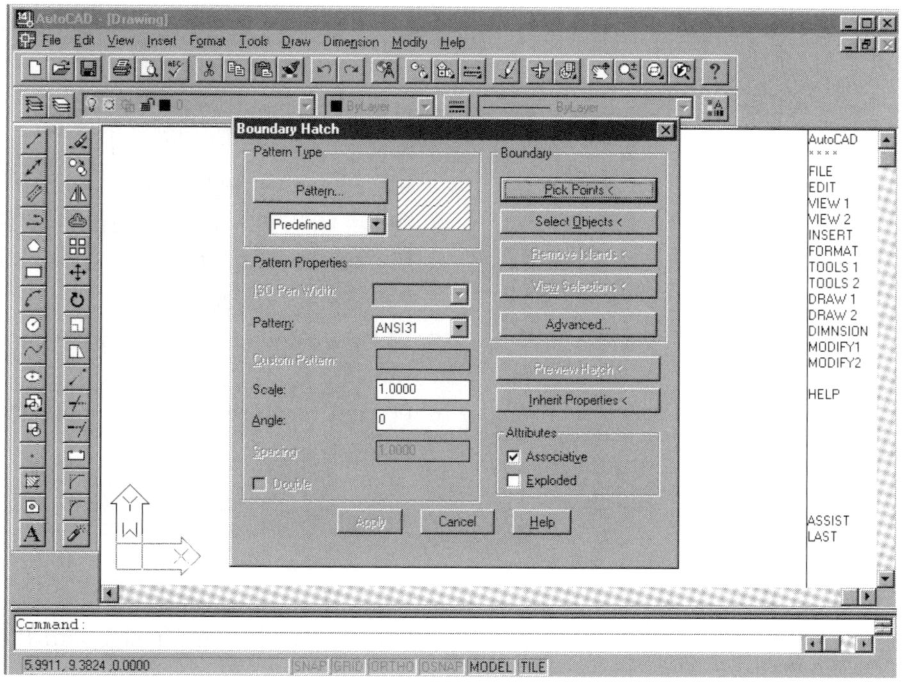

Figure 2–8
Boundary Hatch dialog box.

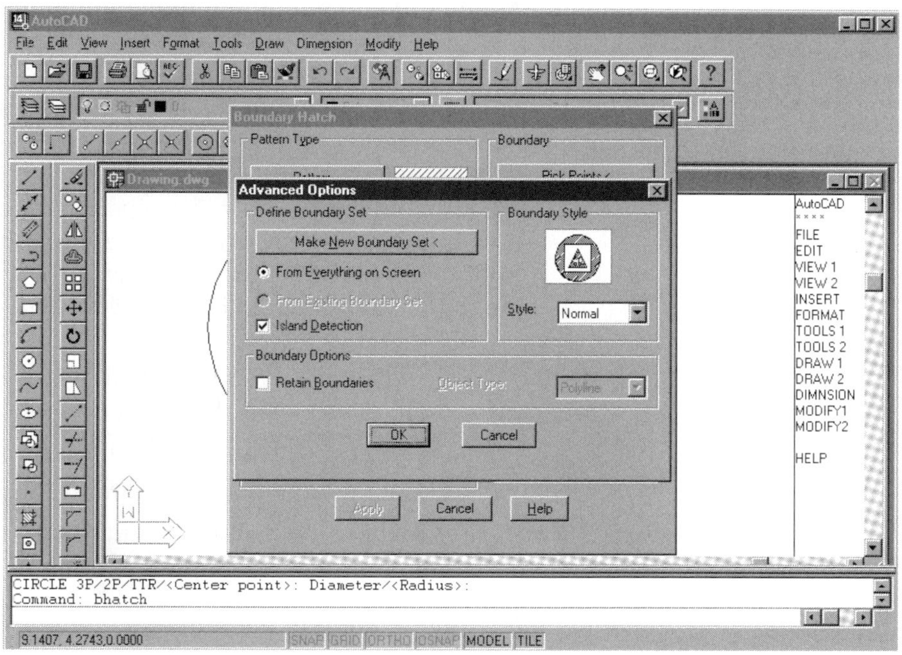

Figure 2–9
Hatch Advanced Options dialog box.

TRY THIS

Hatch a circle using the Bhatch command.

1. Create a circle with a center point of 3,3 and a radius of 2.
2. At the command prompt, type Bhatch (boundary hatch).
3. Change the hatch pattern to ANSI33.
4. Pick Select Objects<.
5. Pick the edge of the circle and right click on the mouse, or press <Enter>.
6. Preview hatch to check the angle and scale of the pattern.
7. Press Apply.

Hatch patterns are defined as graphic objects, so the more hatches a drawing has, the larger the file size and the longer it takes to regenerate a drawing.

Text

The text command provides the option for placing text on the drawing. Three commands can be used to enter text, namely, typing text at the command prompt, selecting Text from the Draw pull-down menu, or selecting MTEXT or DTEXT from the screen menu. One of the first prompts under the text command asks you to specify the starting point of the text on the drawing. You must also determine the justification style that you will use from the options that are available. Text justification options are shown at the command prompt in Figure 2–10. These options include:

Align	Provides the option of aligning the text to an object.
Fit	Fits the text between two points.
Center	Bases center of text on a selected point.
Middle	Centers text around a selected point.
Right	Justifies text to the left of a picked point.
TL	Top Left
TC	Top Center
TR	Top Right
ML	Middle Left
MC	Middle Center
MR	Middle Right
BL	Bottom Left
BC	Bottom Center
BR	Bottom Right

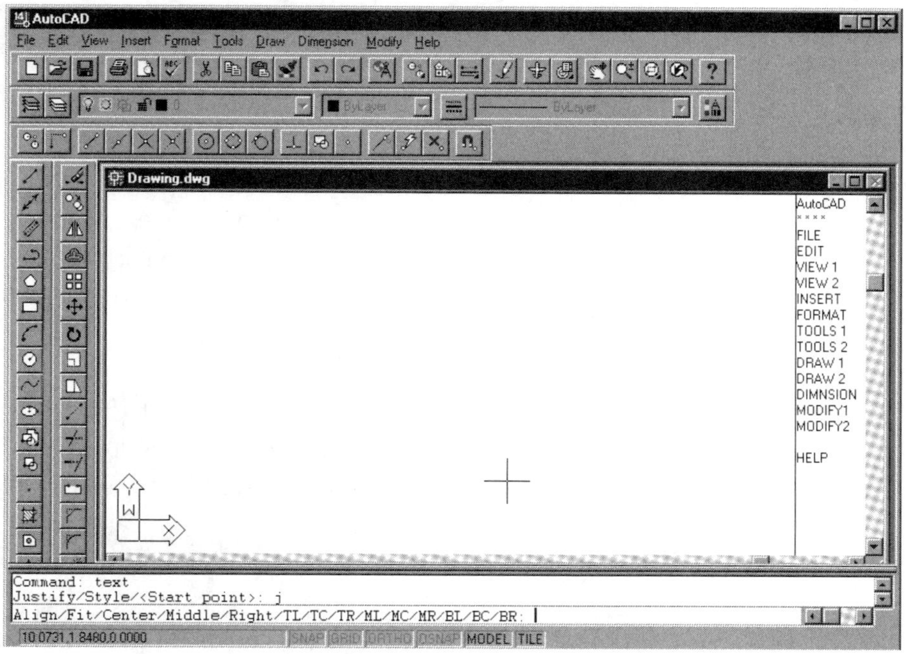

Figure 2–10
Text justification options.

Text size also must be entered after the justification option has been selected. The rotation of the text can also be changed if the text is to be rotated. The default value for text rotation is (0) based on the X axis.

Another option is to set the text style. Figure 2–11 is one dialog box that contains a variety of text styles. From the Format pull-down menu, select Text Style in order to view this dialog box.

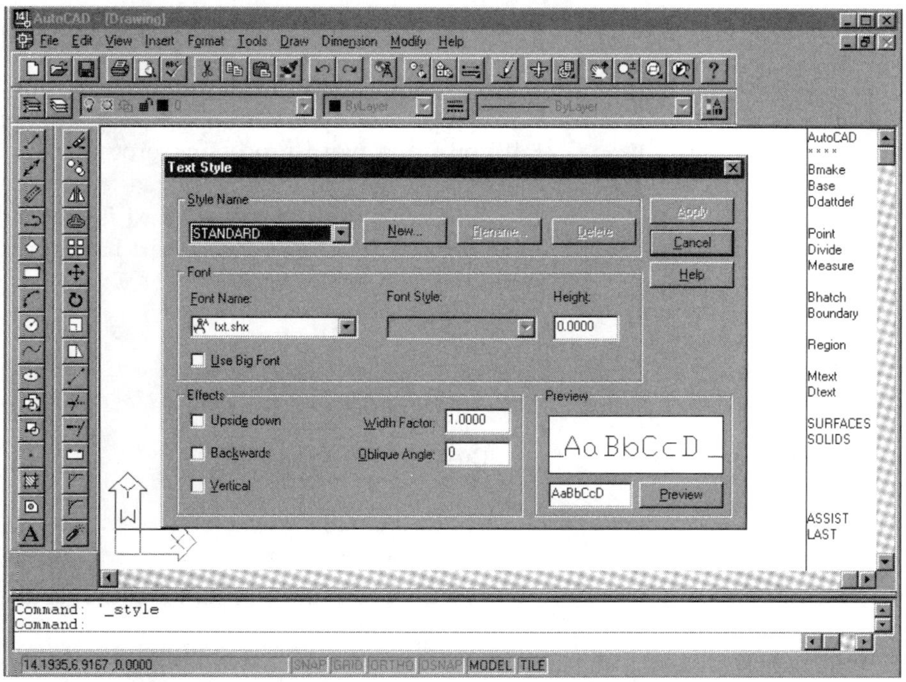

Figure 2–11
Text Style dialog box.

TRY THIS

Create a line of text.

1. From the Draw menu, select Text.
2. Select the Single line text option.
3. Click on the starting point for the first character. If you press the <Enter> key, the text entry point will default to the last text you entered.
4. Specify the text height.
5. Specify the text rotation. (Accept the default.)
6. Enter the text. (Type any line of text.)
7. When you select <Enter> on a blank line, you exit the text command.

The **Dtext** command stands for dynamic text. If you use this command, your characters appear on the screen as you type them. If you use the Text command, the characters will not appear until you are finished typing and exit the command.

If you need to create or import text in paragraph form, use the Multiline (Mtext) text command. When using this command, you will have to define the space in which you want to place the text. You do this by selecting opposite corners of a text box. The command sequence is:

Command: Mtext

Specify first corner:

Specify opposite corner or Height/Justify/Rotation/Style/Width:

After you have selected the opposite corner, a dialog box appears in which you can type your text or import your text from a word processor file. If you use a word processing program to create a file, you should save the text in ASCII text format.

An advantage of using Mtext is that individual words or characters can be formatted. Also, Multiline text has more editing options than either Dtext or Text.

TRY THIS

Create multiline text.

1. From the Draw menu, select Text and then at the next menu select Multiline Text.
2. Specify the first corner of the rectangle in which you want to place the text.

3. Specify the width of the text boundary by moving the pointing device to the left or right of the insertion point and clicking.
4. Specify the text flow by dragging the pointing device either up or down. Click when you have determined the approximate height.
5. Enter the text in the Multiline Text Editor, allowing it to wrap naturally to the next line.

Rectangle

A rectangle is a four-sided object that is constructed out of a polyline. The lines that make up a rectangle are joined at the endpoints. You cannot edit one line without affecting the other lines. Since the lines of a rectangle are polylines, they can have width assigned to them. When selecting the **Rectangle** command, you must pick opposite corners in order to create the image (see Figure 2–12). If you know the coordinates of two diagonal corners, you can type them in at the command prompt in order to create the rectangle. Rectangle options include Chamfer, Elevation, Fillet, Thickness, and Width. If Chamfer is selected, the size of the chamfer must be specified. The Elevation option allows for changing the elevation from its current setting to a new setting. The Fillet option allows you to determine corner radii of the four corners.

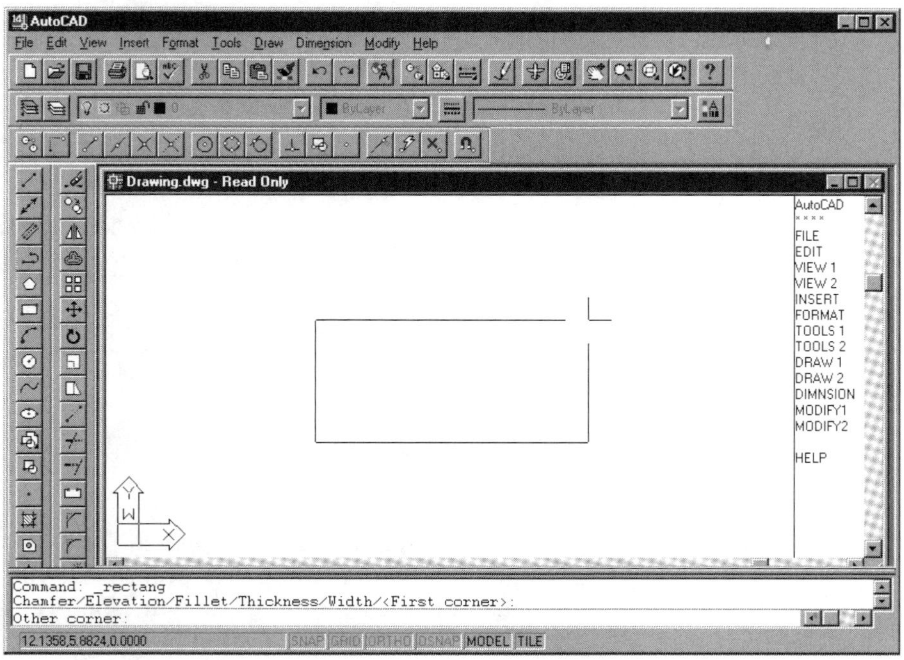

Figure 2–12
Rectangle command.

Try This

Create a rectangle that is 5 × 3 units in size.

1. From the Draw pull-down menu, select **Rectangle.**
2. Type **F** for fillet, and enter a radius of **.25.**
3. Type **W** for width, and enter a value of **.03.**
4. Enter a starting point of **2,2.**
5. Enter an ending point of **7,5.**

Donut

The **donut** command allows you to create a solid filled circle that has a hole in the center. In order to create a donut you must know the outside and inside diameter of the object. For instance, Figure 2–13 depicts a donut that has an outside diameter of 1″ and an inside diameter of .5″.

Try This

Create several donuts of varying sizes.

1. From the Draw pull-down menu, select Donut.
2. Set the inside diameter to .75.
3. Set the outside diameter to 1.25.
4. Select a point to place the donut in the drawing.
5. Press <Enter> twice to cancel and restart the command.
6. Change the diameters to different values, and place these new donuts on the drawing.

Solid

The **solid** command is used to fill a closed object, either triangular or quadrilateral in shape. The solid area will show only if the Fillmode command is on. In order to start the solid command, type or enter solid at the command prompt, or select Surfaces from the Draw pull-down menu, then 2D Solid (see Figure 2–14).

After selecting the Solids command, you must answer a series of prompts in order to successfully create the solid. You must select points on the object to create a solid surface.

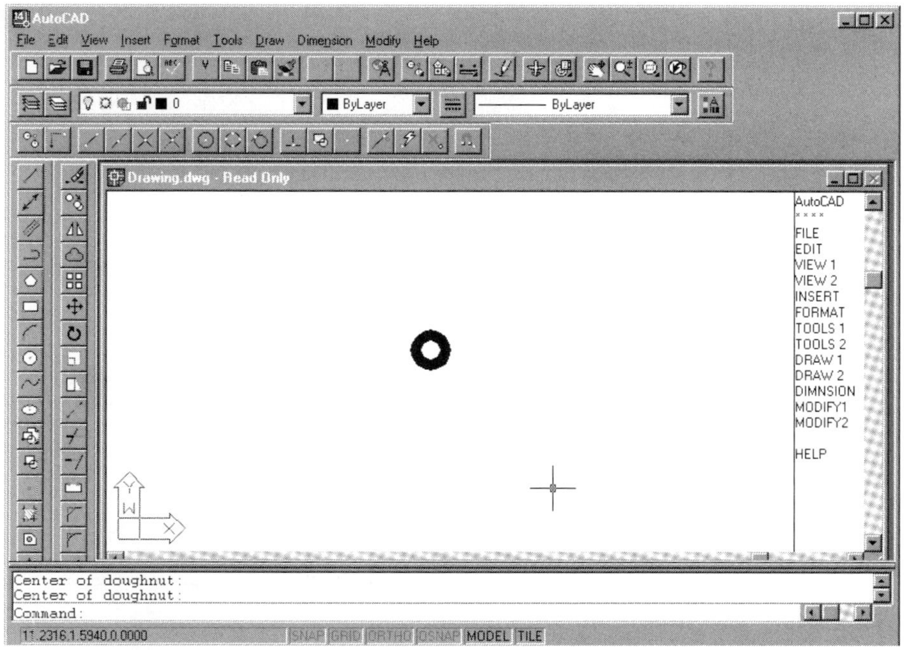

Figure 2–13
Donut command.

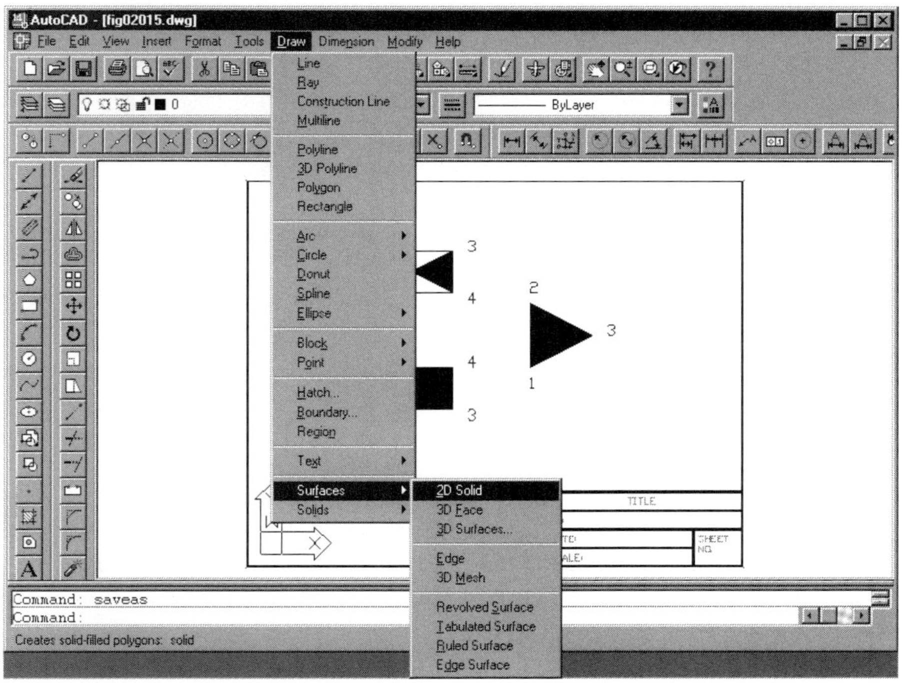

Figure 2–14
2D Solid command from the Draw pull-down menu.

Command:	Solids
First Point:	(must select a point on the object)
Second Point:	(must select a point on the object)
Third Point:	(must select a point on the object)
Fourth Point:	(must select a point on the object)

Press <Enter> to exit the command.

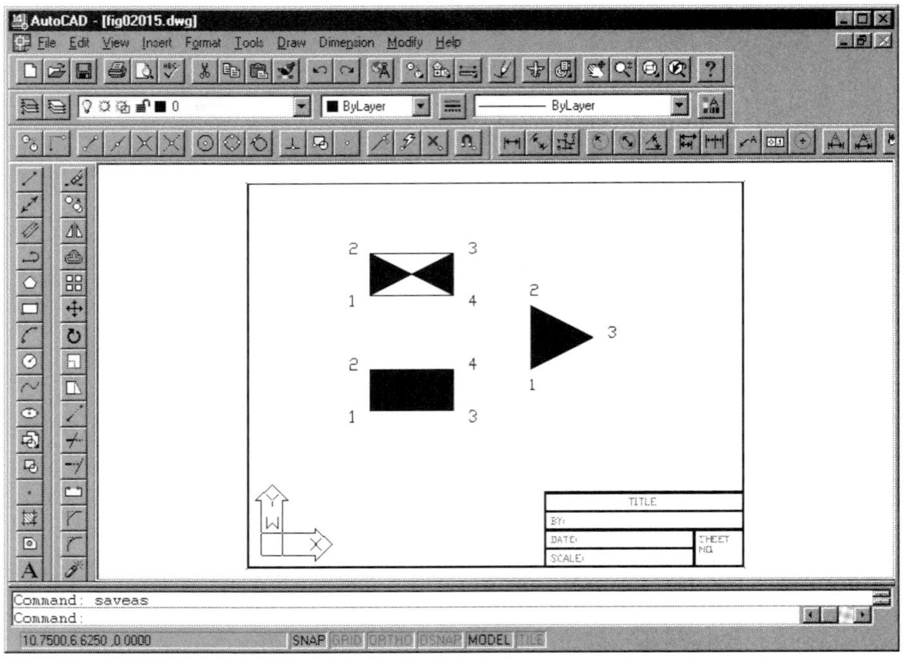

Figure 2–15
2D solid examples.

Figure 2–15 shows three examples for creating a 2D solid. The numbers on each object represent the sequence of picked points.

Chapter 2 ■ Activities

There are four drawing activities associated with this chapter. The first two activities involve the creation of two border template files, one for A-size paper and one for B-size paper. Activities 3 and 4 deal with object creation.

Activity 2–1

Create an A-Size Border Template

The purpose of this activity is for you to create a title block and border for A-size paper (see page 36). The English drawing sheet size for A-size paper is 11″ × 8.5″. When you take into consideration the mechanical limits of most plotters/printers, you cannot use the full sheet of paper. In this particular activity, you will create an A-size border and title block that measure 10″ × 7.7″.

ACTIVITY STEPS:

1. Open the AutoCAD software and select Start from Scratch.
2. From the Format pull-down menu, select Drawing Limits.
3. Accept the default (press <Enter>) of 0,0 for the lower left corner.
4. Type 10,7.7 <Enter> at the Command: prompt to change the settings for the upper right-hand corner.
5. Type z <Enter> then a (all) <Enter> to zoom to full screen.
6. Double click on the MODEL (model space) button at the bottom of the screen to switch to paper space (ps).
7. Type mview (mv) then 0,0 and <Enter> at the First point: prompt.
8. At the Other corner: prompt, type 10,7.7 <Enter>.

   A rectangular box should be showing on the screen. This is a viewport box.
9. Type z (zoom) <Enter> then a (all) <Enter> to zoom full screen in paper space.
10. From the Format pull-down menu, select Drawing Limits. The limits must be reset in paper space. Set the limits to 0,0 and 10, 7.7.
11. Type z (zoom) <Enter> then a (all) <Enter> to zoom full screen.
12. From the Draw pull-down menu, select Polyline to start the pline command.
13. At the From point: prompt, enter 0,0.

14. At the Endpoint of line: prompt, enter w (width) <Enter>.
15. At the Starting width: prompt, type .03 <Enter>.
16. Accent the default ending width by pressing <Enter>. It should read .03.
17. At the prompt Endpoint of line:, type 10,0 <Enter>.
18. At the prompt Endpoint of line:, type 10,7.7 <Enter>.
19. At the prompt Endpoint of line:, type 0,7.7 <Enter>.
20. At the prompt Endpoint of line:, type c (close). An outside borderline should be visible.
21. Press <Enter> to restart the Polyline command.
22. At the prompt From point:, type 6,0 <Enter>.
23. At the prompt Endpoint of line:, type @1.5<90 <Enter>.
24. At the prompt Endpoint of line:, type @4<0 <Enter> two times.
25. The Command: prompt line should be blank. There should be a rectangular box in the lower right corner of the drawing screen.
26. Press <Enter> to restart the Pline command.
27. At the From point: command, type 6, .375 <Enter>.
28. At the Endpoint of line: command, type 9, .375 <Enter>.
29. Press <Enter> twice, once to exit the command and once to restart the command.
30. At the From point: command, type 6, .75 <Enter>.
31. At the Endpoint of line: command, type 10, .75 <Enter>.
32. Press <Enter> twice, once to exit the command and once to restart the command.
33. At the From point: command, enter 6, 1.125 <Enter>.
34. At the Endpoint of line: command, type 10, 1.125 <Enter>.
35. Press <Enter> twice, once to exit the command and once to restart the command.
36. At the From point: command, type 9,0 <Enter>.
37. At the Endpoint of line: command, type 9, .75 <Enter>.
38. Press <Enter> to exit the Pline command.
39. From the File pull-down menu, select Save.
40. Name the drawing Borda and change the **Saveas type** to .dwt.

    The title block and borderlines for an A-size sheet of paper should be complete.

In the second part of this activity you will add text to the title block.

1. At the command prompt, type z (zoom). Use the cursor crosshairs to create a window around the title block in the right corner of the drawing.
2. From the Tools pull-down menu, select Drawing Aids. Change the Snap setting for X and Y to .0625″. Be sure to check the ON box for the snap. The cursor will move at .0625″ intervals.
3. Change the Grid setting for X and Y to .25″. Be sure to check the ON box for the snap. The grid points should be displayed at .25″ intervals.

4. From the Format pull-down menu, select Layer. The Layer dialog box should now appear.
5. In the Layer dialog box, select New. Type Text as the new layer. In this same dialog box and in the same row as the Text layer, select the black square next to the word Continuous. This square represents the color assigned to this layer. After you have selected the square, a Color dialog box should appear. At the top of the dialog box is a row labeled Standard Colors. Click on the color blue. Press <OK> to exit the Color dialog box. The square next to the word Continuous should now appear blue.
6. If the layer Text is not highlighted, click on the word Text. Near the center and top of the dialog box there is a button that makes the layer you have highlighted current. Click on it to make Text the current layer. The current layer name should appear to the right of the word Current.
7. Click <OK> to exit the Layer dialog box.
8. At the command prompt, type Text. For a Starting point: pick a point in the lower right section of the title block. With the snap on, you should be able to move the cursor crosshairs to a point that is two snap points above the bottom line and two snap points from the left vertical line. Press <Enter>.
9. At the Text height: prompt, type .125 <Enter>.
10. Leave the Rotation angle at 0. Press <Enter>.
11. At the Text: prompt, type Scale: <Enter>. Repeat the Text command and place text similar to that in the example (Figure 2–16).
12. Save the drawing before exiting.

ACTIVITY 2–2

Create a B-Size Border Template

The purpose of this activity is for you to create a title block and border for B-size paper (see page 39). The English drawing sheet size for B-size paper is 17″ × 11″. When you take into consideration the mechanical limits of most plotters/printers, you cannot use the full sheet of paper. In this particular activity, you will create a B-size border and title block that measures 15.5″ × 10″.

ACTIVITY STEPS:

1. Open the AutoCAD software and select Start from Scratch.
2. From the Format pull-down menu, select Drawing Limits.
3. Accept the default (press <Enter>) of 0,0 for the lower left corner.
4. Type 15.5,10 <Enter> at the Command: prompt to change the settings for the upper right-hand corner.
5. Type z <Enter> then a (all) <Enter> to zoom to full screen.
6. Double click on the MODEL (model space) button at the bottom of the screen to switch to paper space (ps).

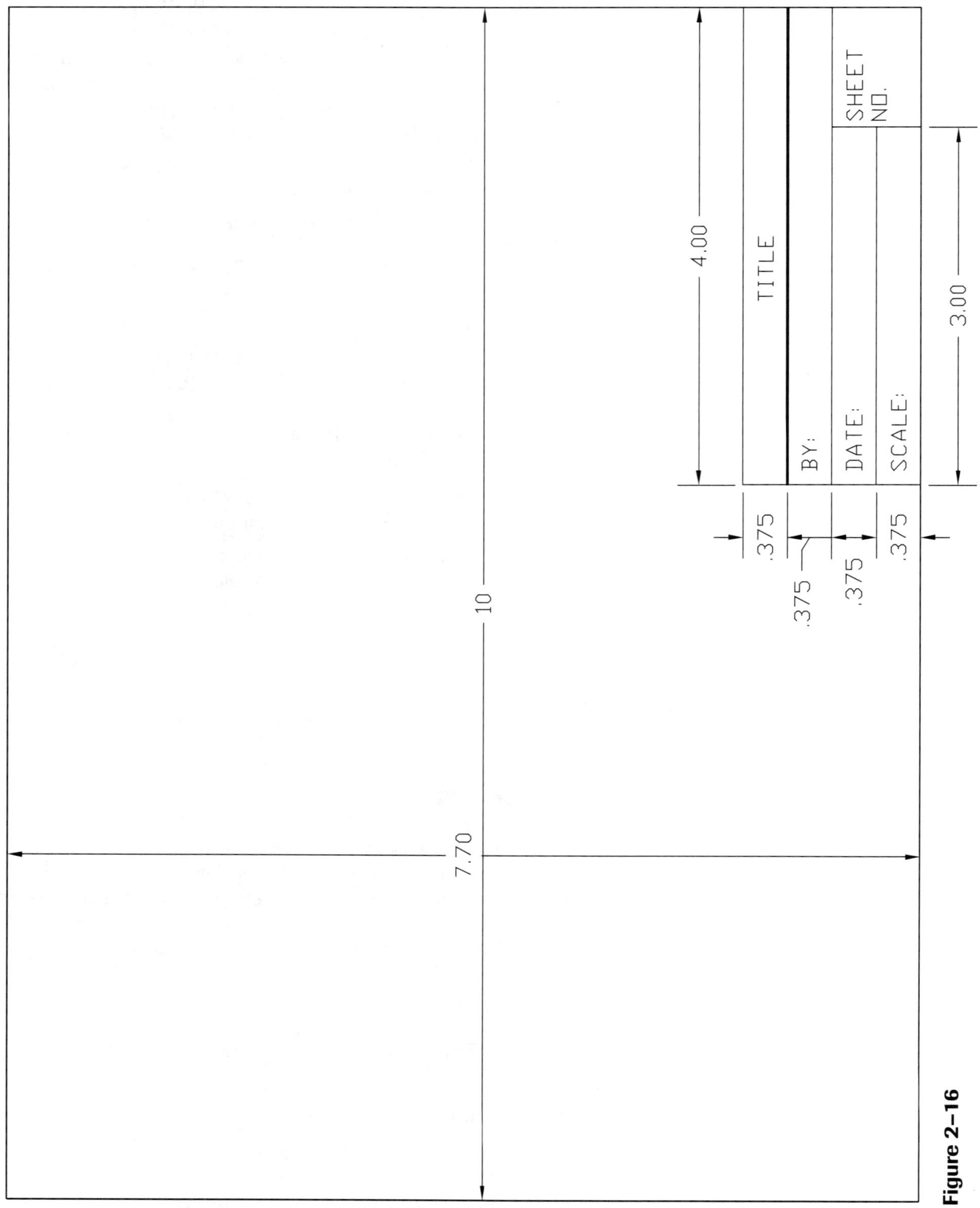

Figure 2–16

7. Type mview (mv) then 0,0 and <Enter> at the First point: prompt.
8. At the Other corner: prompt, type 15.5,10 <Enter>. A rectangular box should be showing on the screen. This is a viewport box.
9. Type z (zoom) <Enter> then a (all) <Enter> to zoom full screen in paper space.
10. From the Format pull-down menu, select Drawing Limits. The limits must be reset in paper space. Set the limits to 0,0 and 15.5,10.
11. Type z (zoom) <Enter> then a (all) <Enter> to zoom full screen.
12. From the Draw pull-down menu, select Polyline to start the pline command.
13. At the From point: prompt, enter 0,0.
14. At the Endpoint of line: prompt, enter w (width) <Enter>.
15. At the Starting width: prompt, type .03 <Enter>.
16. Accent the default ending width by pressing <Enter>. It should read .03.
17. At the prompt Endpoint of line:, type 15.5,0 <Enter>.
18. At the prompt Endpoint of line:, type 15.5,10 <Enter>.
19. At the prompt Endpoint of line:, type 0,10 <Enter>.
20. At the prompt Endpoint of line:, type c (close). An outside borderline should be visible.
21. Press <Enter> to restart the pline command.
22. At the prompt From point:, type 11.5,0 <Enter>.
23. At the prompt Endpoint of line:, type @1.5<90 <Enter>.
24. At the prompt Endpoint of line:, type @4<0 <Enter> two times.
25. The Command: prompt line should be blank. There should be a rectangular box in the lower right corner of the drawing screen.
26. Press <Enter> to restart the Pline command.
27. At the From point: command, type 11.5, .375 <Enter>.
28. At the Endpoint of line: command, type 14.5, .375 <Enter>.
29. Press <Enter> twice, once to exit the command and once to restart the command.
30. At the From point: command, type 11.5, .75 <Enter>.
31. At the Endpoint of line: command, type 15.5, .75 <Enter>.
32. Press <Enter> twice, once to exit the command and once to restart the command.
33. At the From point: command, enter 11.5, 1.125 <Enter>.
34. At the Endpoint of line: command, type 15.5, 1.125 <Enter>.
35. Press <Enter> twice, once to exit the command and once to restart the command.
36. At the From point: command, type 14.5,0 <Enter>.
37. At the Endpoint of line: command, type 14.5, .75 <Enter>.
38. Press <Enter> to exit the pline command.
39. From the File pull-down menu, select Save.
40. Name the drawing Bordb and change the File type to .dwt.

    The title block and borderlines for a B-size sheet of paper should be complete.

In the second part of this activity you will add text to the title block.

1. At the Command: prompt, type z (zoom). Use the cursor crosshairs to create a window around the title block in the right corner of the drawing.
2. From the Tools pull-down menu, select Drawing Aids. Change the Snap setting for X and Y to .0625″. Be sure to check the ON box for the snap. The cursor will move at .0625″ intervals.
3. Change the Grid setting for X and Y to .25″. Be sure to check the ON box for the snap. The grid points should be displayed at .25″ intervals.
4. From the Format pull-down menu, select Layer. The Layers dialog box should now appear.
5. In the Layer dialog box, select New. Type Text as the new layer. In this same dialog box and in the same row as the Text layer, select the black square next to the word Continuous. This square represents the color assigned to this layer. After you have selected the square, a Color dialog box should appear. At the top of the dialog box is a row labeled Standard Colors. Click on the color blue. Press <OK> to exit the Color dialog box. The square next to the word Continuous should now appear blue.
6. If the layer Text is not highlighted, click on the word Text. Near the center and top of the dialog box there is a button that makes the layer you have highlighted current. Click on it to make Text the current layer. The current layer name should appear to the right of the word Current.
7. Click <OK> to exit the Layer dialog box.
8. At the command prompt, type Text. For a Starting point: pick a point in the lower right section of the title block. With the snap on, you should be able to move the cursor crosshairs to a point that is two snap points above the bottom line and two snap points from the left vertical line. Press <Enter>.
9. At the Text height: prompt, type .125 <Enter>.
10. Leave the Rotation angle at 0. Press <Enter>.
11. At the Text: prompt, type Scale: <Enter>. Repeat the Text command and place text similar to that in the example (Figure 2–17).
12. Save the drawing before exiting.

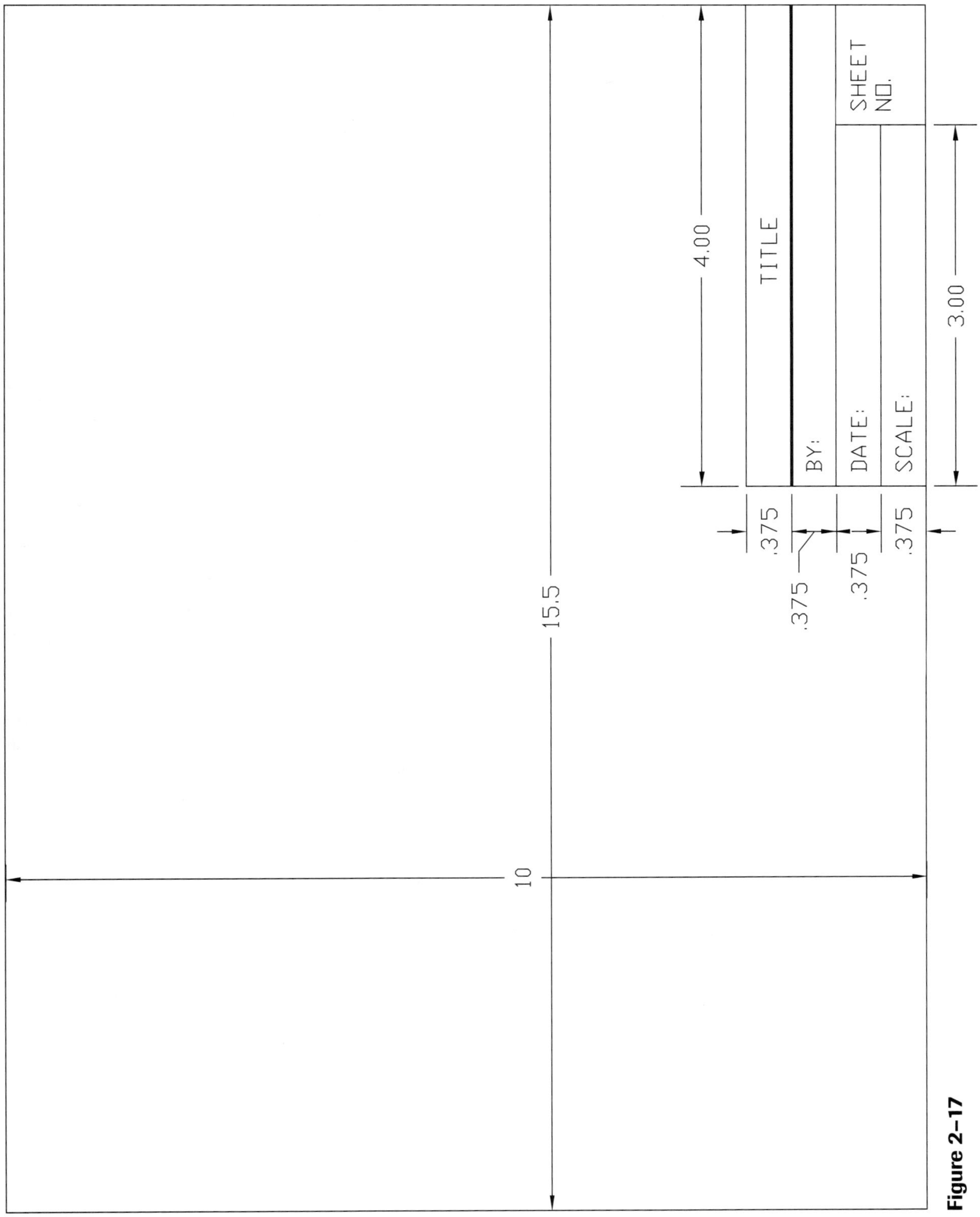

Figure 2–17

ACTIVITY 2–3

Entities Drawing

Plotter paper size: A

Suggested settings:	Grid	.25″
	Snap	.125″
	Layers (3)	**0** (default border)
		Object, Linetype continuous, Color: black
		Text, Linetype continuous, Color: blue
	Units	Decimal

Hints:

1. At the Start Up dialog box, select Use a Template. Load the template file Borda.
2. Switch to model space before changing any of the listed settings. Make the suggested settings, and be sure to create the layers listed. All text height is .125″.
3. Review Figure 2–18. Use the pull-down menu, the floating toolbar, and the screen menu, or type in the command to create the objects. Make sure to create the drawing objects with the accompanying text in model space. Both the pline and the rectangle have line widths of .03″. The donut has an inside diameter of .5″ and an outside diameter of 1. The only objects that should exist in paper space are the borderlines and the border text.
4. Switch to paper space to update the text in the Title block with the appropriate information. You have to be in paper space in order to edit the objects that were created in paper space. The name of the drawing is ENTITIES.
5. Once you have completed the drawing, you can exit the drawing editor in two different ways. Before exiting, always save the drawing. From the File pull-down menu select Exit. At the Command: prompt type quit. If you have made any changes, you will be asked if you want to save those changes.
6. To save your drawing without leaving the drawing editor, type save and press <Enter>. At this point you must give your file a name. Be sure to include the drive designation.

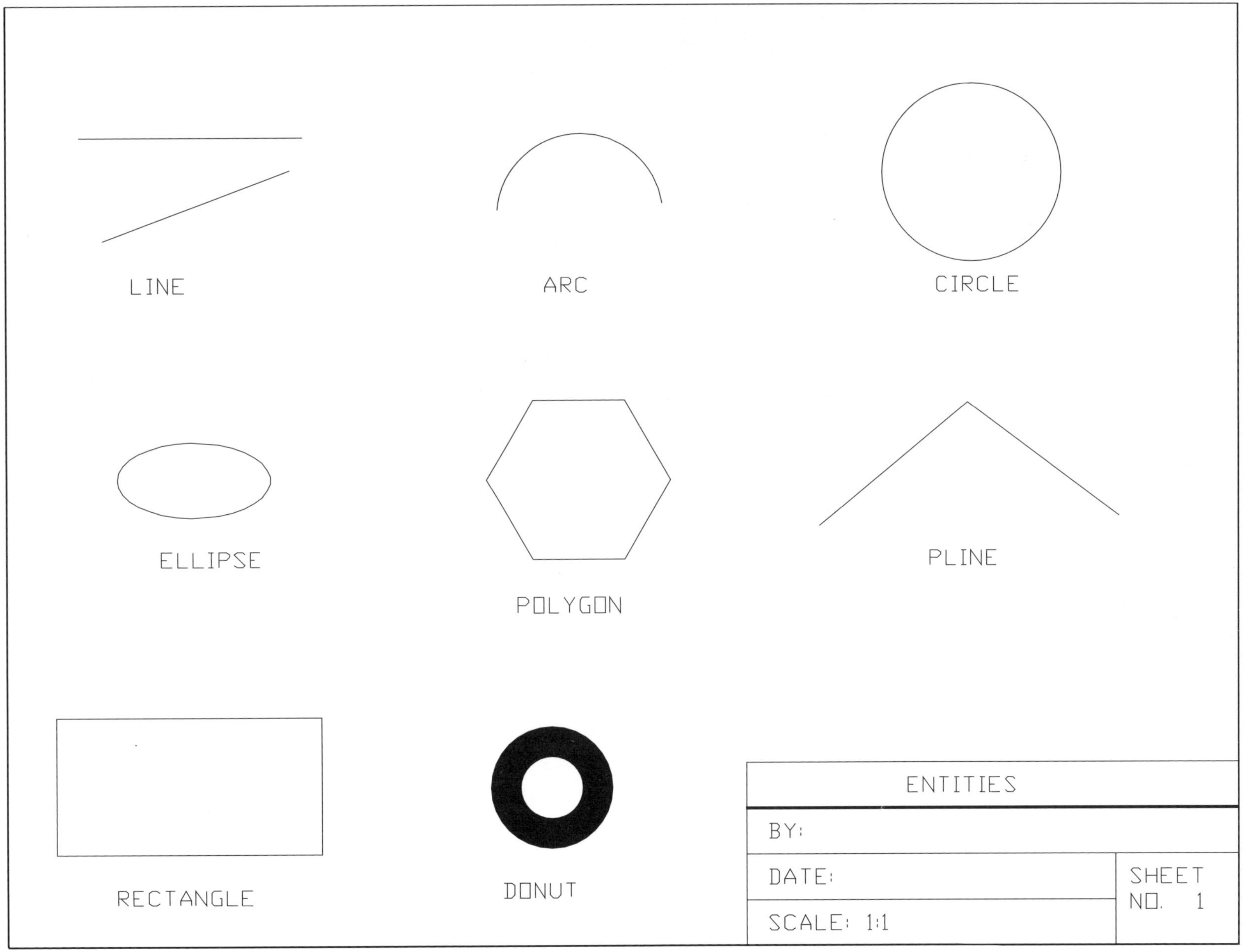
LINE
ARC
CIRCLE
ELLIPSE
POLYGON
PLINE
RECTANGLE
DONUT
ENTITIES
BY:
DATE:
SCALE: 1:1
SHEET
NO. 1

Figure 2–18

ACTIVITY 2–4

Drawing Shim

Plotter paper size: A

Suggested settings:	Grid	.25″
	Snap	.125″
	Layers (3)	**0** (default border)
		Object, Linetype continuous, Color: black
		Text, Linetype continuous, Color: blue
	Units	Decimal

Hints:

1. At the Start Up dialog box, select Use a Template. Load the template file Borda.
2. Switch to model space before changing any of the listed settings. Make the suggested settings, and be sure to create the layers listed.
3. Review Figure 2–19. Use the pull-down menu, the floating toolbar, and the screen menu, or type in the command to create the objects. Make sure to create the drawing objects with the accompanying text in model space. **Note:** The spacing between the objects is 1.5″. **Do not** include dimensions on the drawing.
4. Switch to paper space to update the text in the Title block with the appropriate information. You have to be in paper space in order to edit the objects that were created in paper space. The name of the drawing is SHIM. Name the file you save SHIM also.
5. Once you have completed the drawing, you can exit the drawing editor in two different ways. Before exiting, always save the drawing. From the File pull-down menu select Exit. At the Command: prompt type quit. If you have made any changes, you will be asked if you want to save those changes.

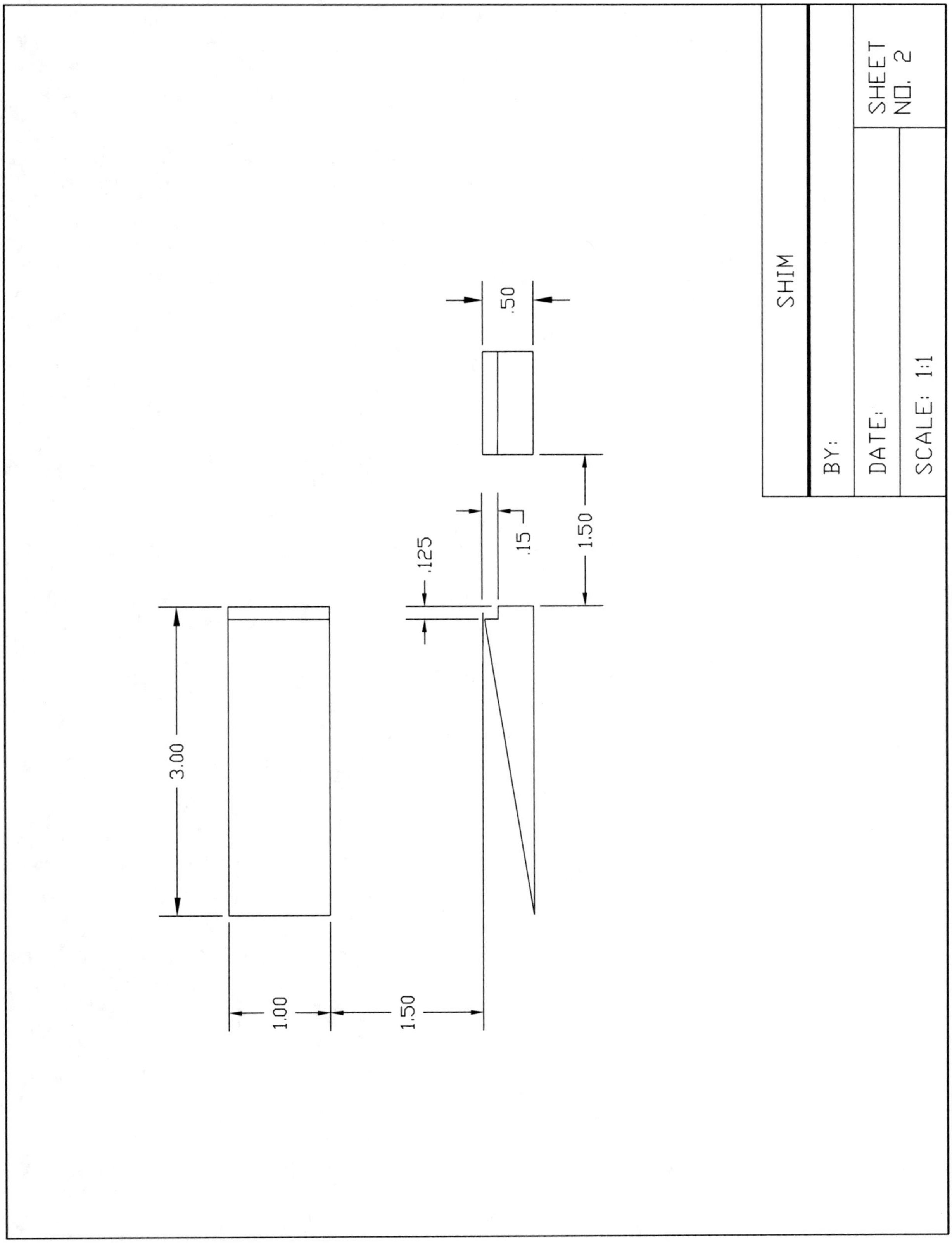

Figure 2–19

CHAPTER

3

Drawing Aids

AFTER READING THIS CHAPTER, YOU WILL BE ABLE TO:

- Use AutoCAD R14 commands that aid in setting up a drawing sheet.

KEY CONCEPTS:

Grid

Limits

Snap

Units

When working in the drawing editor and doing drawing layout, it is beneficial to set certain parameters to aid in producing a drawing. This chapter reviews some of the more common drawing aids that can be used to correctly set up a drawing.

LIMITS

The **Limits** command is linked to the size of the drawing. Drawing limits refer to the electronic drawing screen that determines the actual size of the drawing area on which an object is created. Two different limits must be set: those in model space and those in paper space. Images are drawn full size, so the limits in model space are set to allow for creating images full size. For example, if you were drawing a house that measured 40′ × 30′, you might set the limits at 60′ × 40′.

Paper space limits are typically the same size as the sheet of paper on which the drawing will be printed or plotted. However, paper space limits must allow for the mechanical controls of the plotter. When the limits in model space are different from the limits of paper space, a zoom ×P factor has to be entered in model space so that the drawing will be plotted at the correct size and scale.

Drawing limits can be set from the Format pull-down menu (see Figure 3–1) or through the Use a Wizard options of Quick Setup or Advanced Setup.

The word limits can also be typed at the command prompt in order to set drawing size. When typed, two relative coordinate points must also be set. Typically the lower left corner is left at 0,0 and the upper right point is set to an (X,Y) point that allows a drawing to be drawn at full size, or the (X,Y) point relates to the size of the sheet of paper on which the drawing will be printed (see Figure 3–2). Limits can be set or changed any time during the drawing process.

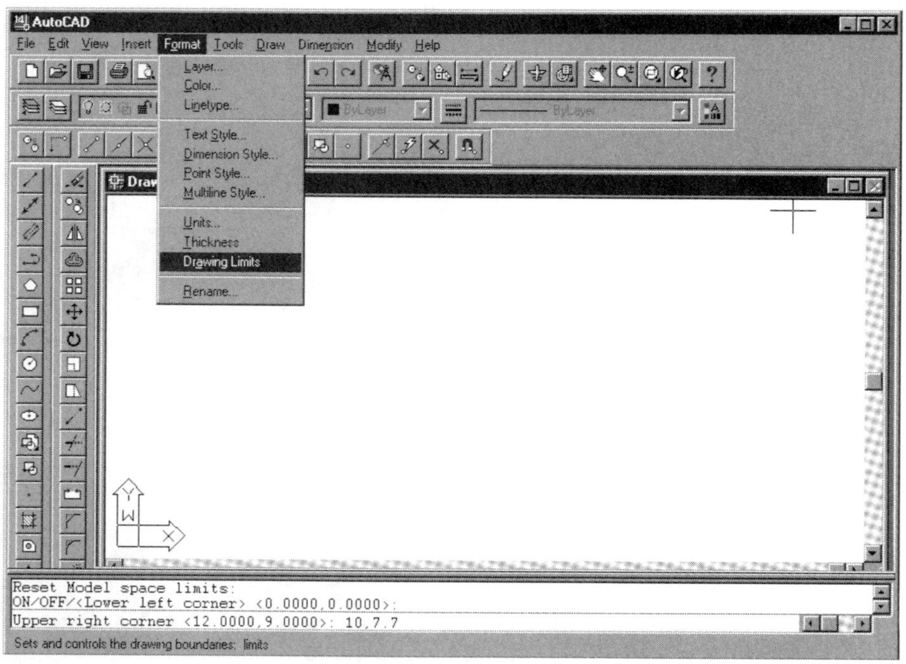

Figure 3–1
Drawing Limits command.

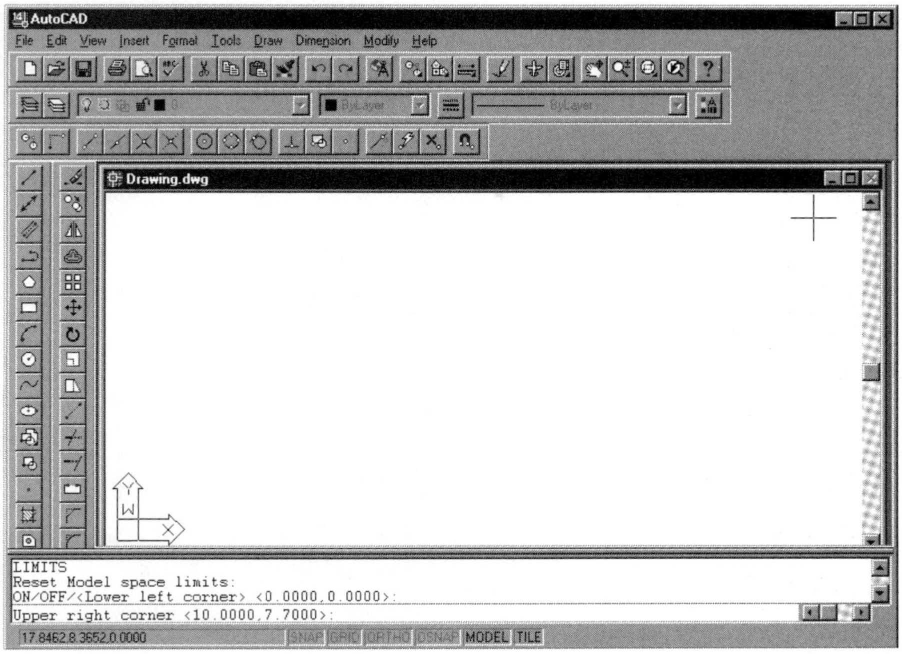

Figure 3-2
Entering limits at the command prompt.

TRY THIS

Practice setting the limits in both model space and paper space.

1. Open AutoCAD.
2. In the Start Up dialog box, select Use a Template.
3. Open the Bordb template from Activity 2-2.
4. Make sure you are in model space (ms) and select Drawing Limits from the Format pull-down menu.
5. At the command prompt, check to see the limits setting.
6. The lower left corner should be at 0,0.
7. The upper right corner should be 15.5,10.
8. Switch to paper space (ps) and check the limit settings.
9. The lower left corner should be at 0,0, and the upper right corner should be 15.5,10.

UNITS

The **Units** command determines the format of the presentation of the information. There are five different formats in which the information can be expressed, namely, Scientific, Decimal, Engineering, Architectural, and Fractional.

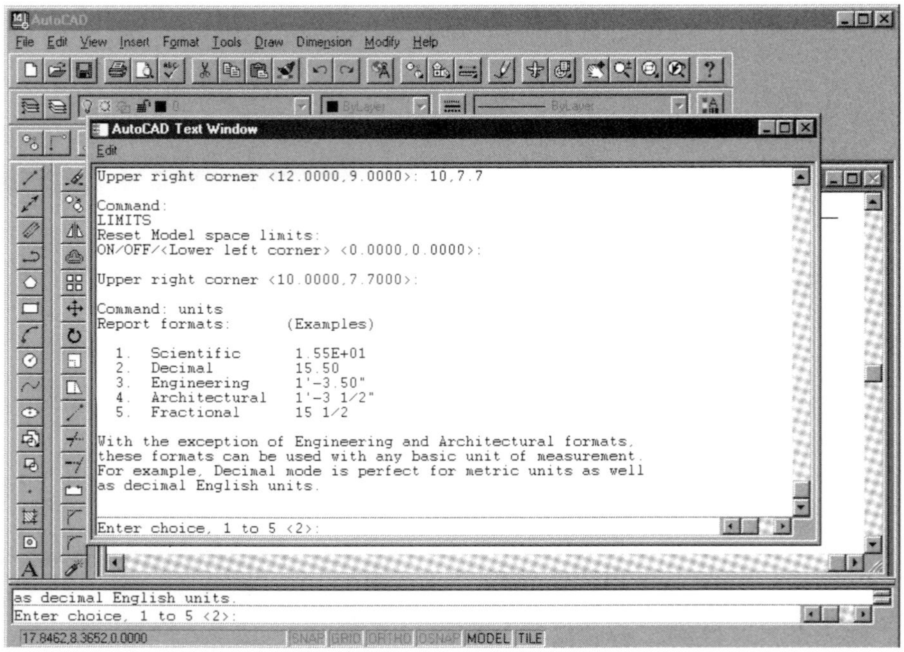

Figure 3–3
Units dialog box.

Units are set through the Use a Wizard options of Quick Setup or Advanced Setup. When units is entered at the command prompt, a text screen appears and displays the following prompts (see Figure 3–3):

Report formats:	**(Examples)**
1. Scientific	1.55E+01
2. Decimal	15.50
3. Engineering	1′-3.50″
4. Architectural	$1'$-$3\frac{1}{2}''$
5. Fractional	$15\frac{1}{2}$

Enter choice, 1 to 5 <current>:

Enter a value (1–5) or press <Enter>

AutoCAD prompts for decimal precision if the scientific, decimal, or engineering format was specified:

Number of digits to right of decimal point (0 to 8) <current>:

Enter a value (0–8) or press <Enter>

AutoCAD prompts for the denominator of the smallest fraction if the architectural or fractional format was specified:

Denominator of smallest fraction to display
(1, 2, 4, 8, 16, 32, 64, 128, or 256) <current>:

Enter a value (1, 2, 4, 8, 16, 32, 64, 128, or 256) or press <Enter>

AutoCAD prompts for angle formats and precision:

Systems of angle measure:	(Examples)
1. Decimal degrees	45.0000
2. Degrees/minutes/seconds	45d0′0″
3. Grids	50.0000g
4. Radians	0.7854r
5. Surveyor's units	N 45d0′0″ E

Enter choice, 1 to 5 <current>:
Enter a value (1–5) or press <Enter>
Number of fractional places for display of angles (0 to 8) <current>:
Enter a value (0–8) or press <Enter>

AutoCAD prompts for the direction for angle 0:

Direction for angle 0:

East	3 o'clock	=	0
North	12 o'clock	=	90
West	9 o'clock	=	180
South	6 o'clock	=	270

Enter direction for angle 0 <current>:
Enter a value or press <Enter>

The default direction for 0° is to the right—east quadrant, or 3 o'clock. The default direction for positive angular measurement is counterclockwise.

Do you want angles measured clockwise? <current>
Enter y or n or press <Enter>
(Autodesk, Inc., 1997)

Units also can be selected from the Format pull-down menu (see Figure 3–4).

TRY THIS

Practice setting up drawings with different units.

1. Open the AutoCAD software program.
2. In the Start Up dialog box, select Use a Template.
3. Open the Bordb template from Activity 2-2.
4. From the Format pull-down menu, select Units.
5. Select Architectural and set the Precision to $\frac{1}{8}''$.
6. Select OK to exit the Units control dialog box.

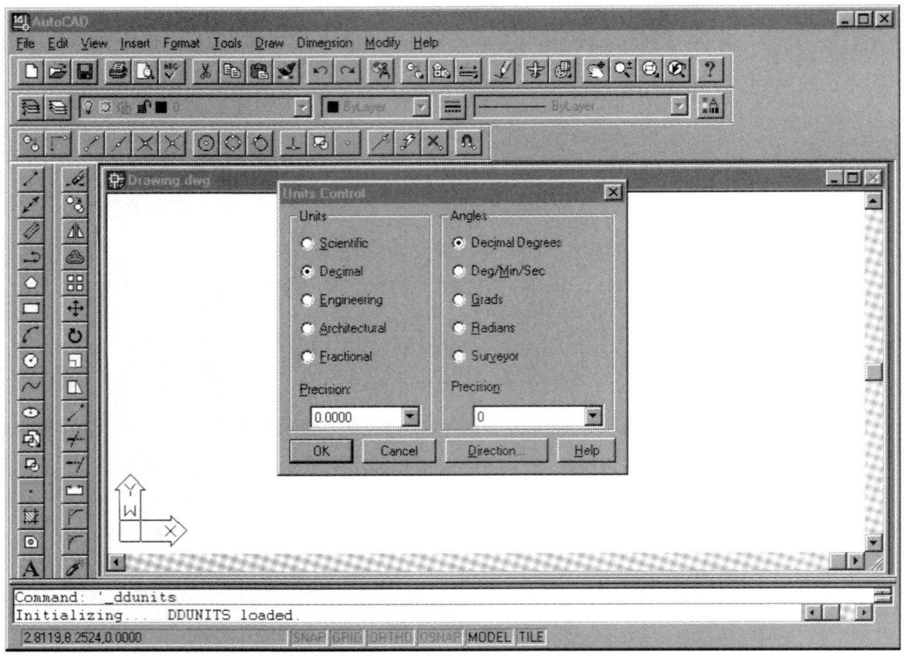

Figure 3–4
Units dialog box.

7. Check the coordinate readout display along the bottom of the screen. It should read in feet and inches.
8. Change your Snap settings to $\frac{1}{4}$". Move the cursor display on the screen; it should move in $\frac{1}{4}$" if the snap is on.

Repeat the preceding steps and try changing the units to Engineering, Scientific, and Fractional. When you exit the drawing editor, answer No when asked to save changes.

GRID

The **grid** is used for visual reference. The distance between grid points is based on the size of the electronic drawing sheet. Grid points are not plotted and are not part of the drawing or any drawing object. The shortcut key for toggling the grid on/off is F7. When the grid is turned either on or off, an automatic redraw occurs, and any **blip marks** that are on the screen are removed. The grid can also be turned on/off by double clicking on the GRID button located at the bottom of the drawing editor screen.

A **blip mark** is a temporary mark in the shape of a plus sign (+) that appears where you specify a point.

In order to access the grid through the pull-down menu, select Tools and then Drawing Aids. The dialog box should appear as shown in Figure

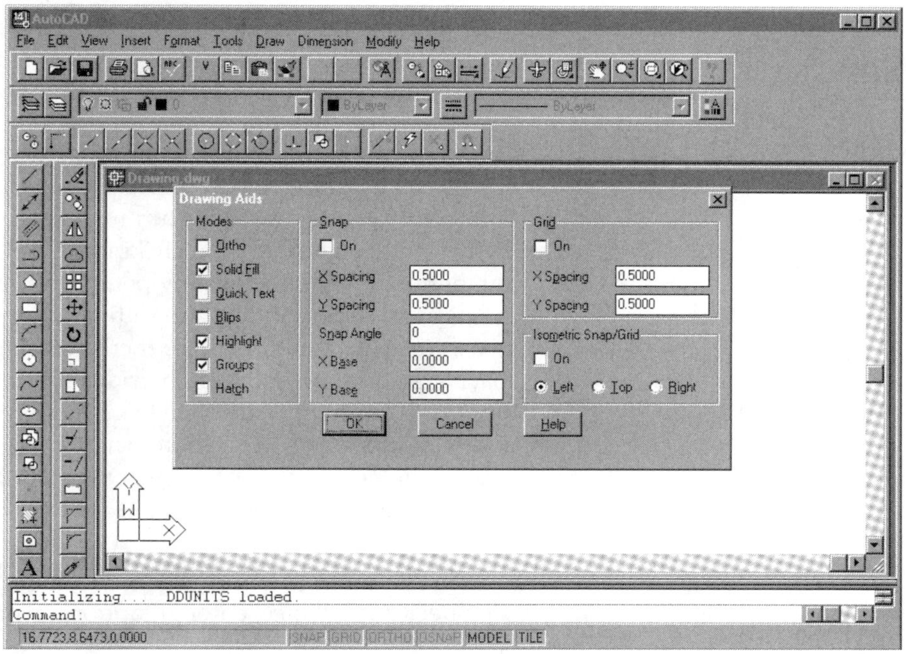

Figure 3–5
Drawing Aids dialog box.

3–5. By clicking in the appropriate boxes, you can enter numerical values for both grid spacing and snap spacing. You can also set grid options by typing grid at the command prompt.

Separate grids exist for model space and paper space, and the grid spacing can be set differently for each.

TRY THIS

Practice setting the grid to different values.

1. Open AutoCAD.
2. In the Start Up dialog box, select Use a Template.
3. Open the Borda template from Activity 2–1.
4. Make sure you are in model space.
5. From the Tools pull-down menu, select Drawing Aids.
6. Select the On box to turn the Grid on.
7. For the X Spacing enter 0.5.
8. For the Y Spacing enter 0.5.
9. Select OK to exit the dialog box.

Grid points should appear that are spaced 0.5 unit apart. Repeat the activity and set the Grid to various values. Try setting the Grid to a value of 0.0625. What message did you get at the command prompt?

SNAP

The **Snap** command limits cursor movement to specific intervals. If drawing objects can be drawn based on snap points, it is much easier to edit and position them. The toggle key for turning the snap on/off is F9. The snap can also be turned on/off by double clicking on the SNAP button located at the bottom of the drawing editor. Any points you enter can be locked into alignment by the snap setting if the snap setting is set to accommodate the incremental measurements. Typically, snap increments are of a lesser value than the grid spacing setting. Also, the snap grid can be rotated with different settings for the X and Y spacing. Any change in the snap grid affects only the coordinates of new points. AutoCAD ignores snap mode in perspective views.

At the command prompt, enter snap. The command prompt line should then change and appear as follows:

Snap spacing or ON / OFF / Aspect / Rotate / Style <current>:

Specify a distance, enter an option, or press <Enter> (see Figure 3–6).

Snap increments also can be set in the Drawing Aids dialog box.

TRY THIS

Practice setting the Snap values to different increments to view their effect on cursor movement and object creation.

1. Open the AutoCAD software program.
2. In the Start Up dialog box, select Use a Template.

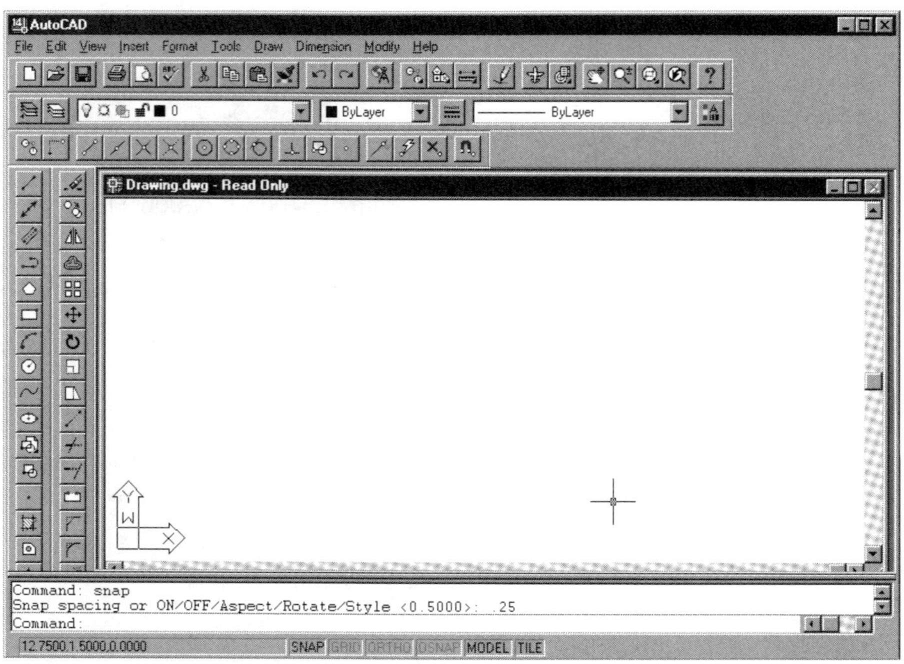

Figure 3–6
Setting snap values.

3. Open the Borda template from Activity 2-1.
4. Make sure that you are in model space.
5. From the Tools pull-down menu, select Drawing Aids.
6. Select the On box to turn the Snap on.
7. Set the X Spacing to 0.25.
8. Set the Y Spacing to 0.25.
9. Select the On box to turn the Grid on.
10. Set the X Spacing to 0.5.
11. Set the Y Spacing to 0.5.
12. Select OK to exit the Drawing Aids dialog box.
13. Move the cursor around on the screen. It should move at 0.25 intervals. Make sure the coordinate readout display located at the bottom is turned on. As you move the cursor around the drawing editor, the readout values in the coordinate display should also change at 0.25 intervals.
14. Create a rectangle that is 3 × 2 units. Since the snap is set to move at 0.25 intervals, you should be able to watch the coordinate display or count grid points to determine the correct size.

Chapter 3 ■ Activity

ACTIVITY 3–1

View the Tutorial on Setting up a Drawing

Open the AutoCAD software program. From the Help pull-down menu select Quick Tour. Click on Drawing with Autocad to gain access to the multimedia menu. Select the Setting Up a Drawing option. View the tutorial to gain a better understanding of how drawings are set up.

CHAPTER

4

Screen Display Commands

AFTER READING THIS CHAPTER, YOU WILL BE ABLE TO:

- Execute commands that affect the visual display.

KEY CONCEPTS:

- Aerial View
- Pan (p)
- Redraw(r)
- Regen
- Zoom (z)

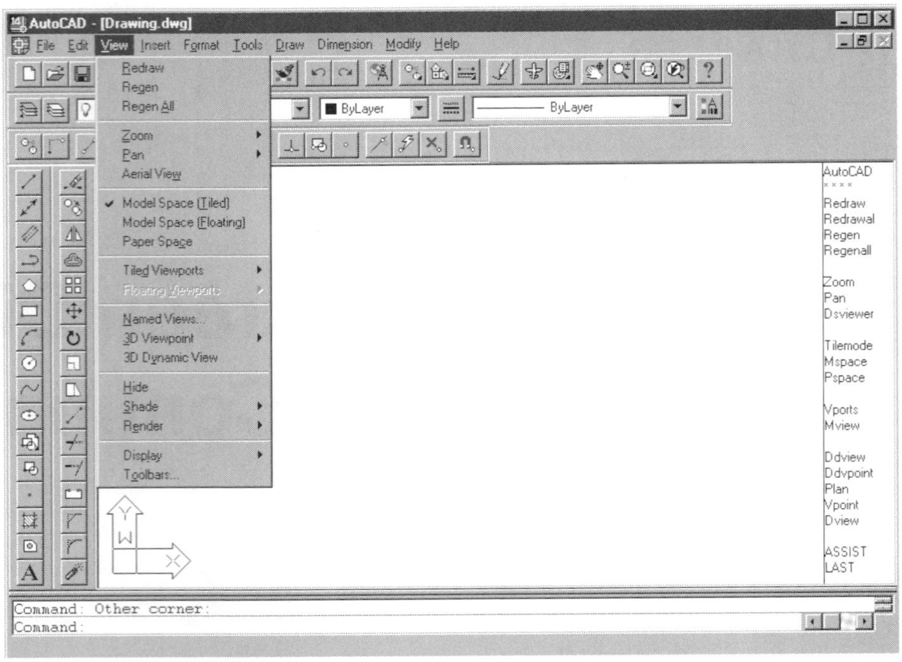

Figure 4–1
View pull-down menu.

To effectively edit a drawing, it is sometimes necessary to enhance or change the visual display of the drawing screen. AutoCAD has several commands that affect the visual display of the drawing editor, namely, Zoom, Pan, Aerial View, Redraw, and Regen.

These commands can be selected from the View pull-down menu, with toolbar icons, or from the screen menu (see Figure 4–1). The English-word equivalent of the command can also be typed at the command prompt line.

ZOOM

The **Zoom** command magnifies or shrinks the drawing on the display screen. Zoom can be selected from the View pull-down menu, or z can be entered at the command prompt. Three zoom icons are also located in the top toolbar. These icons represent Zoom Realtime, Zoom Window, and Zoom Previous (see Figure 4–2).

Figure 4–2
Zoom toolbar icons.

When zoom is entered at the command prompt or Zoom is selected from the View pull-down menu, the following submenu options become available: All/Center/Dynamic/Extents/Previous/Scale(X/XP)/Window/ <Realtime>:. Enter an option, specify a zoom window, enter a scale value, or press <Enter> to turn on real-time zooming. Descriptions of the command options follow:

All	Displays entire drawing limits (whichever is larger).
Center	Specifies center point and new display magnification.
Dynamic	Permits you to pan a box representing the viewing screen around the entire generated portion of the drawing and enlarge or shrink it in a dynamic, graphic manner.

Extents	Displays current drawing content as large as possible.
Previous	Restores previous view.
Window	Designates rectangular area to be drawn as large as possible. (This is the default option.)
numberX	Sets scale relative to current display (1×).
numberXP	Sets scale relative to paper space units (1×P).
Realtime	zoom in or out of the drawing by moving the cursor vertically up or down.

The Zoom command is used extensively to view objects and details in a complex drawing. It is much easier to add objects and details to a drawing if you zoom in on the area where they are to be placed.

PAN

The **Pan** command gives you the option of moving the display window in any direction, without changing its magnification. The effect of the pan is similar to using either a vertical or horizontal scroll bar (see Figure 4–3). When either the down arrow or the up arrow is selected in the vertical scroll bar, the screen shifts in the direction of the arrow. Moving the arrow in a horizontal scroll bar would move the view to either the left or the right of its current place.

Portions of entities that are not fully displayed on the drawing screen can be displayed with the Pan command. AutoCAD R14 uses the realtime pan option. A hand icon appears when the Pan command is used (see Figure 4-4). In order to use pan, you must select (hold the mouse button down

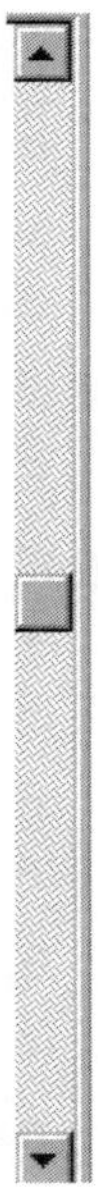

Figure 4–3
Vertical scroll bar.

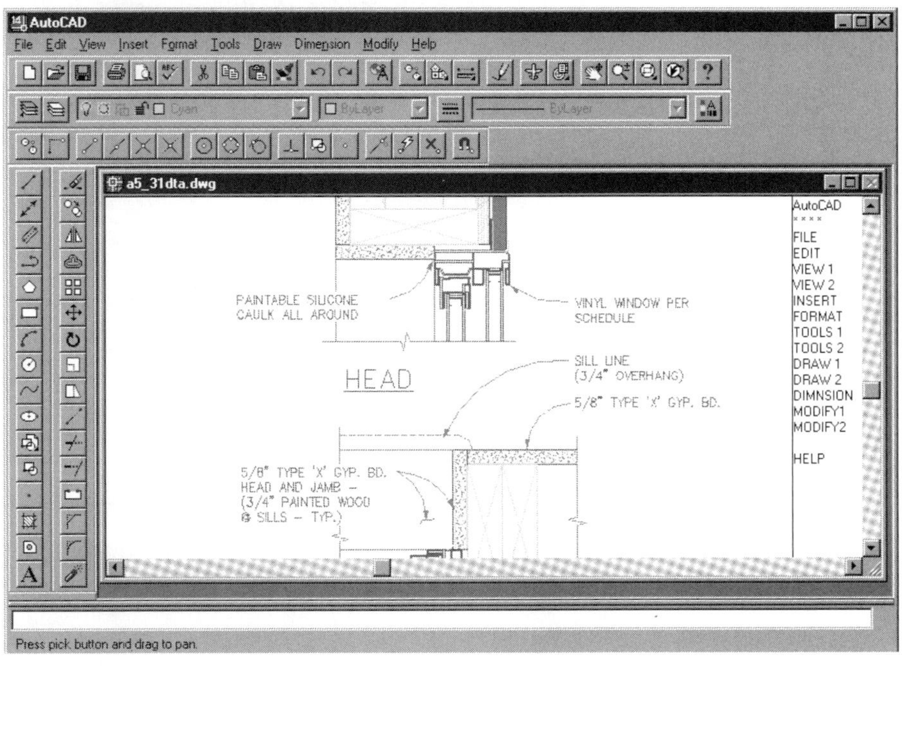

Figure 4–4
Using pan to move to a different point in a drawing.

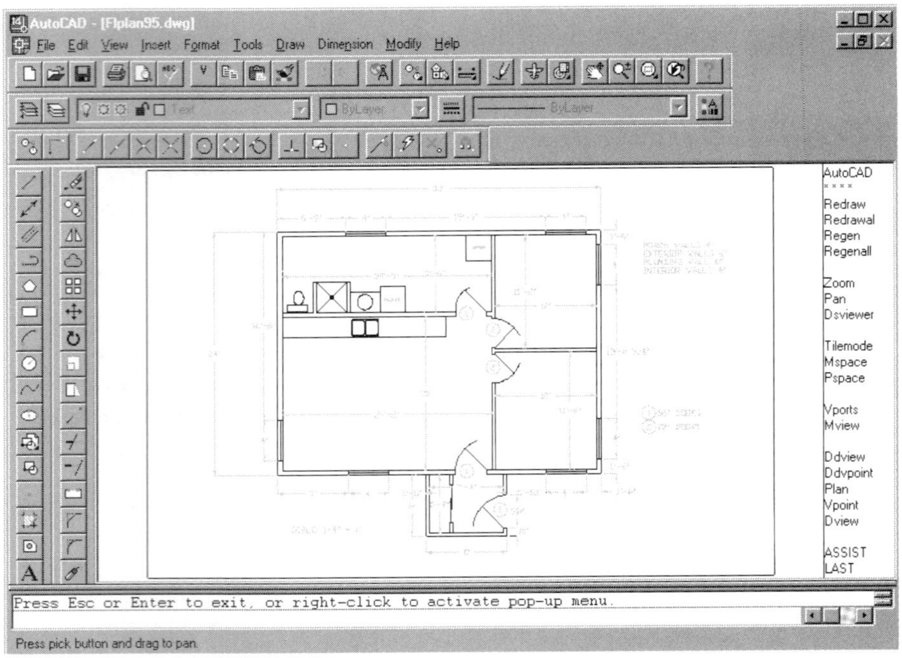

Figure 4–5
Exiting the Pan command.

on) a point in the drawing editor, move the hand icon to a new position, and release the mouse button. To exit the pan, press Esc or Enter, as indicated at the command prompt in Figure 4–5.

Figure 4–6 shows two partial circles being displayed in the drawing editor. The Pan command was used to adjust the screen to show all parts of the circles (see Figure 4–7).

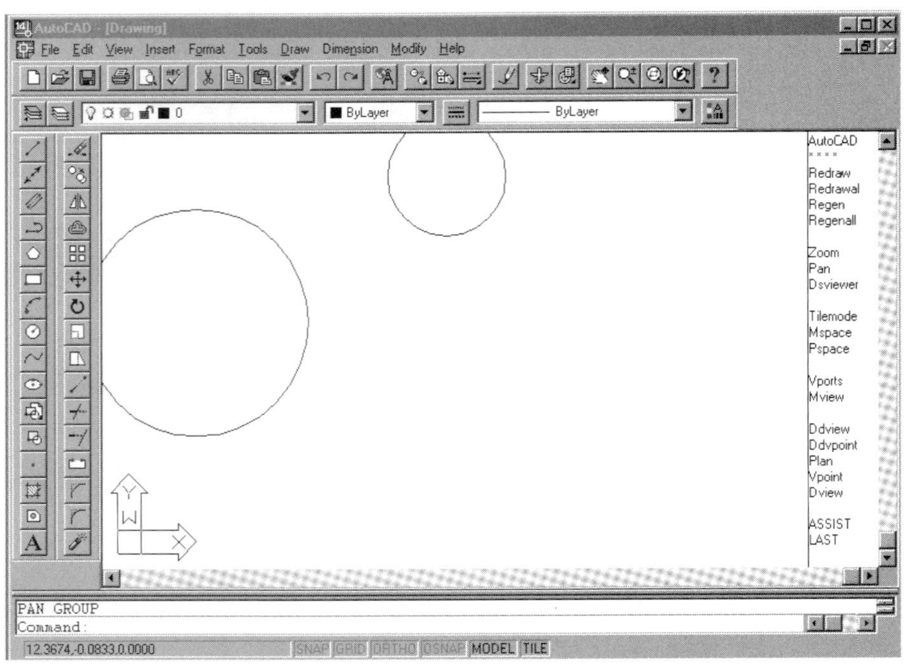

Figure 4–6
Pan command.

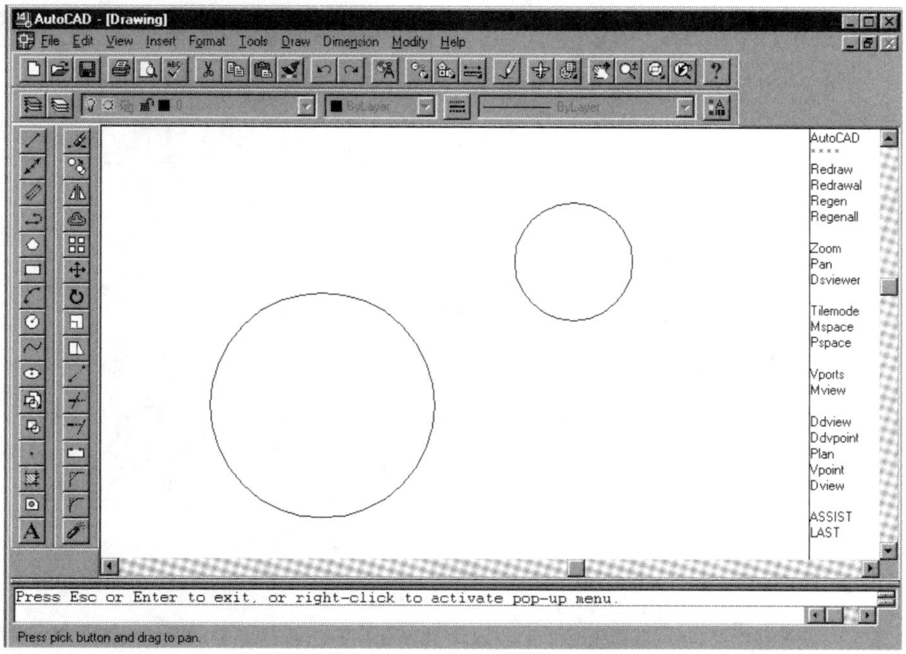

Figure 4–7
Using Pan to adjust the view.

TRY THIS

Open the drawing file pipes.dwg from the AutoCAD/Samples subdirectory and use the realtime pan mode to move about the drawing.

1. Open the existing drawing file pipes.dwg
2. From the View pull-down menu select Pan, then go to the next menu and select Realtime (P, <Enter>).
3. Click and move the hand icon around the drawing to view different parts of the drawing.

AERIAL VIEW

Aerial view is a navigation tool that displays the drawing in a separate window (see Figure 4–8). To access the aerial view, select the icon shown in Figure 4–9, or select Aerial View from the View pull-down menu. If you keep the Aerial View window open, you can zoom and pan without choosing a menu option or entering a command by selecting and moving the pointing device inside the Aerial View window. The pan or zoom view in the drawing responds to the direction of movement of the input device. Pan and zoom icons are also found in the toolbar icon menu of the Aerial View window (see Figure 4–10).

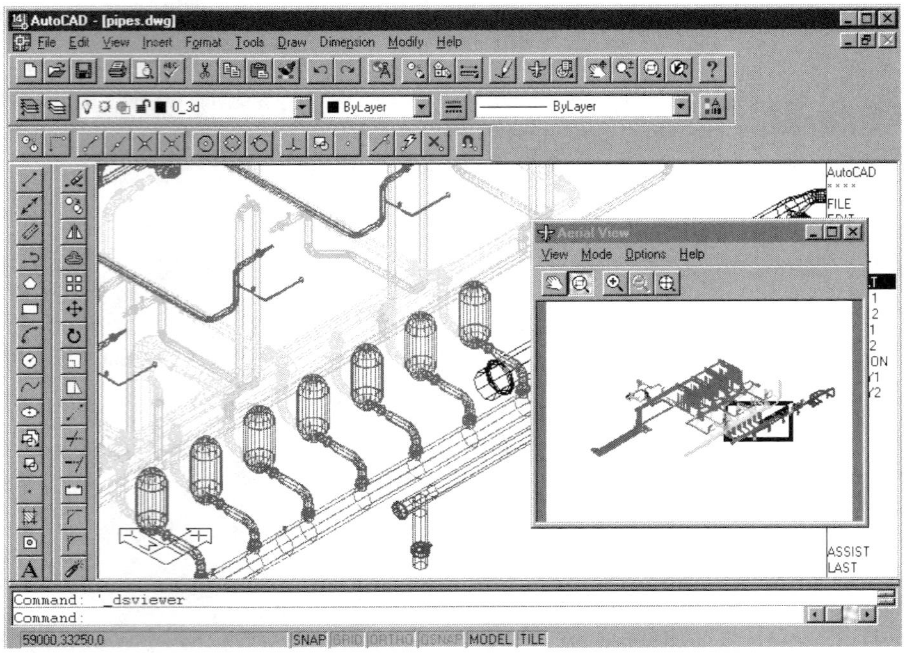

Figure 4–8
Aerial View window.

Figure 4–9
Aerial View icon.

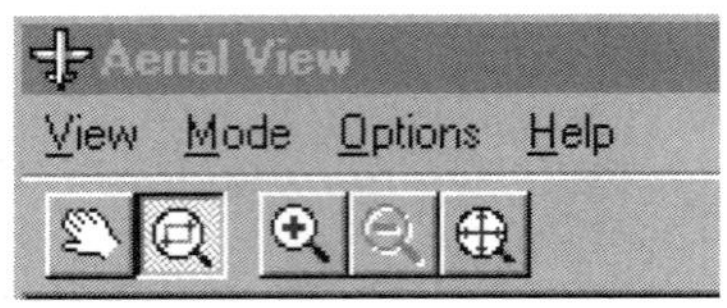

Figure 4–10
Pan and zoom icons in aerial view window.

REDRAW

Any time you create or edit an entity, blip marks appear on the screen. Often the clutter from these blip marks hides part of the drawing entity or creates excess clutter on the screen. The **Redraw** command redraws the current active display screen. When the redraw (r) command is selected, any point entry blips are removed from the screen display. The Redraw command affects only what is seen on the screen; it does not affect any information in the drawing database.

To activate the redraw, choose Redraw from the View pull-down menu, or type command r (redraw) at the prompt.

TRY THIS

See the effects of the Redraw command on the drawing screen.

1. Open AutoCAD and start a drawing from scratch.
2. At the command prompt, type Blipmode, then <Enter>, On.

3. From the Draw pull-down menu select Polygon.
4. Draw an eight-sided polygon.
5. Use the erase command to delete the polygon and then press <Enter>.
6. There should be three blip marks on the screen.
7. Type r (redraw).
8. The blip marks should disappear from the screen.

REGEN

The **Regen** command regenerates the drawing in the active display by recalculating all the entities in the drawing database for optimum display and object selection. Any entities that have been edited, erased, or purged are affected by the Regen command. Regeneration occurs automatically when you change the display of your drawing with some of the zoom or pan operations.

To activate regeneration, choose Regen from the View pull-down menu, or type regen at the command prompt.

ACTIVITY 4–1

View the Tutorial on Improved Interactive Display

Open AutoCAD. Select Start from Scratch to open the drawing editor. From the Help pull-down menu, select What's New. Select the second-row menu option Improved Interactive Display and watch the short tutorial. You should gain a better understanding of the realtime pan and zoom options.

ACTIVITY 4–2

Practice Using the Aerial View Option

Open AutoCAD. Select Open a Drawing, find the Azimuth drawing in the AutoCAD Samples directory, and open it. From the View pull-down menu, select Aerial View. Practice zooming in on various parts of the drawing by moving the window in the Aerial View dialog box (see Figure 4–11).

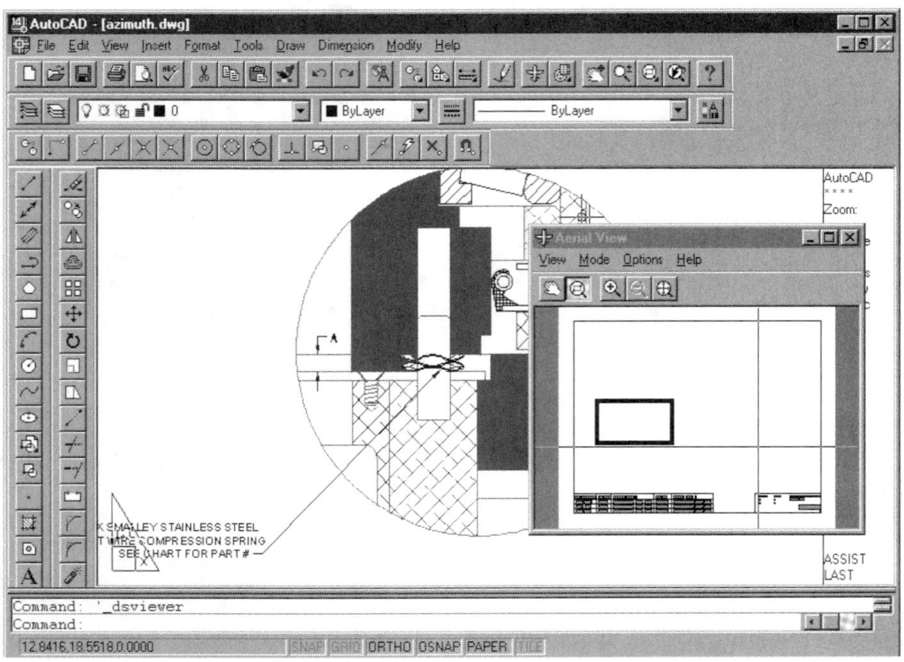

Figure 4–11
Aerial view.

CHAPTER

5

Object Snaps

AFTER READING THIS CHAPTER, YOU WILL BE ABLE TO:

- Use Osnap (object snaps) for locating objects.

KEY CONCEPTS:

Apparent Intersection (appint)
Center (cen)
Endpoint (endp)
Insert (ins)
Intersect (int)
Midpoint (mid)
Nearest (nea)
Node
Perpendicular (per)
Quadrant (qua)
Quick
Tangent (tan)

INTRODUCTION

Object snaps are functions that help locate objects by snapping exactly to specific points on an existing object.

AutoCAD has several drawing aids that have been built into the program to help you create accurate, precise drawings. One group of functions that is extremely valuable for creating accurate drawings is the Osnap (object snaps) functions. These are functions that help locate objects by snapping exactly to specific points on existing objects. For example, you can snap to the center point of a circle, the midpoint of a line, or the intersection of two lines. The various Osnap functions are listed in the Key Concepts. The object snaps are an easy way to locate the exact position of an object without knowing coordinate points.

The object snaps functions can be typed in at the command prompt, selected from the toolbar, or selected from the screen menu on the right side of the drawing editor. Typically, the OSNAP toolbar is not displayed. In order to display the OSNAP toolbar icon, go to the View pull-down menu and select Toolbars. The dialog box for the various toolbars that can be displayed appears. Selecting the OSNAP toolbar produces the screen shown in Figure 5–1.

Object Snap Functions

Endpoint (endp)	Snaps to the closest endpoint of an object such as a line or arc.
Midpoint (mid)	Snaps to midpoint of a line or arc.
Intersect (int)	Snaps to the intersection of objects such as lines, circles, arcs, and splines.
App Int (appint or app)	Snaps to the intersection of two objects that do not intersect each other in 3D space but might appear to on the screen.
Center (cen)	Snaps to the center of an arc, circle, or ellipse.
Quadrant (qua)	Snaps to the closest quadrant of an arc, circle, or ellipse. Another way to say it will snap to the 0, 90, 180, 270 degree points.
Node (node)	Snaps to a point drawn with the Point command.
Insert (ins)	Snaps to the insertion point of a block, shape, text, attribute, or attribute definition.
Perpend (per)	Snaps to a point that forms a perpendicular alignment with another object. Used with lines, circles, ellipses, splines, and arcs.
Tangent (tan)	Snaps to the point on a circle or arc that when is connected, forms a line tangent to that point (Autodesk, Inc., 1997).
Nearest (nea)	Snaps to a point that is closest to the specified point.
Quick (qui)	Snaps to the nearest point it can find.
None (none)	Turns off the object snap mode.

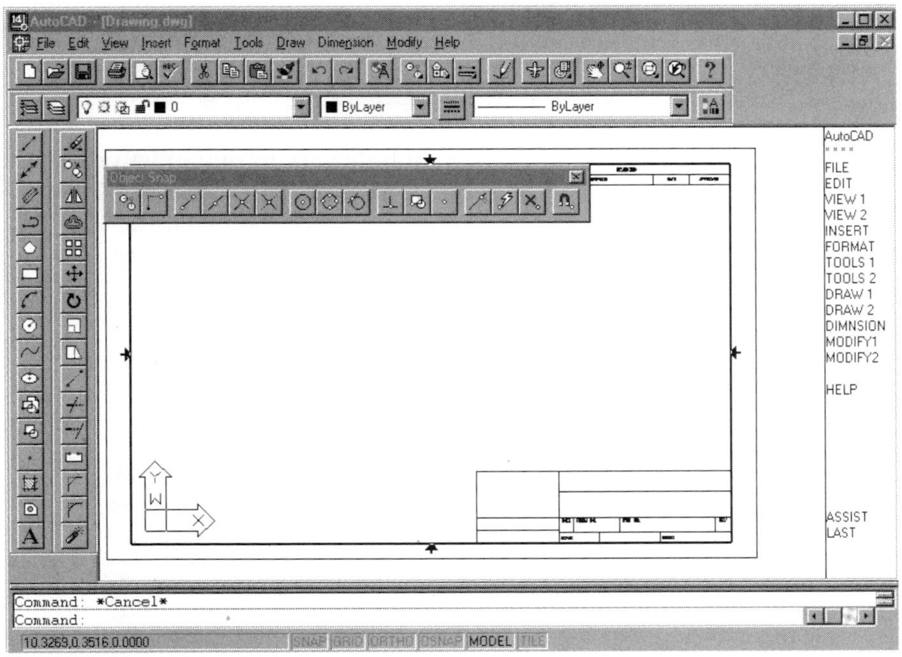

Figure 5–1
Osnap toolbar.

Running object snap-One or more object snaps that are on continuously.

An object snap that is on continuously is called a **running object snap**. More than one object snap can be turned on at one time. In order to turn a running object snap on, go to the Tools pull-down menu and select Object Snap Settings. A dialog box similar to the one in Figure 5–2 should appear. Pressing the F3 function key will also cause the Running Osnap dialog box to appear. Click in each blank box to turn on that particular Osnap.

Now, let us examine some of the most important osnap functions.

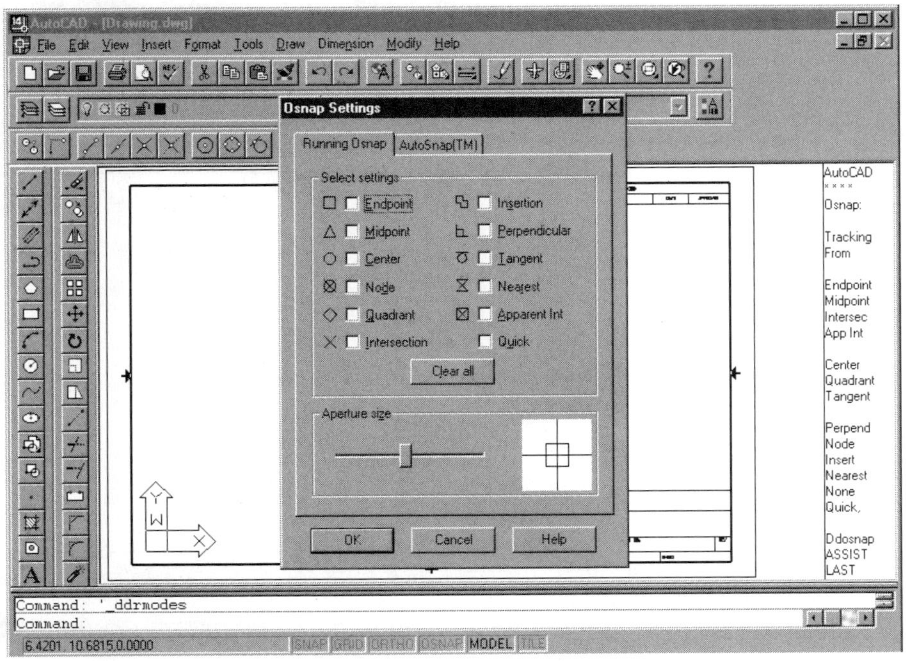

Figure 5–2
Osnap settings dialog box.

ENDPOINT

It is often necessary to find exact points after you have edited a drawing or created entities. In the example in Figure 5–3, an arc was to be drawn from the endpoint of two parallel lines. The easiest way to find the start and endpoint of the arc is to use the **Endpoint** Osnap function, using the following procedure.

Command: Arc (a)	
Center/(Start Point):	endp (When the cursor is moved near the endpoint of each line, it is easy to select where the arc will start and end.)
Center/End/(Second Point):	endp
End Point:	Select a point with the pointing device.

TRY THIS

Create an arc of any size, and draw two lines from the endpoints of the arc.

1. Use the Advanced Setup wizard.
2. In Step 5 make sure you set your paper size to 15.5 × 10.
3. In Step 6 select the ANSI_B.dwt template.

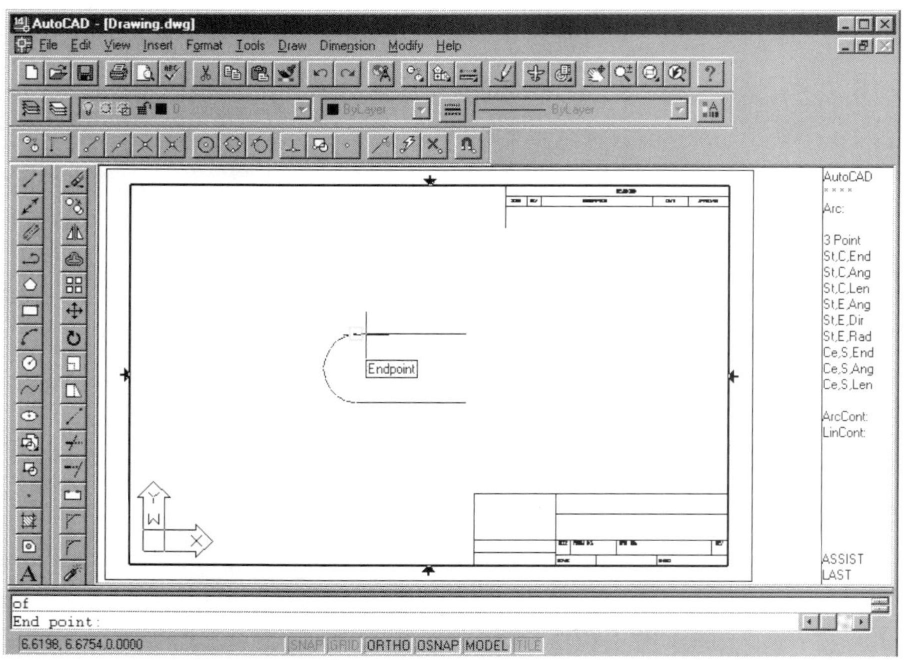

Figure 5–3
Using Osnap Endpoint to connect an arc to two lines.

4. Using the Arc toolbar icon, create an arc near the center of the drawing editor.
5. Draw two lines, each 1″ long, from each endpoint of the arc. Locate the endpoints of each arc with the **endp Osnap** command.

MIDPOINT

The **Midpoint (mid)** object snap command is used to snap to the middle of objects such as arcs and lines. It is used when you want to create a line or other object from the midpoint of an existing arc or line. In Figure 5–4 a horizontal line was to be drawn across the middle of the rectangle. Osnap Midpoint (mid) was used to find the starting point of the line as well as the endpoint of the line. When the cursor was placed at any point on the line, the midpoint was automatically located. The midpoint was indicated by a yellow triangle-shaped icon.

The command sequence for creating the horizontal line in the rectangle in Figure 5–4 was as follows:

Command:	l (line)
LINE From point:	mid (midpoint) Select any point on the right vertical line.
To point:	mid (midpoint) Select any point on the left vertical line.
To point:	<Enter>

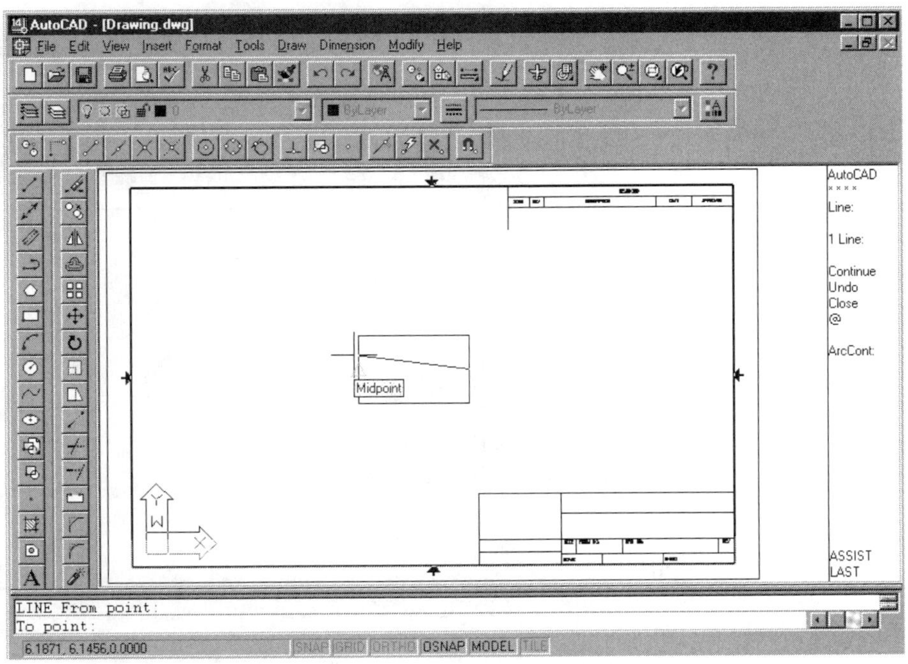

Figure 5–4
Using Osnap Midpoint.

TRY THIS

Create two horizontal lines 2.75″ long and draw a vertical line from the midpoint of each line. Draw the horizontal lines from two different X plane coordinates.

1. Use the Advanced Setup wizard to create a border and title block (ANSI_B) for a B-size (17 × 11) drawing. Set the paper size to 15.5 × 10.
2. Set the grid spacing to 0.5.
3. Set the snap to 0.25.
4. Select the line icon.
5. At the From point: command, enter 3,3.
6. At the To point: command, type 5.75, 3.
7. Press <Enter> twice (once to cancel the command and once to restart the command).
8. At the From point: command, enter 5,5.
9. At the To point: command, type 7.75, 5.
10. Press <Enter> twice (once to cancel the command and once to restart the command).
11. At the From point: command, type mid and select any point on the lower line.
12. At the To point: command, type mid and select any point on the upper line.

Your drawing should look similar to Figure 5-5.

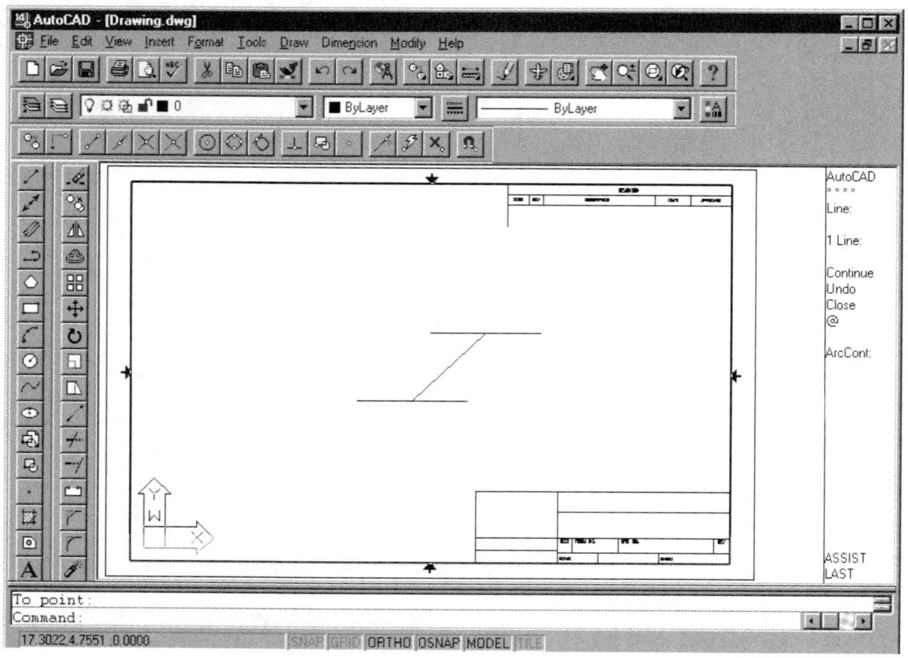

Figure 5-5
Using Osnap Midpoint to draw a line between two parallel lines.

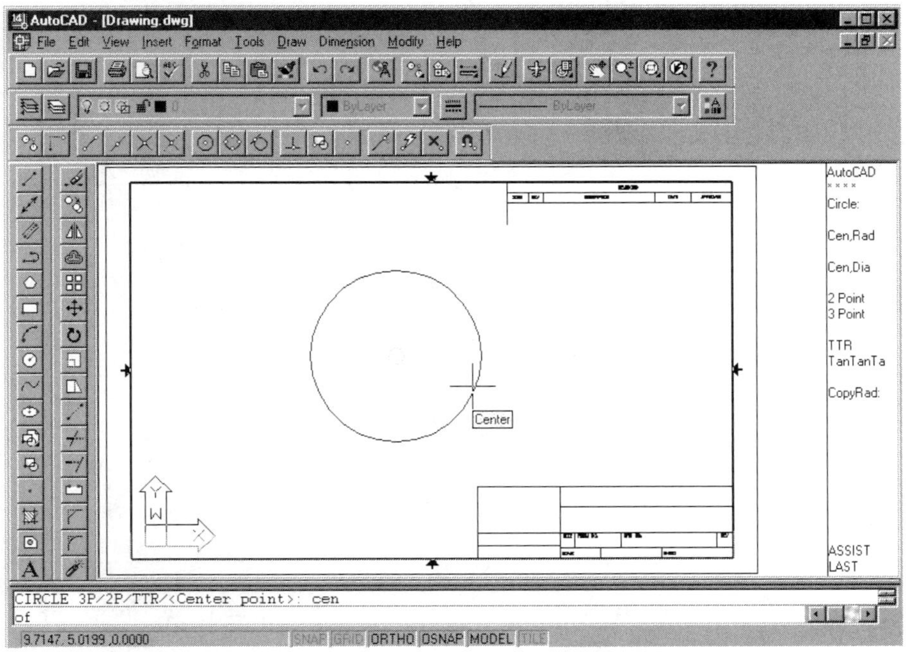

Figure 5–6
Locating the center of the circle with Osnap Center.

CENTER

The **Center (cen)** object snap command is useful for locating the centers of arcs, circles, or true ellipses. In order to snap to the center of an object, you must select some part of the visible entity. In Figure 5–6, the center (cen) object snap is being used to locate a smaller circle inside a larger circle. Both circles will have the same center.

INTERSECTION

The **Intersection (int)** object snap command snaps to the intersections of objects such as lines, circles, arcs, and splines. If you want to create an entity from the point where two objects intersect, the intersection (int) object snap will automatically find the intersection. In Figure 5–7, a diagonal line was drawn from the intersection of the horizontal and perpendicular. Osnap Intersection (int) was used to locate the point where the two objects crossed each other.

TRY THIS

Draw four diagonal lines from the intersection of two 6″ lines that are perpendicular to each other.

1. Use the Advanced Setup wizard to create a border and title block (ANSI_B) for a B-size (17 × 11) drawing. Set the paper size to 15.5 × 10.

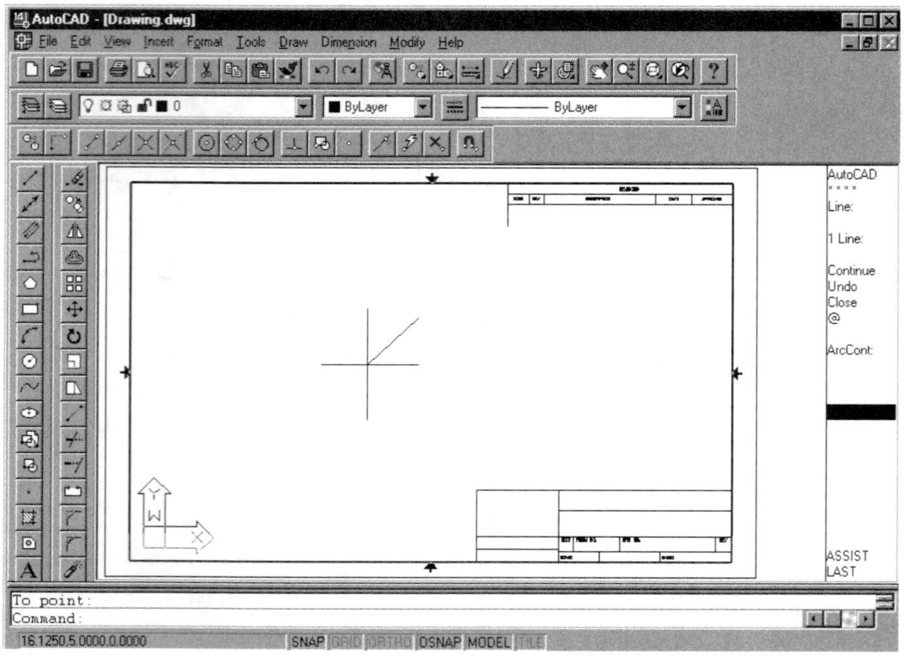

Figure 5–7
Intersection osnap.

2. Set the grid spacing to 0.5.
3. Set the snap to 0.25.
4. Create two 6″ lines whose intersection is 8,5.
5. Use intersec object snap to draw four 3″ diagonal lines that bisect each quadrant and whose common endpoint is the intersection of the original horizontal and perpendicular lines.

Your object should look similar to Figure 5–8.

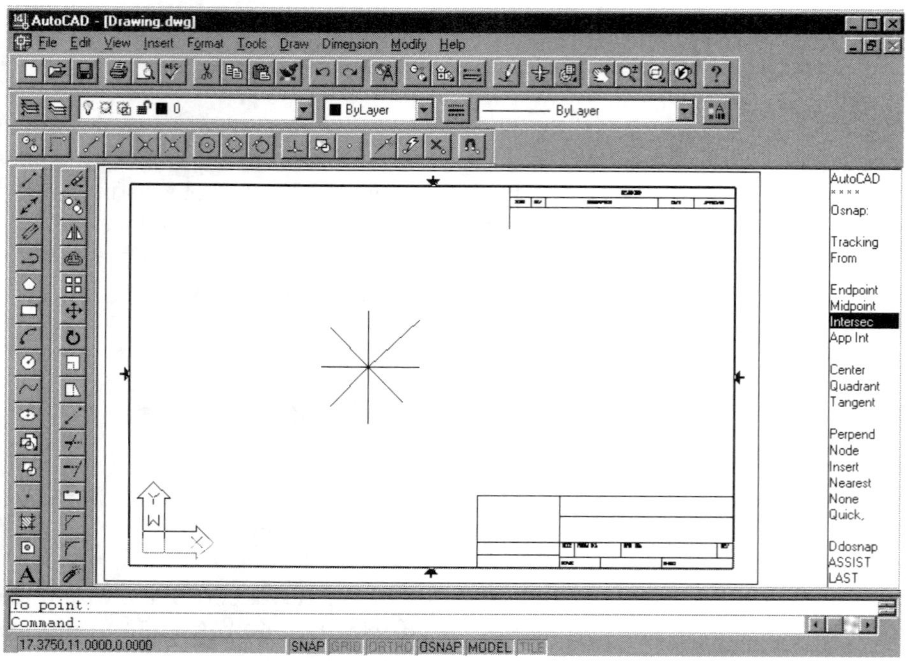

Figure 5–8
Using Osnap Intersec to create multiple lines from an intersection.

PERPENDICULAR

The **Perpend (per)** object snap command snaps to a point that is perpendicular (90°) to another object or to an imaginary extension of that object. The perpendicular object snap can be used to find a starting point or an ending point.

TRY THIS

Use the Perpend object snap to intersect a line at a 90° angle.

1. Start AutoCAD.
2. Select Start from Scratch at the Start Up dialog box.
3. Draw a line 3″ long at a 45° angle. Start the line at 4,4.
4. Draw another line with the starting point of 6.5,4.
5. Use the Perpendicular (per) object snap to connect to the original line.

The drawing should look similar to Figure 5–9.

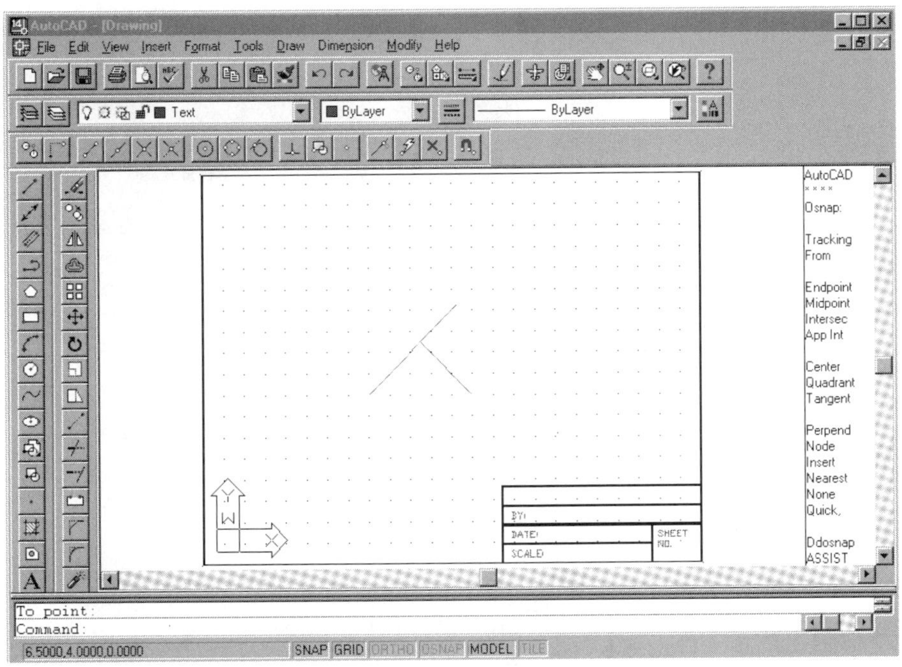

Figure 5–9
Using Osnap Perpend to create a perpendicular line.

QUADRANT

The **Quadrant (qua)** object snap command is used to snap to the closest point of an arc, circle, or ellipse. There are four quadrants, thus four quadrant points: 0, 90, 180, and 270.

TRY THIS

Create two circles of dissimilar sizes and draw lines connecting the circles using quadrant object snap.

1. Start AutoCAD.
2. From the Start Up dialog box, select Start from Scratch.
3. Create two circles. Place the center point of one circle at 2.5,3 with a radius of 1. Place the center of the second circle at 6,3 with a radius of .5.
4. Using the quadrant object snap command, draw a line from the 90° quadrant point of each circle.
5. Using the quadrant object snap command, draw a line from the 270° quadrant point of each circle.

The drawing should look similar to Figure 5–10.

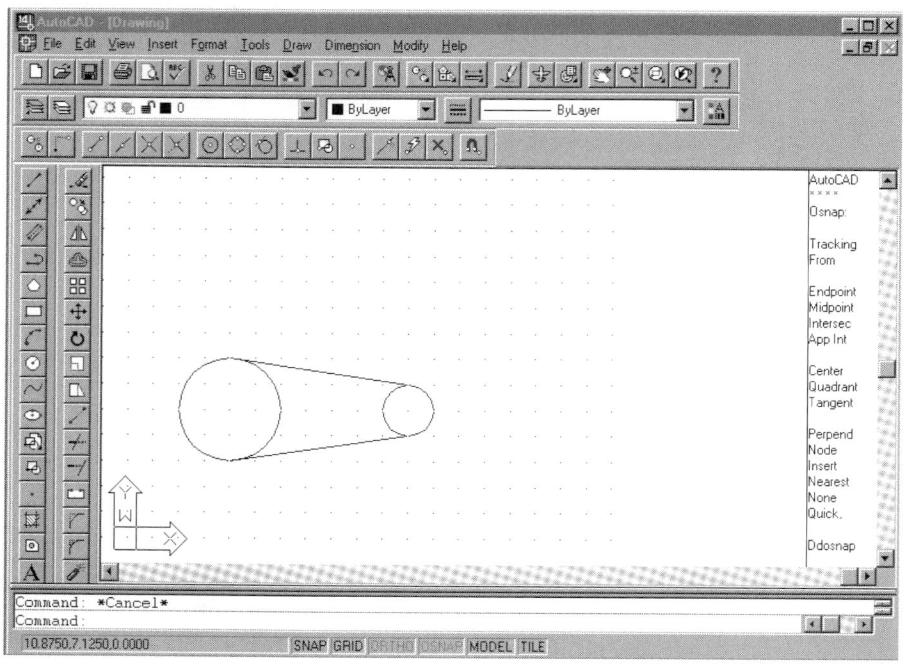

Figure 5–10
Using Osnap Quadrant to draw lines between two circles.

TANGENT

The **Tangent (tan)** object snap command snaps to the point of a circle or arc, that when connected to the last point creates a line tangent to that object (AutoDesk, 1997). For instance, if you want to draw a line tangent to a circle from a point, use the tangent object snap when selecting the circle or arc to which you want to connect. In Figure 5–11, two lines tangent to a circle were drawn from a single point.

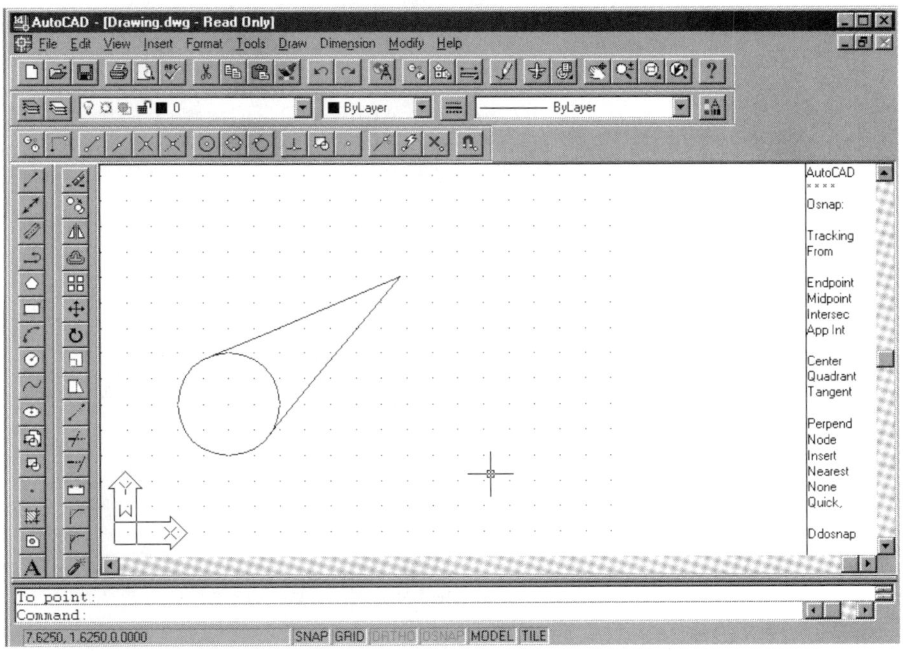

Figure 5–11
Using Osnap Tangent to draw lines tangent to a circle from a point.

Activity 5–1

View a Multimedia Presentation on Quick Precision Drawing

Open the AutoCAD software program and select Start from Scratch. Select What's New from the Help pull-down menu. At the main menu, select Quick Precision Drawing. Finally, select Object Snap Enhancements. Let the multimedia presentation run on its own, or step through the presentation at a pace you prefer.

Activity 5–2

Practice Using Object Snaps

This activity was designed for you to practice your use of object snaps by replicating the drawing in Figure 5–12 on p. 75. Be sure to label all entities. Use the following procedure:

1. Start AutoCAD, and at the Start Up dialog box, select Use a Template.
2. Select the A-size template you created in Chapter 2.
3. Check your layer settings to be sure they are set correctly.
4. Draw all entities in model space.
5. Place all geometric figures on the OBJ layer.
6. Place all text on the TXT layer.
7. When you have finished drawing, save the activity as Act5-1.

Plotter Paper Size:	A	
Suggested Settings:	Grid	0.50″
	Snap	0.125″
	Layers (7)	**0** (default border)
		Cen, Linetype center, Color: cyan
		Dim, Linetype continuous, Color: green
		Hid, Linetype hidden, Color: magenta
		Object, Linetype continuous, Color: black
		Tbk, Linetype continuous, Color: red
		Text, Linetype continuous, Color: green

Hints:

1. Open your border template file for an A-size drawing. After it has loaded, use the SAVEAS command to rename the drawing file ACT5-1. Use Figure 5–12 on p. 75 as the model for the drawing.
2. Make sure you are in model space before you begin drawing the objects.
3. Be sure to check layer settings before you begin to draw or enter text.
4. Use the Osnap commands to create the entities.
5. Remember to save the drawing.

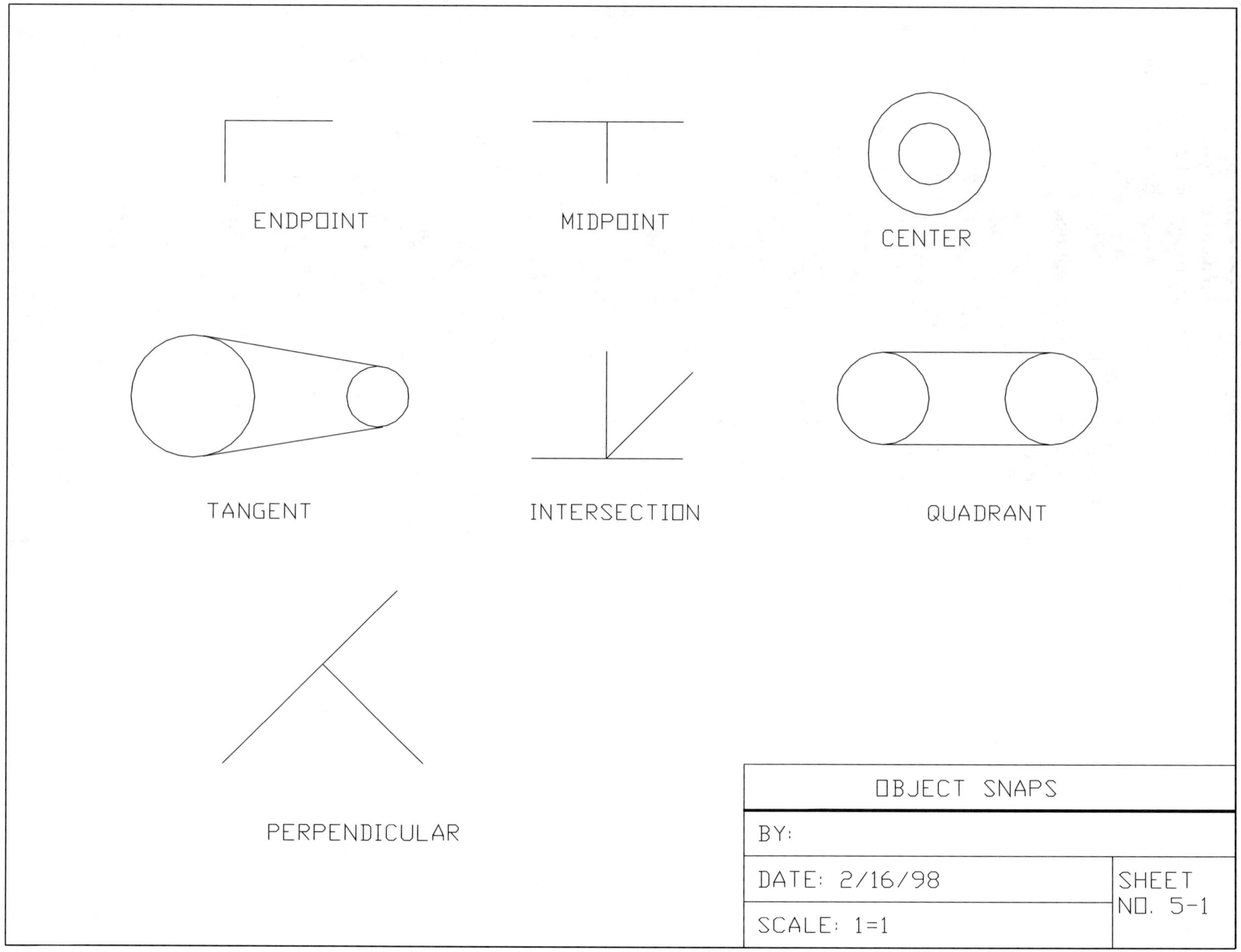

Figure 5–12
Activity 5–2

CHAPTER

6

Edit Commands

AFTER READING THIS CHAPTER, YOU WILL BE ABLE TO:

- Understand and use various editing commands to make changes to your drawing(s).

KEY CONCEPTS:

- Array
- Break
- Chamfer
- Copy (Co)
- Ddedit
- Erase (E)
- Explode
- Extend
- Fillet
- Mirror
- Move (M)
- Offset
- Oops
- Pedit
- Rotate
- Scale
- Stretch
- Trim

EDITING ENTITIES

In the design phase of creating a drawing, it is sometimes necessary to edit the objects created. There are several commands in AutoCAD for editing. Common editing commands include Break, Ddedit, Erase, Explode, Extend, Move, Oops, Pedit, Rotate, Scale, Stretch, and Trim. Edit commands can be selected from the Modify pull-down menu (see Figure 6–1), from two options, **Modify1** and **Modify2**, in the screen menu, or from the modify toolbar (see Figure 6–2).

SELECTION SETS

Before objects can be edited, a selection set needs to be created. A selection set may be a single object or a group of objects. A variety of selection modes are available for creating a selection set, as described in the following list:

All	Selects all entities on thawed layers. To use the filter list, you must define Point1 and Point2 as dummy arguments.
Crossing	Selects objects within and crossing a rectangular area whose corners are defined by Point1 and Point2.
CrossingPolygon	Selects objects within and crossing an area defined by an array of points in Point1. To use the filter list, you must define Point2 as a dummy argument.

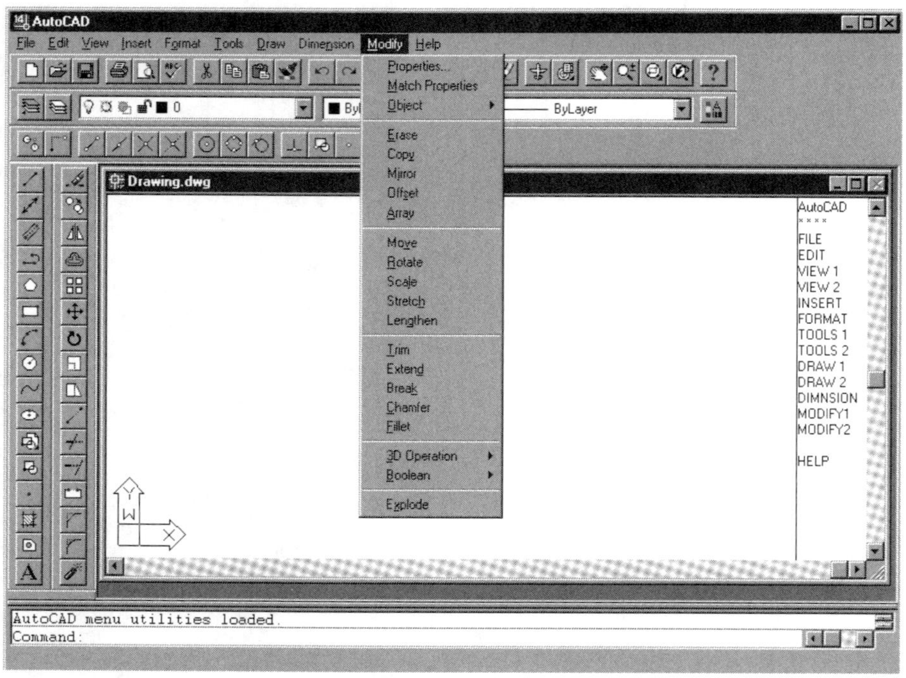

Figure 6–1
Modify pull-down menu.

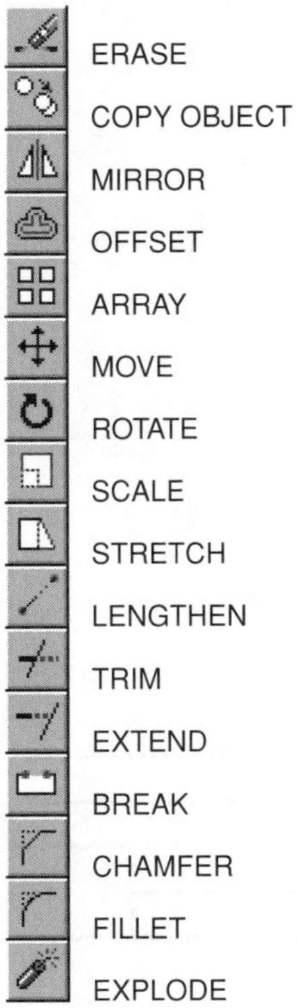

Figure 6–2
Modify toolbar.

Fence	Selects all entities crossing a selection fence. Point1 contains an array of points defining the fence. To use the filter list, you must define Point2 as a dummy argument.
Last	Selects the most recently created visible entity. To use the filter list, you must define Point1 and Point2 as dummy arguments.
Previous	Selects the most recent selection set. This mode is ignored if you switch between paper and model space and attempt to use the selection set. To use the filter list, you must define Point1 and Point2 as dummy arguments.
Window	Selects all entities completely inside a rectangular area whose corners are defined by Point1 and Point2.
WindowPolygon	Selects objects within a polygon defined by an array of points in Point1. To use the filter list, you must define Point2 as a dummy argument.

The two most common methods for selecting objects are to use the pickbox (see Figure 6–3) or to use a window that is created when an edit command is selected.

A **selection window** is rectangular in shape, and the objects within the window are defined by picking two opposing corners. Typically the entire object must be enclosed within the window for it to be selected. However, various window options affect how objects will be selected within a window. For example, in Figure 6–4 we wanted to erase some of the smaller interior rectangles, so we used the following sequence:

Command: E (erase)

Select Objects: pick point (The lower left corner of the window was selected.)

Select Objects: Other corner: pick point (The upper right corner was selected.)

All the entities located within the rectangular box would be erased when the commands were executed.

If a **crossing window (c)** is used, any part of an object that is located within the rectangular window set is selected. This means that even if part of the object was outside the window set, it would still be selected. The **pickbox** is used to select single entities.

If objects are selected before the editing command is used, **grips** (blue boxes that indicate control points) appear on the entity selected. In Figure 6–5

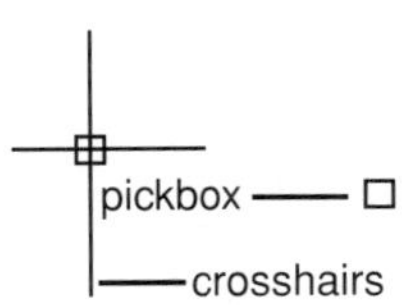

Figure 6–3
Pickbox symbol.

When you choose an editing command, AutoCAD prompts you to select objects and replaces the crosshairs with a pickbox. You select individual objects with the pointing device or by using the methods described in this section.

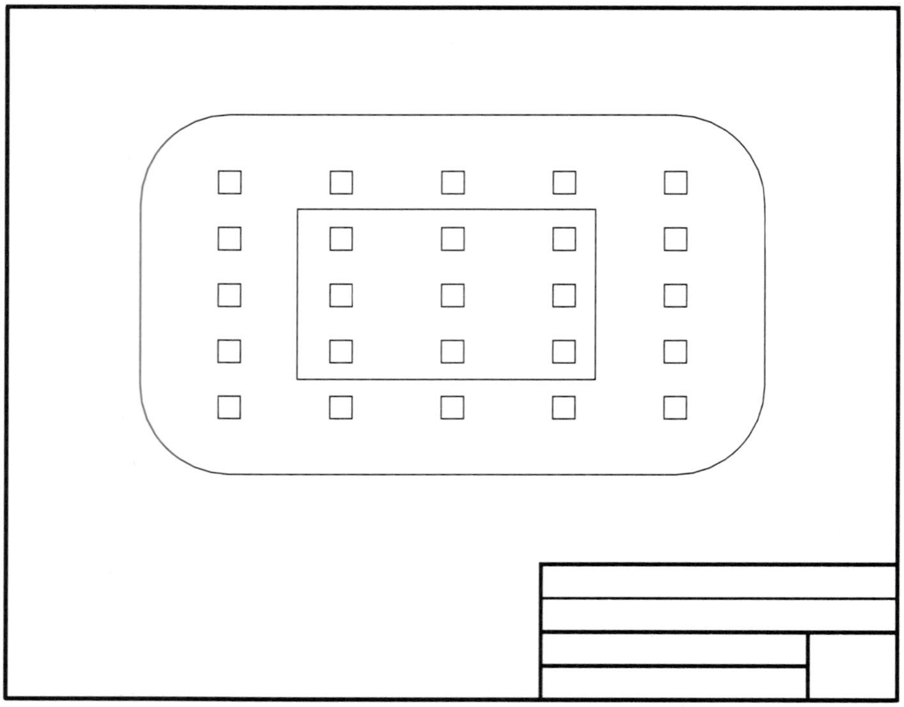

Figure 6–4
Making a window selection set.

there are three blue grip boxes. The line on which the boxes appear was selected prior to the selection of an editing command. Grips mark control locations on a selected object. Grips can be turned on or off by selecting **Grips** in the Tools pull-down menu. Once the object has been selected, you can select the editing command that you want to use.

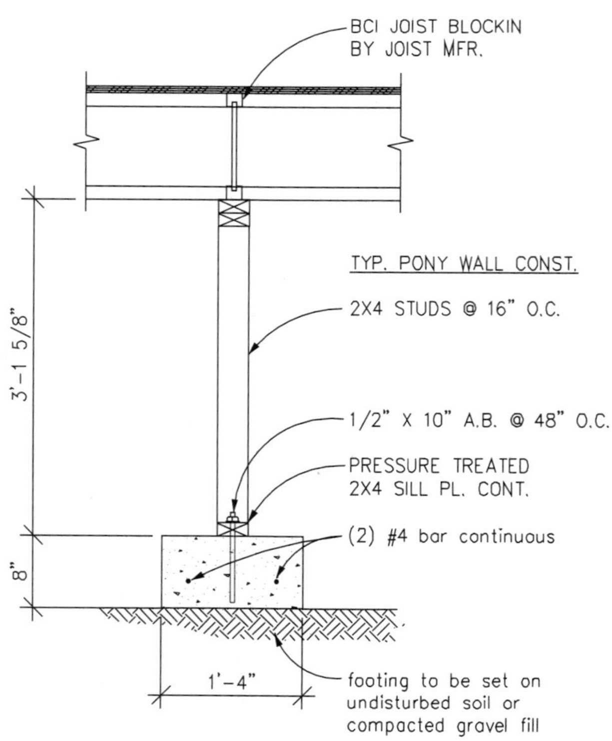

Figure 6–5
Grips.

EDIT COMMANDS

Break

To **break** an entity means to remove a portion of the entity between two points. If the Break command is used to remove a portion of a circle, the order in which points are picked will determine what part of the entity remains. Figure 6–6 illustrates the difference that direction makes in the selection of break points. If you break a circle, it changes to an arc by deleting the portion from the first point to the second, going counterclockwise. In order to break an object, select the object by pointing to it. The break begins at the selection point and ends at the second point selected.

To **break** an entity means to remove a portion of the entity between two points.

TRY THIS

Break two circles, one in a clockwise direction and the other in a counter-clockwise direction.

1. Open a new AutoCAD drawing, using Start from Scratch.
2. Create two circles 2″ in diameter. Position them like those shown in Figure 6-6.
3. From the Modify pull-down menu, select Break.
4. Break the circle on the left using a clockwise motion, left to right.
5. Break the circle on the right using a counterclockwise motion, right to left.

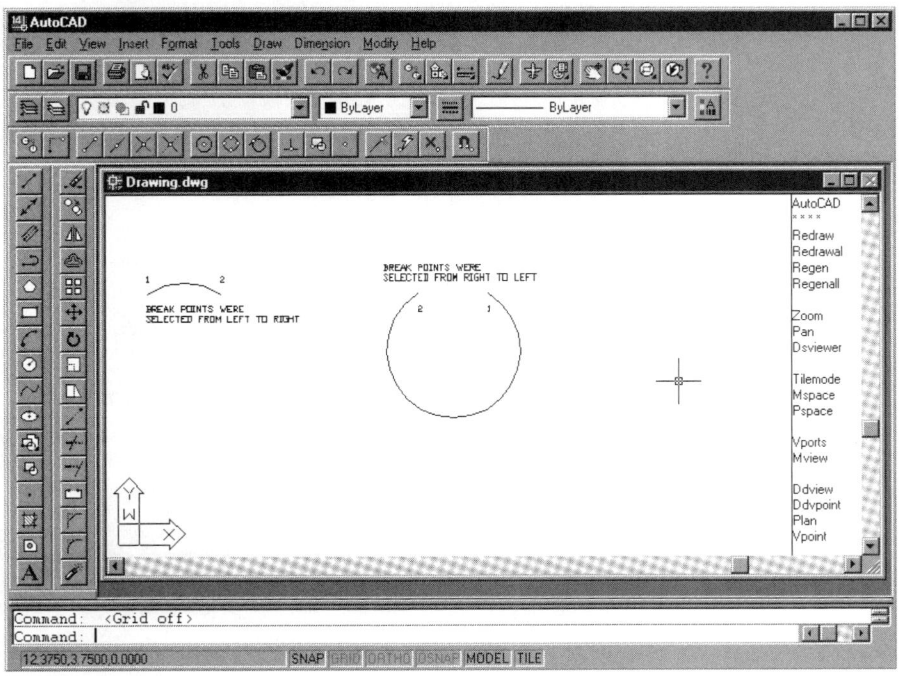

Figure 6–6
Using the Break command to break a circle.

Erase/Oops

The **Erase** command deletes objects. If erase is used to delete an object drawn with the line command, single lines of the object will be deleted. However, an object drawn with a polyline or a form thereof is considered a group and if it is selected, all parts of the object disappear (see Figure 6–7). The shortcut key for erase is (E).

The opposite of the erase command is **Oops**. If an object or portion of an object is mistakenly erased, the Erase command can be undone by typing oops. The Oops command can be used only immediately after the Erase command. As seen in Figure 6–7, the Oops command is found in the screen menu with the erase command.

TRY THIS

Use the Erase command to delete objects, and use the Oops command to undo the Erase command.

1. Open a new AutoCAD drawing, using Start from Scratch.
2. Draw two lines perpendicular to each other.
3. Draw a rectangle using the Rectangle command.
4. From the Modify pull-down menu, select Erase.
5. Using the pixel box that represents the cursor, select either the horizontal or the perpendicular line to delete it.
6. Also pick one line on the rectangle to erase the whole object.

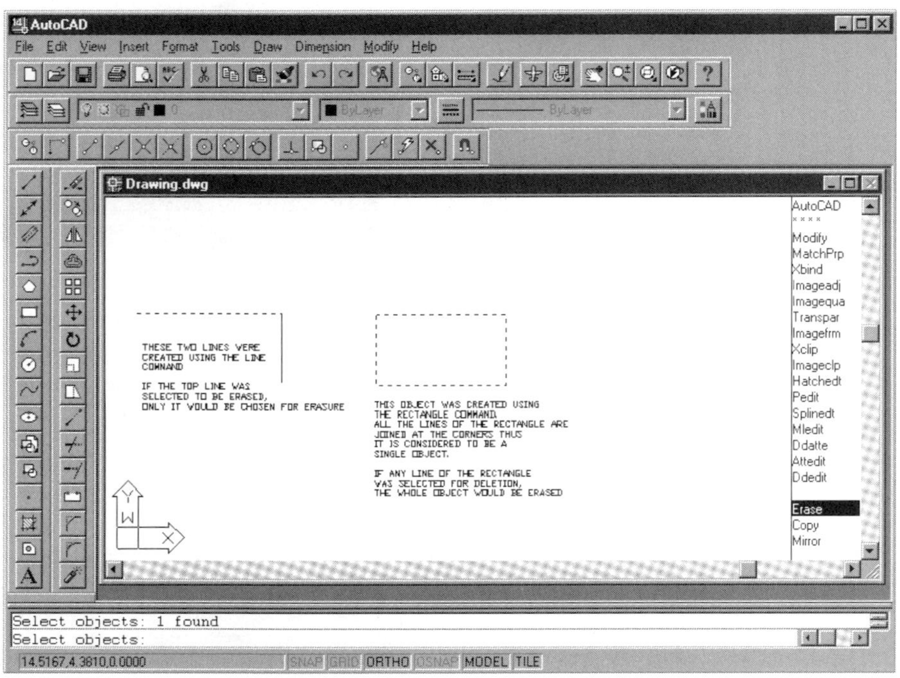

Figure 6–7
Erasing a single line and a rectangle that is a polyline.

7. Press <Enter> to complete the command.

Depending on the line that you selected, it should disappear as should the rectangle when you press <Enter> to finish the command.

Explode

Explode separates a compound object into individual objects.

The **Explode** command is used to edit a compound object. A compound object comprises more than one AutoCAD object. For example, an object that is created with a polyline is a compound object. Common 2D objects that are exploded for editing purposes include solids, blocks, dimensions, multilines, and polylines. In the previous example a rectangle was erased when one line of the rectangle was selected. If the rectangle was exploded instead, then it would comprise four separate lines, not a polyline.

TRY THIS

Explode a rectangle.

1. Open a new AutoCAD drawing, using Start from Scratch.
2. From the pull-down Draw menu, select Rectangle.
3. Create a rectangle that has a lower left corner at 1,1 and an upper right corner of 5,4.
4. From the Modify pull-down menu, select Explode.
5. Using the pixel box, pick one line of the rectangle.
6. From the Modify pull-down menu, select Erase.
7. Using the pixel box, pick on any line of the rectangle. Only that line should be erased, not the whole rectangle.

Extend

Extend lengthens one object to join another.

The **Extend** command allows an object to be lengthened to join another. Extend is used when one object falls short of another and the objects need to be joined. Executing the command requires the selection of a boundary edge first (see Figure 6–8) and then an object or portion of an object (see Figure 6–9) that will intersect the boundary selected.

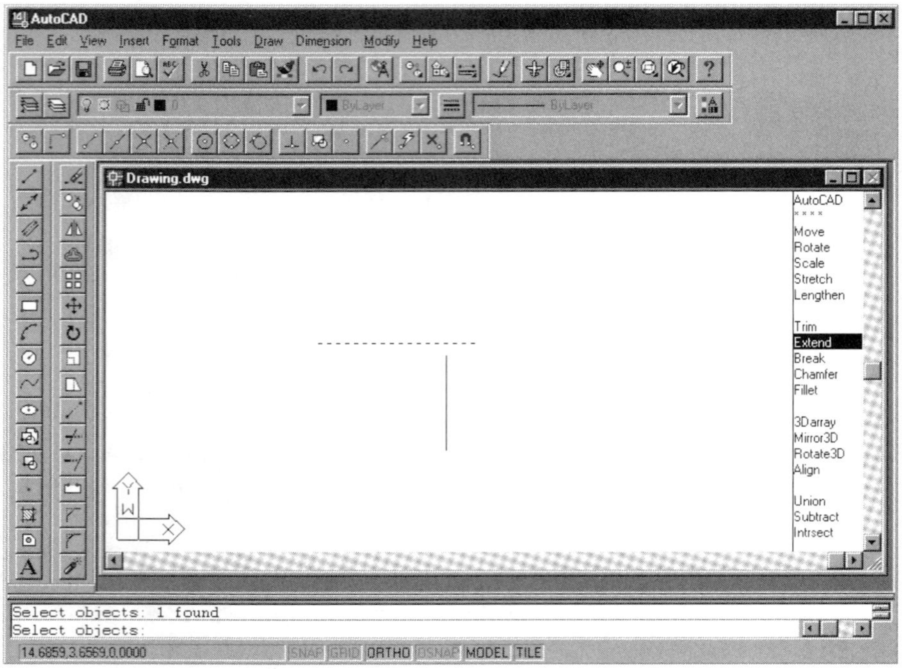

Figure 6–8
Selecting a boundary edge for the Extend command.

TRY THIS

Draw two lines that do not touch or do not close an object.

1. Open a new AutoCAD drawing, using Start from Scratch.
2. From the Draw pull-down menu, select Line to create two lines. Make sure the lines do not intersect or touch one another, as in Figure 6–8.
3. From the Modify pull-down menu, select Extend.

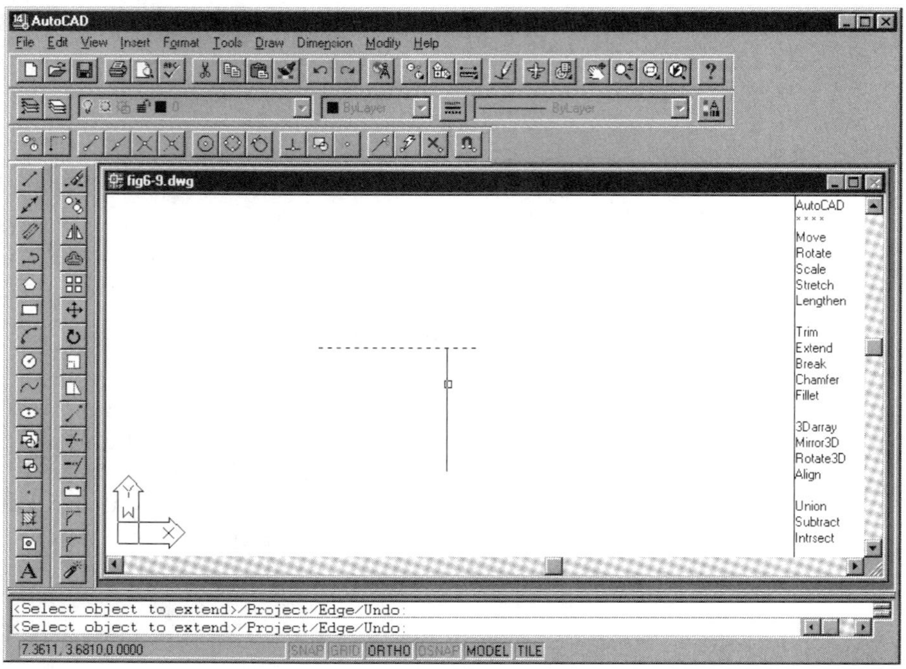

Figure 6–9
Extending a line to intersect the boundary edge.

4. In Figure 6–8, the horizonital line is the boundry line, and the vertical line would be the entity extended to meet the horizonital line.
5. Select the horizontal line as the boundary edge.
6. Select the vertical line as the line to extend.

After completion of the command, the vertical line should be touching the horizontal line.

Trim

The **Trim** command is used for editing objects in a drawing so they end precisely at a "cutting edge." One or more other objects in the drawing define a cutting edge. The Trim command is often used where portions of an object extend past a boundary edge. The command sequence for trim is as follows:

Command: Trim <Enter>

Select Objects: Pick a cutting edge (entity that acts as a boundary line). <Enter>

<Select object to trim>/Project/Edge/Undo: Select that portion of the entity you want to trim. <Enter>

In Figure 6–10 the two vertical parallel lines were chosen as the cutting edges or planes. Since it was determined that the horizontal line between the two vertical lines was to be removed, that portion of the line between the two vertical lines was selected. The result is depicted in Figure 6–11.

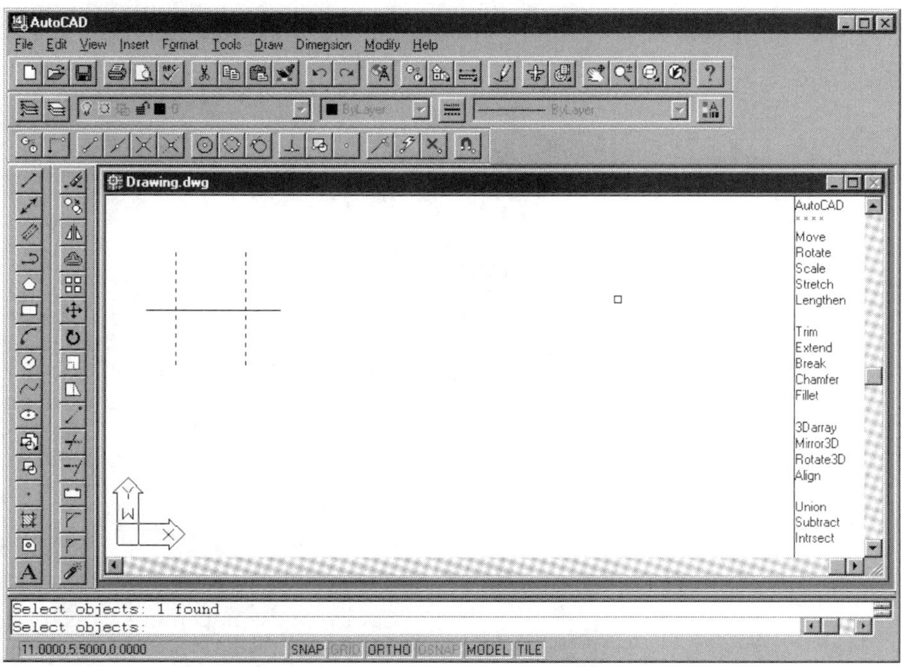

Figure 6–10
Selecting cutting-plane lines.

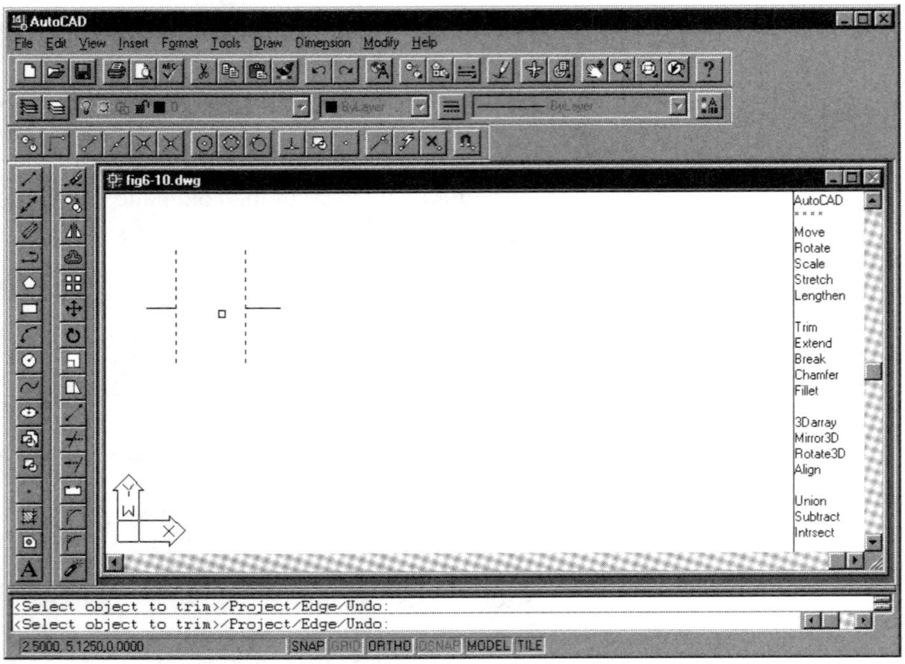

Figure 6–11
Using the Trim command to remove lines between two cutting planes.

TRY THIS

Create a tic-tac-toe pattern and trim it so that all you have left is a rectangle.

1. Open a new AutoCAD drawing, using Start from Scratch.
2. From the pull-down Draw menu, select Line or Multiline to create the tic-tac-toe pattern.
3. After the pattern has been created, go to the Modify pull-down menu and select Trim.
4. Select the appropriate cutting planes and trim lines to end up with a rectangle.

Move

The **Move** command is used to move one or more objects to a new location. A single keystroke **(m)** activates the move command. At the command prompt, enter move or select Move from the Modify pull-down menu. The command sequence is as follows:

Command: m

Select objects: Use an object selection method.

Base point or displacement: Specify a base point (1).

Second point of displacement: Specify a point (2), or type movement displacement using polar coordinates.

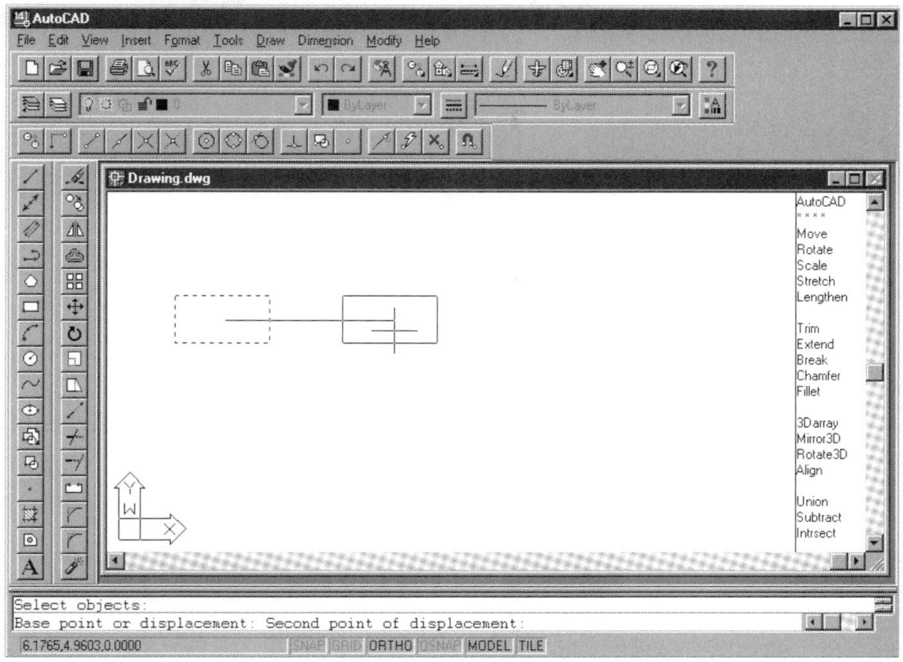

Figure 6–12
Move command.

The two points you specify define a displacement direction that indicates how far the selected objects are to be moved and in what direction (see Figure 6–12).

TRY THIS

Move an object a certain distance.

1. Open a new AutoCAD drawing, using Start from Scratch.
2. Draw a 2″-diameter circle with a center point at 3,3.
3. From the Modify pull-down menu, select Move.
4. Pick the circle and move it a distance of 1″ using a polar coordinate reading of @1″<0.

The circle should move 1″ to the right of its original position.

Rotate

Objects or parts of objects often have to be repositioned based on a certain point. The **Rotate** command rotates an object around a selected point (base point).

Select Rotate from the Modify pull-down menu or at the command prompt, type rotate.

Command: Rotate

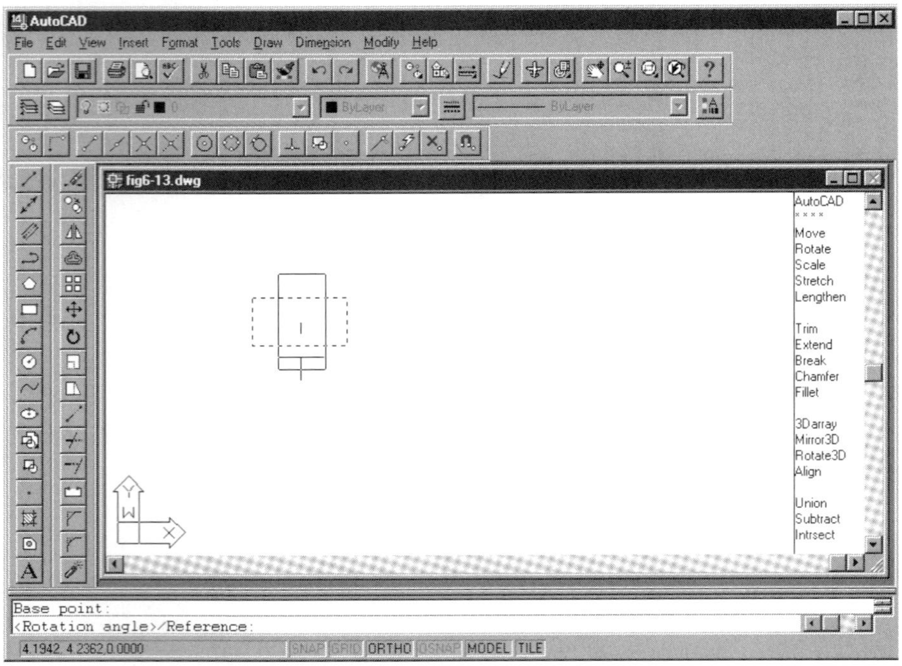

Figure 6–13
Rotating a rectangle.

Select objects: Use an object selection method.

Base point: Specify a point (1).

<Rotation angle>/Reference: Specify an angle or press <Enter> return.

After selection of the second point, the object should rotate to its new position (see Figure 6–13).

TRY THIS

Create a square and rotate it 45°.

1. Open a new AutoCAD drawing, using Start from Scratch.
2. From the icon toolbar on the left side of the drawing editor, select Rectangle.
3. Create a square with an origin point at 1.5,1.5 that is 3″ × 3″.
4. From the Modify2 screen menu, select Rotate:.
5. Click on any line of the rectangle.
6. Press <Enter> at the Select object: prompt after you have selected the object.
7. At the Base point: prompt, pick near the center of the square.
8. At the Rotation angle: prompt, type 45 then <Enter>.

The square should now appear on the screen rotated at a 45° angle.

Scale

Often it is necessary to resize an object. Rather than redrawing an object to meet specifications, you can use the **Scale** command to change object size. From the Modify pull-down menu, select Scale or at the command prompt, type scale.

Command: Scale

Select objects: Use an object selection method.

Base point: Specify a point (1) around which the object will be scaled.

<Scale factor> / Reference: Specify a numerical value or <Enter>.

The image in Figure 6–14 was scaled by dragging the mouse to a certain point and then picking at a point that was close to the appropriate size. In most instances, to get an accurate size, you would type in a scale value at the command prompt.

TRY THIS

Create a circle that is 3″ in diameter and scale it by a factor of 0.75.

1. Open a new AutoCAD drawing, using Start from Scratch.
2. Select Circle from the toolbar on the left side of the drawing editor.
3. Type 4,4 as the center point of the circle.
4. Enter 1.5 as the radius of the circle.
5. From the screen menu on the right, select MODIFY2.

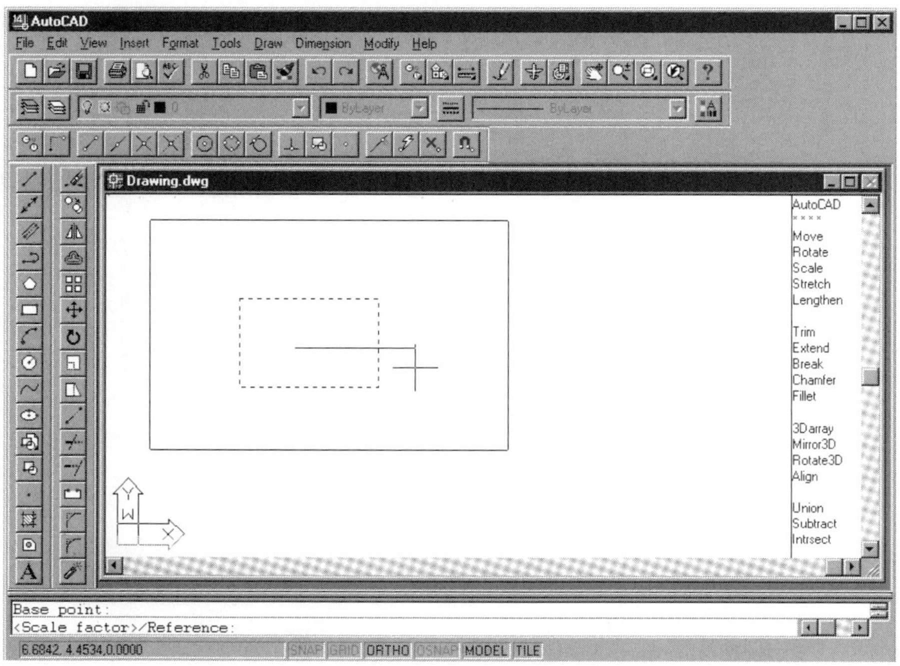

Figure 6–14
Scaling a rectangle.

6. Then select Scale:.
7. At the Select object: prompt, pick on the circle at any point.
8. Press <Enter>.
9. Type cen at the Base point: prompt.
10. Pick any point of the circle.
11. At the Scale/Reference point: prompt, type 0.75.

The circle should shrink in size to 75% of its original size.

Stretch

To **stretch** an object is to enlarge or shrink a portion of a drawing. The Stretch command is used with lines, arcs, traces, solids, polylines, and 3D Faces. Portions of an object to stretch are typically selected with a crossing window. Parts of the object called anchor points are left in place and are not within the selection set of the crossing window. The command sequence for stretch is as follows:

> Command: Stretch
>
> Select object: Select the object parts of the object to be stretched by using a crossing window to leave unselected points anchored.
>
> Base point: Pick a base point.
>
> Pick a new point that you want object stretched to, or type in direction and distance (see Figures 6–15 and 6–16).

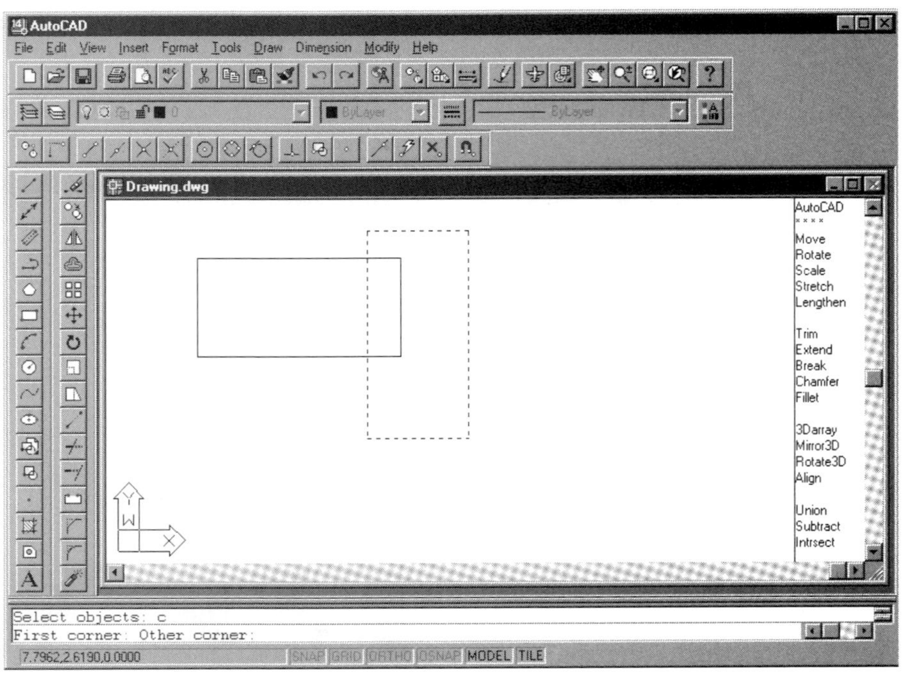

Figure 6–15
Stretching a rectangle.

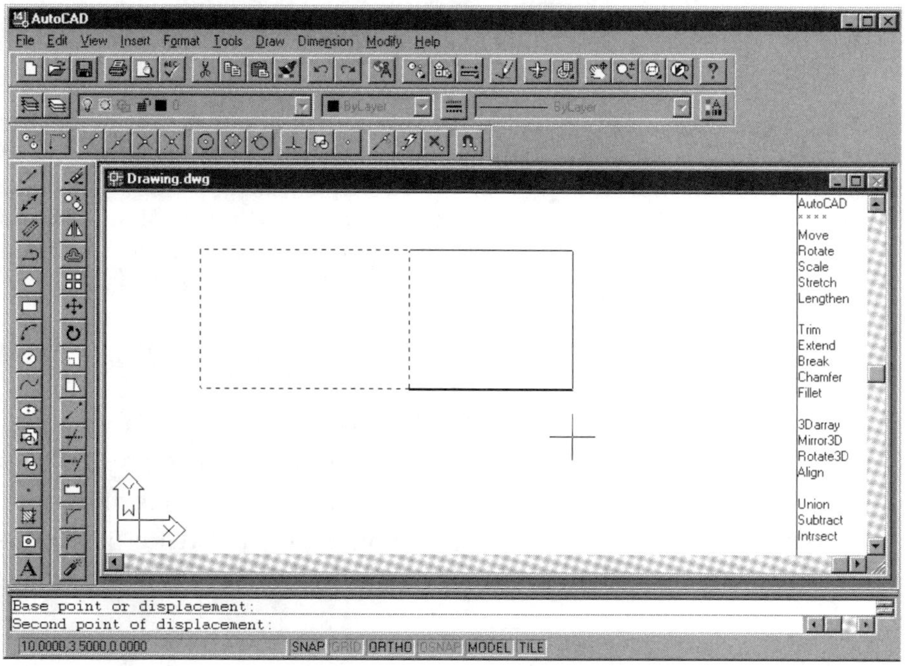

Figure 6–16
Stretching the object to a new point.

Figure 6–16 depicts how the object would be stretched. Since this was a rectangle (as such, a polyline) only the right side of the object was selected using a crossing window. A base point was selected, and the object was then stretched to the desired size.

TRY THIS

Draw a line that is 2″ long, then stretch it and make it 4″ longer.

1. Open a new AutoCAD drawing, using Start from Scratch.
2. From the toolbar icon menu, click on the line icon.
3. At the Starting point: prompt, type 1,1.
4. At the To Point: prompt, type @2<0.
5. Press <Enter> to exit the command.
6. From the Modify pull-down menu, select Stretch.
7. Type c (stands for crossing window), press <Enter>.
8. At the First point: prompt, use the input device to pick a point near the right endpoint of the line.
9. At the Second point: prompt, use the input device to pick a point beyond the right endpoint.
10. Press <Enter> at the Select Object: prompt.
11. At the Base point: prompt, pick near the right endpoint of the line.
12. At the Second point: prompt, type @2<0.

Copy

To **copy** objects in a drawing means to create entities that have the same characteristics as the object being copied.

The **Copy** command is used to copy objects in a drawing or to copy objects from one drawing to another. The Copy command is found in the Modify pull-down menu. When you copy an object within a drawing, you will be asked to specify a starting point and an endpoint for the copy. These points are called the **base point** and the **second point of displacement**. Single or multiple copies can be made.

Select Copy from the Modify pull-down menu or at the command prompt, type copy.

Command: Copy

Select objects: to copy, and press <Enter>.

Base point: Any point on the drawing.

<Rotation angle>/Reference: Specify the point of displacement (where you want the copy object to appear on the drawing).

To copy an object several times (see Figure 6–17):

1. From the Modify pull-down menu, select Copy.
2. Select the objects to copy, and press <Enter>.
3. Enter m (multiple).
4. Specify the base point.
5. Specify the second point of displacement.
6. Specify the next point of displacement.
7. Press <Enter> to end the command after placing all the copies that you need.

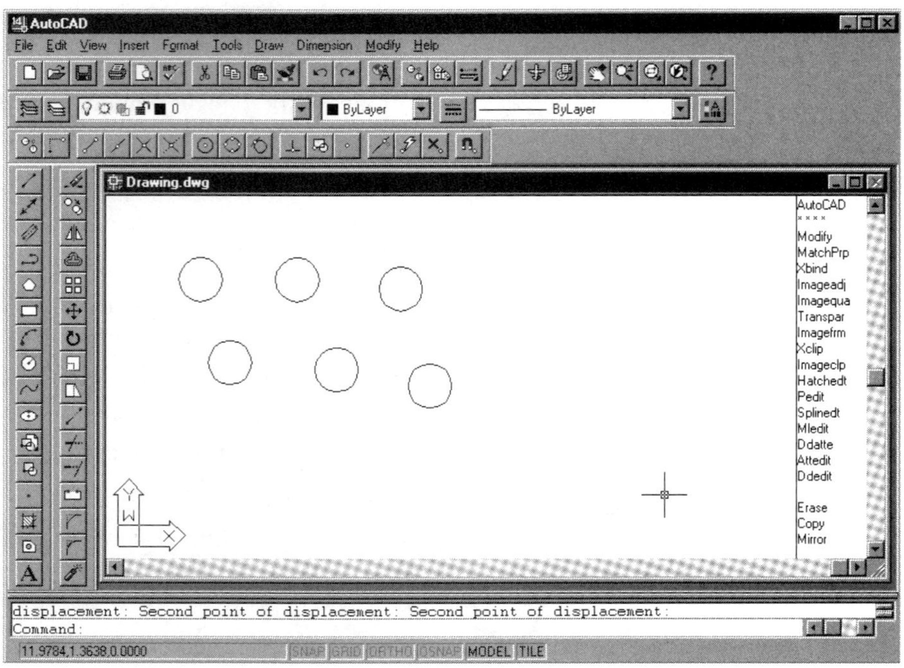

Figure 6–17
Using the Copy command to create multiple copies of an object.

TRY THIS

Create multiple copies of a circle.

1. Open a new AutoCAD drawing, using Start from Scratch.
2. Create a circle that is 2″ in diameter and place it on the drawing.
3. From the Modify pull-down menu, select Copy.
4. At the Select object: prompt, select the circle.
5. Press <Enter> to exit the Select object: prompt.
6. Type m at the Base point/Multiple: prompt.
7. At the Base point: prompt, pick near the center of the circle.
8. Place six more circles in the drawing at random locations.

Objects from an AutoCAD drawing can be copied and placed in another drawing file or application. In order to copy drawing objects, use the copy from the Edit menu or type Ctrl+C (hold down the Ctrl key and type C). Objects are copied to the Clipboard, from where they can be placed in other drawings or applications, as is common with other programs that are used in Windows applications.

Mirror

Drawing objects are typically **mirrored** when half the object is drawn, and the second half is created by mirroring the first half (see Figure 6–18). If an

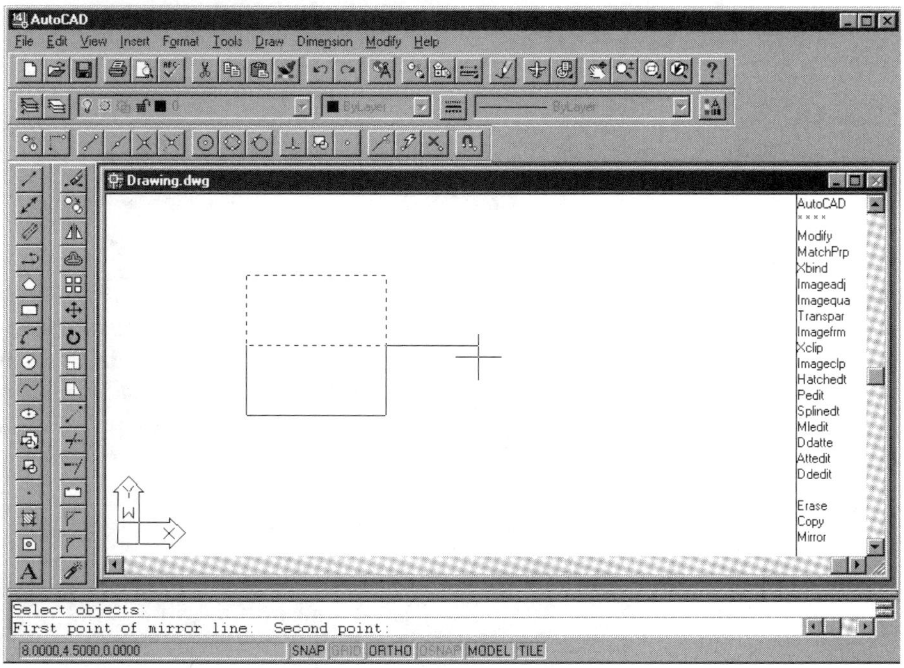

Figure 6–18
Using the Mirror command to mirror a rectangle.

object is symmetrical, it makes sense to draw half the object and mirror it to create the second half. Objects are mirrored around a mirror line that is defined by picking two points. The original mirrored object can be deleted or retained. The Mirror command is most commonly used in the XY plane. The sequence of commands to mirror objects is:

Select the mirror icon from the Modify toolbar.

Select objects: To be mirrored with a window. Command: Mirror

Base point: Specify the first point of the mirror line. Specify the second point of the mirror line.

<Rotation angle>/Reference: Press <Enter> to retain the original object(s).

TRY THIS

Create half of a rectangle, and use the Mirror command to create the other half.

1. Open a new AutoCAD drawing, using Start from Scratch.
2. Use the Line command to create half of a rectangle. Be sure two legs of the rectangle are equal.
3. From the toolbar, select the mirror icon.
4. Using a window for creating the selection set, select the three lines to be mirrored.
5. Press <Enter> to exit the Select objects: prompt.
6. Use Osnap endp to establish the first point of the mirror line. Select the endpoint of the line about which the object will be mirrored.
7. Move the mouse or other input device in the direction that provides the correct mirror results. Select the appropriate point.

Fillet

The **Fillet** command rounds or fillets the edges of two objects.

The **Fillet** command is used to connect two objects (lines) with an arc. Figure 6–19 depicts two perpendicular lines that have a 0.5″ fillet (rounded corner). AutoCAD treats both inside and outside corners as fillets. Common entities that can be filleted include line segments, polyline line segments, circles, arcs, and true ellipses. The fillet radius is the arc radius that connects filleted objects. If a rectangle or polygon is filleted, all corners are filleted the same. Fillet options at the prompt include the following:

Polyline/Radius/Trim/<Select first object>:

The default setting of the fillet radius is (0).

To set the fillet radius and use the fillet command, select Fillet from the Modify pull-down menu.

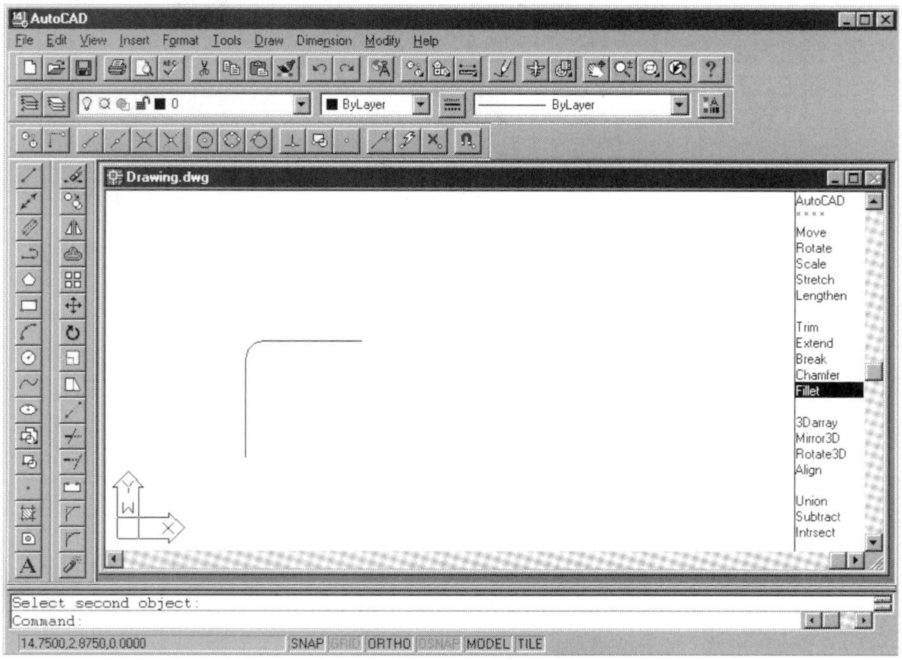

Figure 6–19
Fillet command used to round a corner.

Command: Fillet

Select object: Type the letter r (to set radius value) and press <Enter>.

Base point: Enter the numerical value for the radius.

<Rotation angle>/Reference: Press <Enter> twice to reactivate the fillet command. Select the objects to be filleted.

TRY THIS

Create a fillet with a radius of 0.375″ on four corners of a rectangle.

1. Open a new AutoCAD drawing, using Start from Scratch.
2. Draw a rectangle that measures 2″ × 3″.
3. From the toolbar, select the fillet icon.
4. Change the radius value to 0.375″.
5. Pick near the endpoint of each line to be filleted. Repeat the command for each corner.

Chamfer

The **Chamfer** command creates a beveled corner or edge.

The **Chamfer** command creates a beveled line between two nonparallel objects (see Figure 6–20). However, if the chamfer distance is left at zero, a perpendicular corner is created. Lines and polylines are common objects that are chamfered.

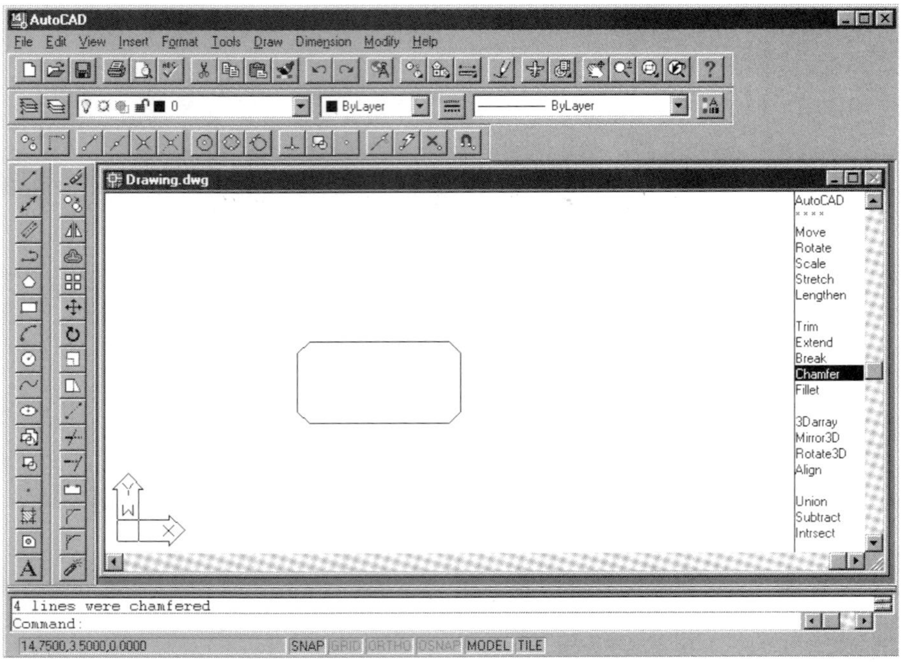

Figure 6–20
A rectangle with chamfered corners.

Chamfer options at the prompt include the following: Polyline/Distance/Angle/Trim/Method:. If a polyline is chamfered, all corners are beveled the same. The chamfer Distance prompt lets you determine the length of each line to be chamfered. Similarly, the chamfer Angle option allows you to determine the angle of each beveled line.

TRY THIS

Create a 2″ × 3″ rectangle using the Rectangle command.

1. Open a new AutoCAD drawing, using Start from Scratch.
2. Create a 2″ × 3″ rectangle using the Rectangle command.
3. From the Modify pull-down menu, select Chamfer.
4. Type D, then <Enter>.
5. At the Enter first chamfer distance: prompt, type 0.25; press <Enter>.
6. At the Enter second chamfer distance: prompt, type 0.25; press <Enter>.
7. Press <Enter> to restart the Chamfer command.
8. Select polyline; press <Enter>.

All corners of the rectangle should be chamfered the same.

Array

The **Array** command allows you to copy an object numerous times at set increments in both the vertical and horizontal directions or around an imaginary circle.

There are two array options, polar and rectangular, that can be used to replicate objects. The Array command allows you to copy an object numerous times at set increments in both the vertical and horizontal directions or around an imaginary circle. The Array command can be activated through the Modify pull-down menu, typed at the command prompt, or selected from either the screen menu or the toolbar. Rectangular arrays are used to array objects in rows (horizontal) and columns (vertical). Both positive and negative values can be entered. A positive value will create copies up and to the right of the original. Negative values will copy down or to the left of the original. Polar arrays are used to array items in a circular pattern. Often, it is more efficient to use the Array command rather than the Copy command when you have multiple objects to create.

If you use the rectangular array, you must specify the number of rows, columns, and the distance between each. If you select a polar array, you must designate the number of objects and the angle through which you want the objects arrayed, and you must specify if the objects are to be rotated.

Figure 6-21 is a drawing in which both a polar and rectangular array were used. A polar array was used to array the four 0.25″-diameter circles. A rectangular array was used to create the text box that identifies the circles and circle diameters.

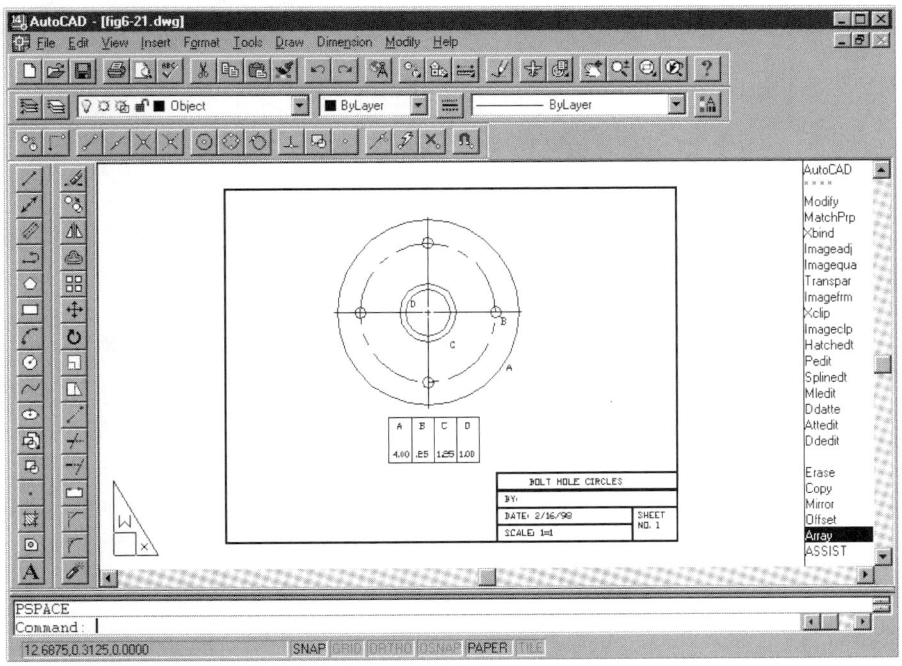

Figure 6–21
A polar and a rectangular array.

TRY THIS

Use polar array to array a line within a circle.

1. Start AutoCAD.
2. Select Use a Template and select the A-size template file you created in Chapter 2.
3. Make sure you are in model space, and create a circle with a center point of 5,5 and a radius of 2.
4. Create a line that has one endpoint of 5,5 and another endpoint that intersects the circle.
5. From the Modify pull-down menu, select Array.
6. Select the line to array it.
7. When prompted to respond to Rectangular/Polar:, enter P.
8. For the center point select the center of the circle. Use the object snap cen to find the circle center.
9. At the Number of items: prompt, enter 30.
10. At the Angle to fill: prompt, accept the default of 360.
11. Respond yes to the prompt asking if the objects are to be rotated.
12. The line should then be arrayed 30 times in the circle.

TRY THIS

Use rectangular array to array a square.

1. Start AutoCAD.
2. Select Use a Template and select the A-size template file you created in Chapter 2.
3. Make sure you are in model space, and use the rectangle command to draw a square that is 1×1.
4. Select the array icon from the toolbar.
5. Select the rectangle at the Select Object: prompt.
6. Enter r for rectangular.
7. At the Number of rows: prompt, enter 2.
8. At the Number of columns: prompt, enter 4.
9. Distance between rows is 2.
10. Distance between columns is 2.

Two rows of squares should appear on the screen (see Figure 6–22). There should also be four columns. The spacing between the rows and columns is 1. In a rectangular array, AutoCAD always reads the lower left point of the entity as the origin point. That is why we entered 2 for the spacing.

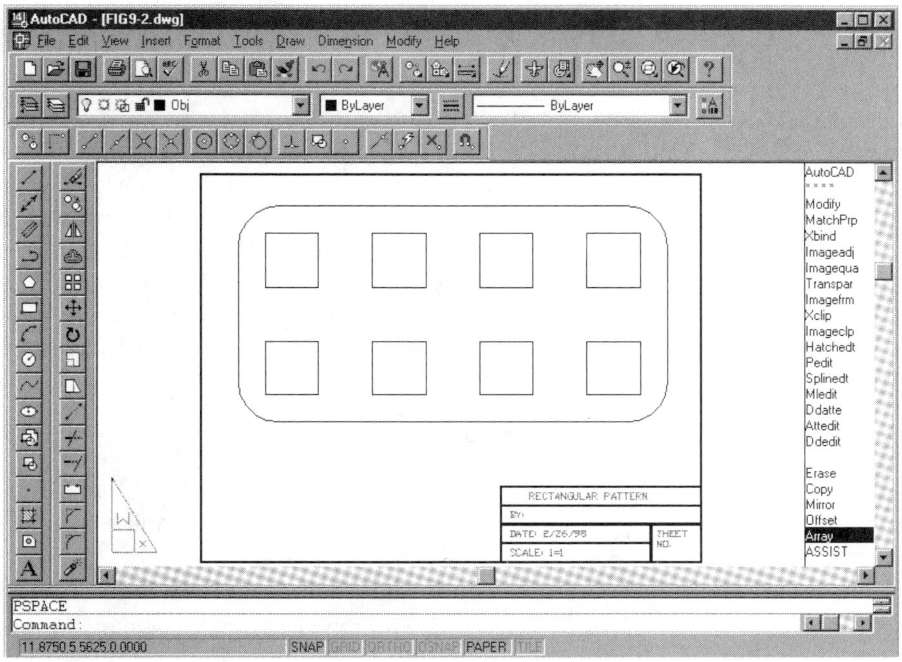

Figure 6–22
Rectangular array of squares.

Offset

When an object is **offset**, a new object is created that is similar to the selected object.

Offset is another command located in the Modify pull-down meu. When an object is offset, a new object is created that is similar to the selected object. Many objects can be offset, including lines, arcs, circles, 2D polylines, and ellipses. When you offset an object, you need to enter a distance and a side of an object to offset. In the example in Figure 6–23, a 4″-diameter circle was offset to the inside 1″ to create a 2″-diameter circle.

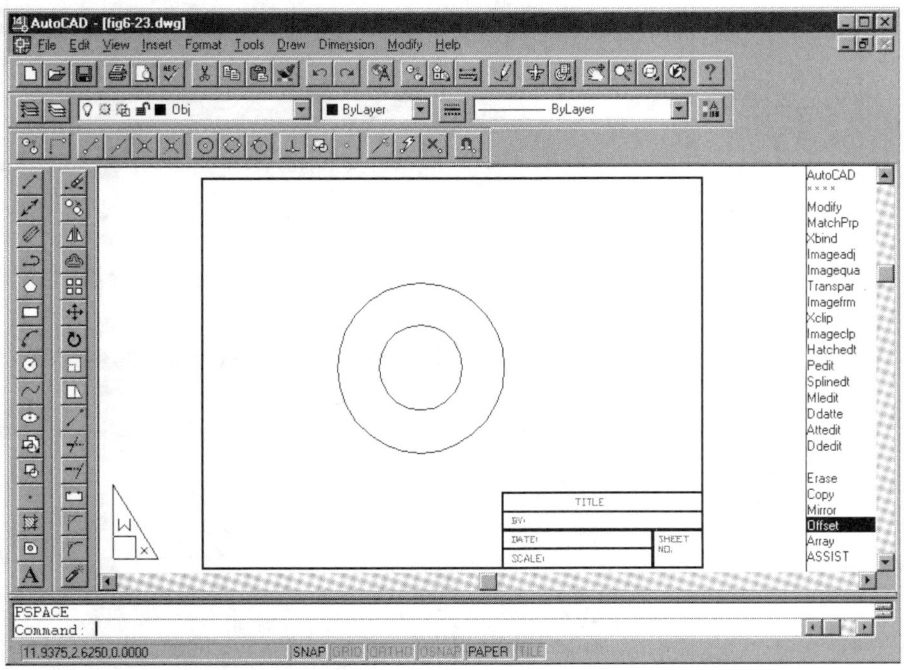

Figure 6–23
Offset of a circle.

Ddedit

The **Ddedit** command is used to edit text.

The editing command for editing text is **Ddedit**. This command is used for editing text that was created with the Text command. It is commonly used to correct misspelled words or text information in the drawing. To execute the command, either select it from the Modify pull-down menu, or type ddedit at the command prompt. Click on the text to be edited. When a dialog box appears with the highlighted text (see Figure 6–24), enter the new text, and press <Enter> when you are finished. The dialog box will close, and the selected text will automatically be changed in the drawing.

TRY THIS

Use the Ddedit command to edit a line of text.

1. Open a new AutoCAD drawing, using Start from Scratch.
2. From the Draw pull-down menu, select Text, then select Single line text.
3. Using your input device, pick the text starting point.
4. Change the size of the text to 0.125″.
5. Leave the rotation angle at (0).
6. At the text prompt type "AutoCAD release 14 is fun to use".
7. Press <Enter> twice to exit the command.
8. Type ddedit at the command prompt.
9. Select the line of text to be edited.
10. Change the text in the dialog box to read, "AutoCAD is fun".

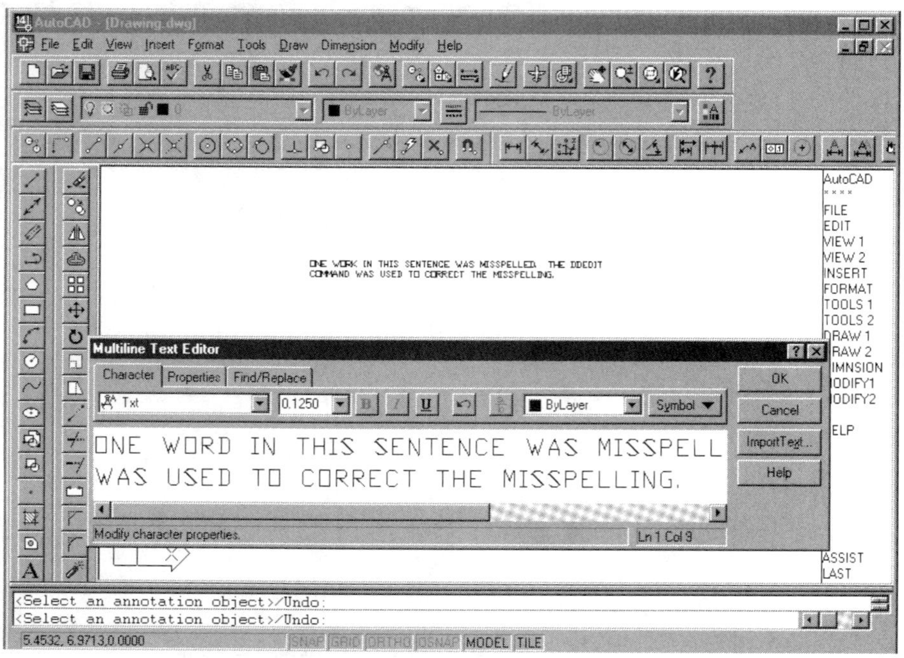

Figure 6–24
Ddedit dialog box.

11. Click OK to change the text in the drawing.
12. Press <Enter> to exit the command.

Pedit (polyedit)

The **Pedit** command is used to edit objects that were made with a polyline.

Objects that are created with polylines require a special editing command, **pedit**. The following options included in the Pedit command: are

Close/Join/Width/Edit vertex/Fit/Spline/Decurve/Ltype gen/Undo/eXit<X>:

Close	Closes a polyline entity; can add a segment to close entity.
Join	Connects dissimilar entities to make one continuous polyline.
Width	Changes the default width of the polyline.
Edit vertex	Edits individual vertices.
Fit	Creates smooth curves that pass between vertices.
Spline	Creates a curve that passes through the first and last vertices. Uses other vertices to pull the curve in one direction or the other.
Decurve	Returns the polyline to its original state.
Ltype gen	Changes the linetype application.
Undo	Reverses the last Pedit command.
eXit	Exits the Pedit command.

Figure 6–25 displays a listing of the pedit commands in the screen menu.

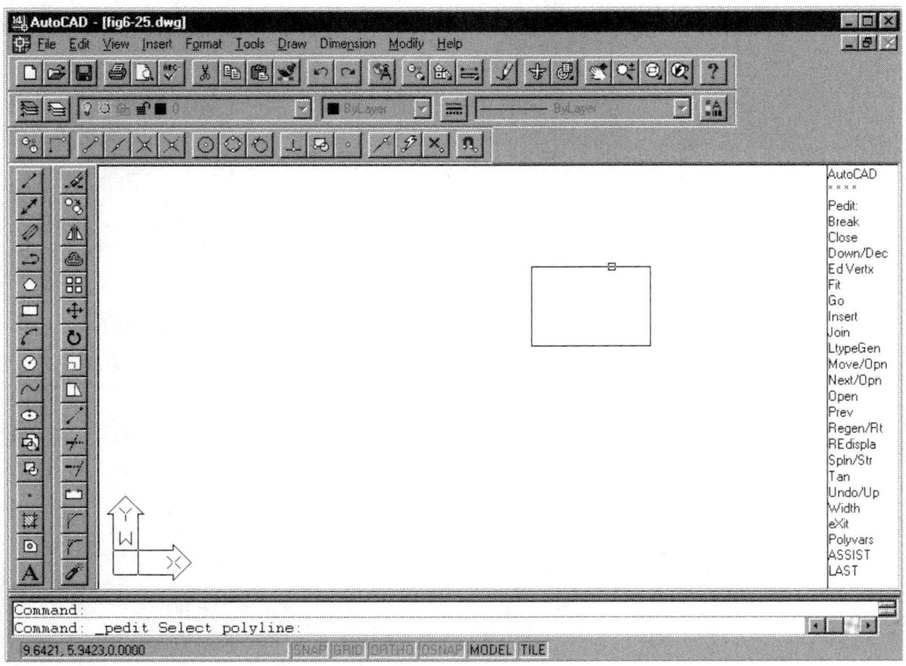

Figure 6–25
Screen menu display of Pedit options.

If the object that you select is not created with a polyline, you will be asked if you want to convert the line to a polyline.

TRY THIS

Create a rectangle and change its line width to 0.05″ using the pedit command.

1. Open a new AutoCAD drawing, using Start from Scratch.
2. From the Draw pull-down menu, select Rectangle.
3. Create a rectangle that has an origin point at 2,2 and an upper right corner point of 6,5.
4. From the screen menu (right side of the drawing editor) select Modify1, then Pedit.
5. Select any line of the rectangle.
6. Type w (width).
7. Type 0.05″ as the width for all line segments.

Chapter 6 ■ Activities

Activity 6–1

Draw a Star

In this activity you will use the Copy and Rotate commands to create a star by copying and rotating a square several times. Make the suggested settings, and create the necessary layers as listed. (To learn how to add layers to a drawing, go to the Help menu and select AutoCAD Help Topics. Click on the Index tab and type the word layers where indicated. Find the add/deleting layers to/from option, and select it. A dialog box should appear with information on how to create layers.) A likeness of the drawing appears in Figure 6–26.

Plotter Paper Size: A

Suggested Settings:	Grid	0.50″
	Snap	0.125″
	Layers (7)	**0** (default border)
		Center (cen), Linetype center, Color: cyan
		Object (obj), Linetype continuous, Color: black
		Hidden (hid), Linetype continuous, Color: magenta
		Tbk (title block), Linetype continuous, Color: red
		Txt (text), Linetype continuous, Color: green
		Dim (dimensions), Linetype continuous, Color: green
	Units	Decimal

Hints:

1. Open your border template file for an A-size drawing. After it has completed loading, use the Saveas command to rename the drawing file ACT6-1.
2. The star consists of 2″ squares drawn in model space. Be sure the snap and grid are set and are On before drawing. Draw one square using the line, rectangle, or polygon command. Copy the original square and rotate it 45°. Move the rotated copy so that it overlays the original square. Now copy both squares and rotate them 22.5°. Move the copied object back so that they overlay the original entity.

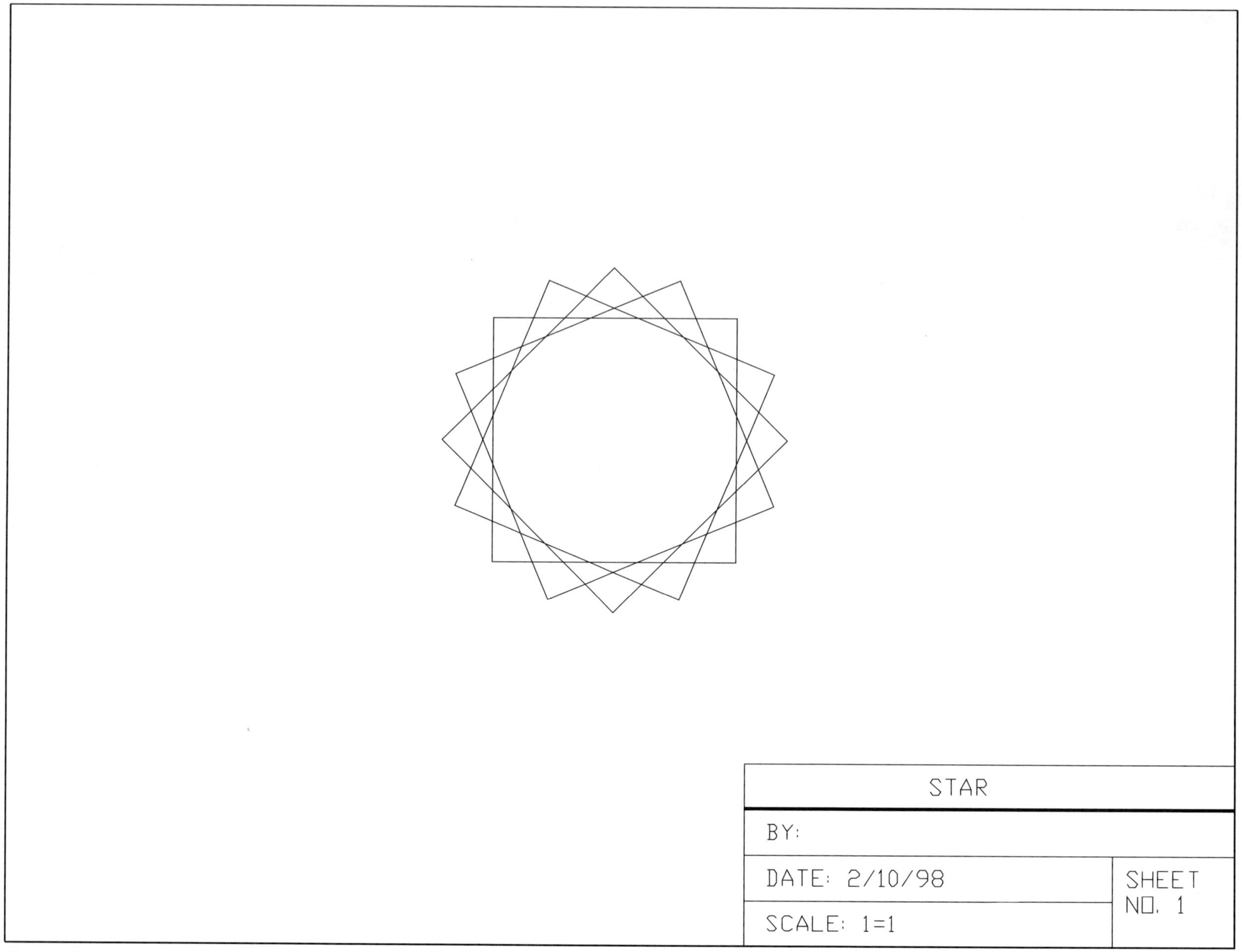

Figure 6–26
Activity 6–1

ACTIVITY 6–2

Draw a Slider Bracket

In this activity you will use the Chamfer and Fillet commands to create two separate objects. Make your settings and create the necessary layers as listed. A likeness of the drawing appears in Figure 6–27.

Plotter Paper Size: A

Suggested Settings:	Grid	0.50″
	Snap	0.125″
	Layers (7)	**0** (default border)
		Center (cen), Linetype center, Color: cyan
		Object (obj), Linetype continuous, Color: black
		Hidden (hid), Linetype continuous, Color: magenta
		Tbk (title block), Linetype continuous, Color: red
		Txt (text), Linetype continuous, Color: green
		Dim (dimensions), Linetype continuous, Color: green
	Units	Decimal

Hints:

1. Open your border template file for an A-size drawing. After it has completed loading, use the Saveas command to rename the drawing file ACT6-2.
2. Make sure you are in model space before you begin drawing the object.
3. In this activity you will draw three views: top, front, and right side. The three views are spaced 1.5″ apart. Dimensions of the object are provided in Figure 6–27.
4. Depending on the layers you created in your A-size template, you may have to add new layers in this object. The linetypes of hidden and center will have to be loaded and assigned to the Hidden and Center layers, respectively. (To load a linetype, type linetype at the command prompt and press <Enter>. The Layer & Linetype Properties dialog box should appear. Select the Linetype tab and click on Load. Select the linetype you want loaded and click OK. Click on the Layer tab. Select the layer to which you want to assign a linetype and click on the linetype that currently is assigned to that layer. A dialog box should appear that lets you select a different linetype for that layer. Select the linetype you want to use for that layer and click OK.)
5. The easiest method for creating the centerlines for the circles is to use Cen in the Dimension pull-down menu. The Dimension menu has several variables that can be changed. In order to create the centerlines in the circle, use the following procedure:

- At the command prompt, enter Dim
- At the Dim command, enter dimcen
- Enter a value of -0.0625 and press <Enter>
- At the Dim command, enter cen
- Select the circle
- The centerline complete with the crosshairs should appear.

6. **Do not** include the dimensions on the drawing.

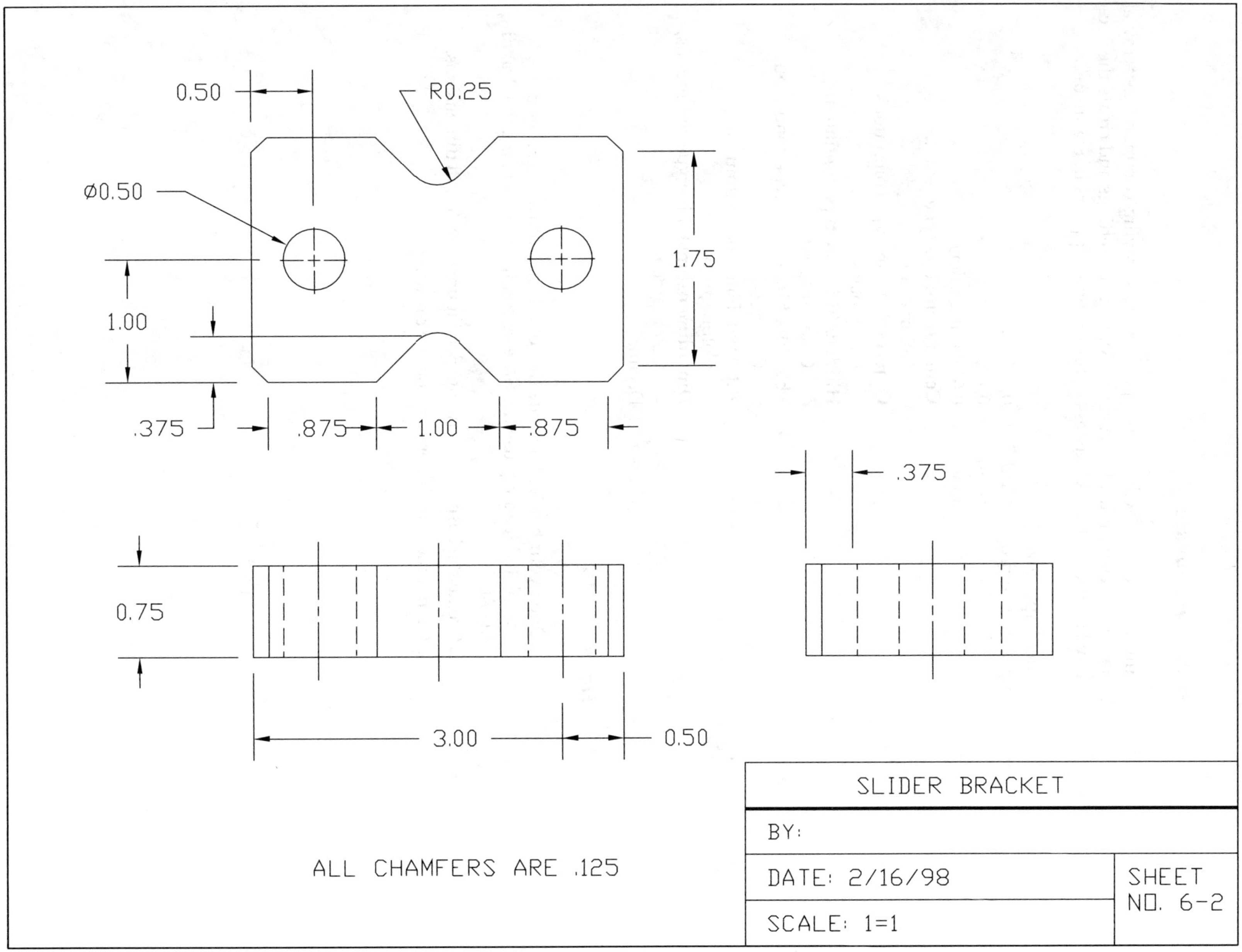

Figure 6–27
Activity 6–2

ACTIVITY 6–3

Draw a Baseplate

In this activity you will use the polar array drawing command to array a series of circles within a larger circle. Make your settings and create the necessary layers as listed. A likeness of the drawing appears in Figure 6–28.

Plotter Paper Size: B

Suggested Settings:	Grid	0.50″
	Snap	0.125″
	Layers (7)	**0** (default border)
		Center (cen), Linetype center, Color: cyan
		Object (obj), Linetype continuous, Color: black
		Hidden (hid), Linetype continuous, Color: magenta
		Tbk (title block), Linetype continuous, Color: red
		Txt (text), Linetype continuous, Color: green
		Dim (dimensions), Linetype continuous, Color: green
	Units	Decimal

Hints:

1. Open your border template file for a B-size drawing. After it has completed loading, use the Saveas command to rename the drawing file ACT6-3.
2. Create the baseplate drawing. See Figure 6–28 for all dimensions.
3. **Do not** include dimensions on the drawing.

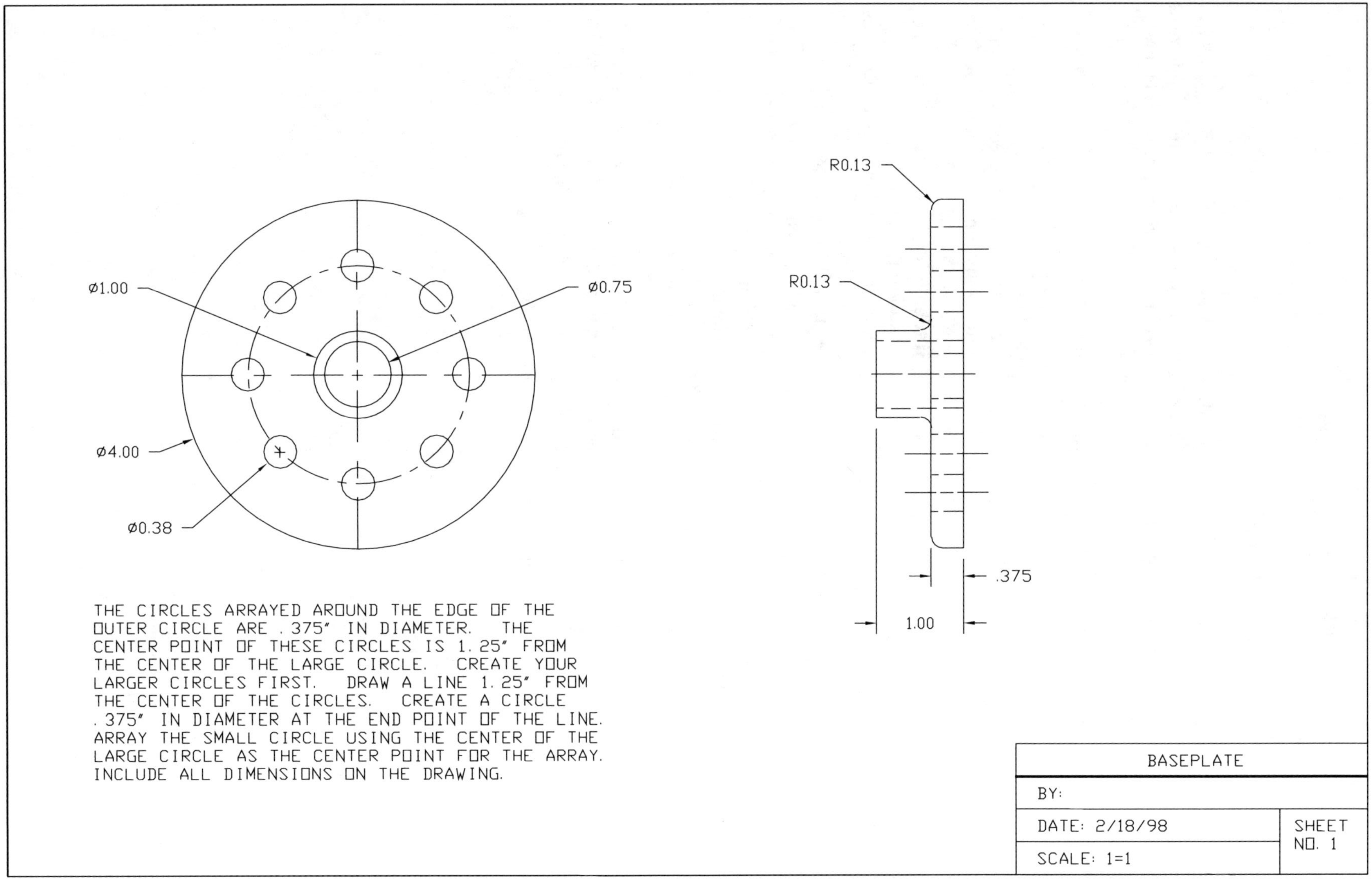

Figure 6–28
Activity 6–3

ACTIVITY 6–4

Draw a Grate

In this activity you will use the rectangular array drawing command to array a series of objects in rows and columns. Make your settings and create the necessary layers as listed. A likeness of the drawing appears in Figure 6–29.

Plotter Paper Size: A

Suggested Settings:	Grid	0.50″
	Snap	0.125″
	Layers (7)	**0** (default border)
		Center (cen), Linetype center, Color: cyan
		Object (obj), Linetype continuous, Color: black
		Hidden (hid), Linetype continuous, Color: magenta
		Tbk (title block), Linetype continuous, Color: red
		Txt (text), Linetype continuous, Color: green
		Dim (dimensions), Linetype continuous, Color: green
	Units	Decimal

Hints:

1. Open your A-size drawing template file. After it has completed loading, use the Saveas command to rename the drawing file ACT6-4.
2. Create the grate drawing. See Figure 6–29 for all dimensions.
3. **Do not** include dimensions on the drawing.

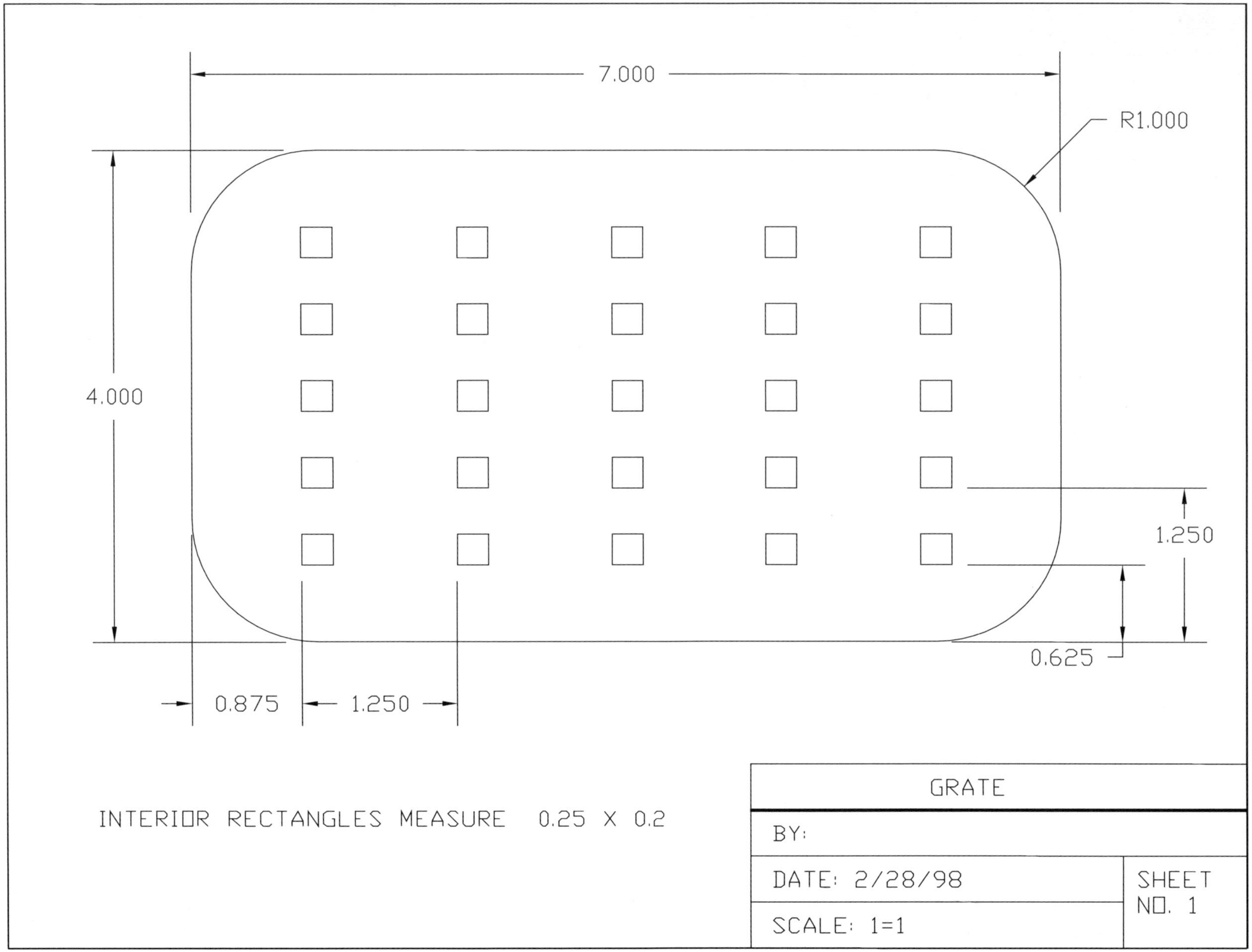

Figure 6–29
Activity 6–4

CHAPTER

7

Using and Creating Template Files

AFTER READING THIS CHAPTER, YOU WILL BE ABLE TO:

- Use template drawing files.
- Use those options associated with layer control.
- Identify typical drawing scales.

KEY CONCEPTS

Drawing Scales
Layers
Template Files

Any time that AutoCAD is opened from the desktop, the Start Up dialog box is displayed. This dialog box contains four options for starting the software, namely, Use a Wizard, Use a Template, Start from Scratch, or Open a Drawing.

If you select Start from Scratch to make a prototype drawing, you will be able to specify the drawing parameters that you want which may include grid, limits, snap, and units. It makes sense to establish drawing parameters in a prototype drawing, since it can continually be reused. Title blocks, borders, and layers are a few of the other items that can be set in a template or prototype drawing, so that this information is consistent from drawing to drawing. Because drawings are printed/plotted on standard sizes of paper, prototype or template drawings can be created for each size of paper used for printing and/or plotting.

USING A TEMPLATE DRAWING FILE

New drawings are based on a template, one created by you or, in some instances, one created by AutoCAD. Any drawing can be used as a template. When templates are used, any changes that are made to the template are saved under a different file name. Template files include settings that are consistent with your particular office standards. These may include:

- Unit type and precision
- Drawing limits
- Snap and grid
- Layer organization
- Title blocks, borders, and logos
- Dimension and text styles
- Linetypes

TRY THIS

Open up a template file to review title block styles.

1. Open AutoCAD.
2. From the startup menu select Use a Template.
3. Open the ANSI_a.dwt template file.
4. Type ps to change to paper space.
5. Zoom in on the Title Block.
6. Above DWG NO, type your name, and set the text height to 0.25″.
7. Fill in the rest of the information in the title block.
8. Save the drawing file under a new name.

In Figure 7–1 the Find File option was used from the Open Existing dialog box window. All template files (.dwt), rather than drawing files (.dwg), were sought. Figure 7–1 displays a partial listing of the template files that exist. The style and size of each template file is determined by the template file name. For example, ANSI_a.dwg is a standard template file established by the American National Standards Institute that fits A-size drawing paper. ISO is the acronym for International Standards Organization.

TRY THIS

Open up a template file to review title block styles.

1. Open AutoCAD.
2. From the startup menu select Use a Template.
3. Open the ISO_A1.dwt template file. This is a metric title block.
4. Switch to model space and check the limits of the drawing. What do they read?
5. How would you scale this drawing to fit A-size paper?

When you use a template file, remember to save the drawing file with a name that is different from the given template file name.

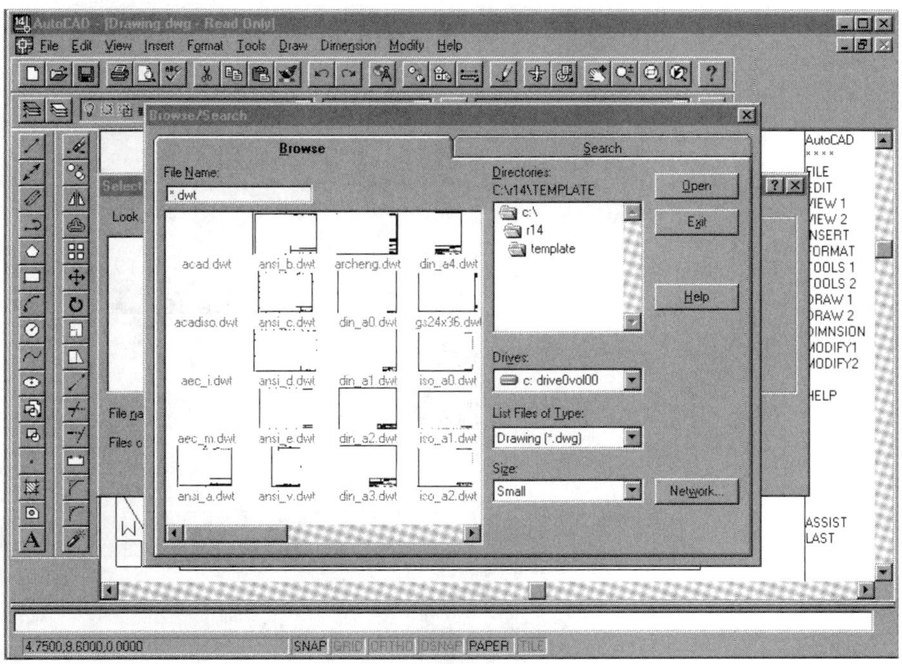

Figure 7–1
AutoCAD R14 template drawing files.

LAYER ORGANIZATION

Layers are primarily an organizational tool in AutoCAD. Each layer has an associated color and linetype. Layers group information by function, and in AutoCAD, layers are sorted alphabetically by name. In any template, any number of layers can be created and saved with the template file. However, certain standards have been created by business and industry for the naming of layers and assigning of layer characteristics. These standards have been developed for manufacturing, architectural/residential, and architectural/mechanical commercial drawings.

Layer characteristics are assigned in the Layer & Linetype Properties dialog box (see Figure 7–2). Color and linetype are the two most common characteristics assigned to a layer. The dialog box appears when you type la at the command prompt, or if you select the Layers icon on the Object Properties toolbar.

The status of the layer you are currently working on is displayed in this toolbar, which is displayed at the top of the drawing editor screen (see Figure 7–3). The various options associated with the Object Properties toolbar are described next.

Make Object's Layer Current	Gives you the option of selecting a layer based on the selection of the object.
Layer	Activates the Layer and Linetype dialog box.
Layers On/Off	Used to turn layers on or off. If the light bulb icon is yellow, the layer is on. If the light bulb icon is grayed out, the layer is off.

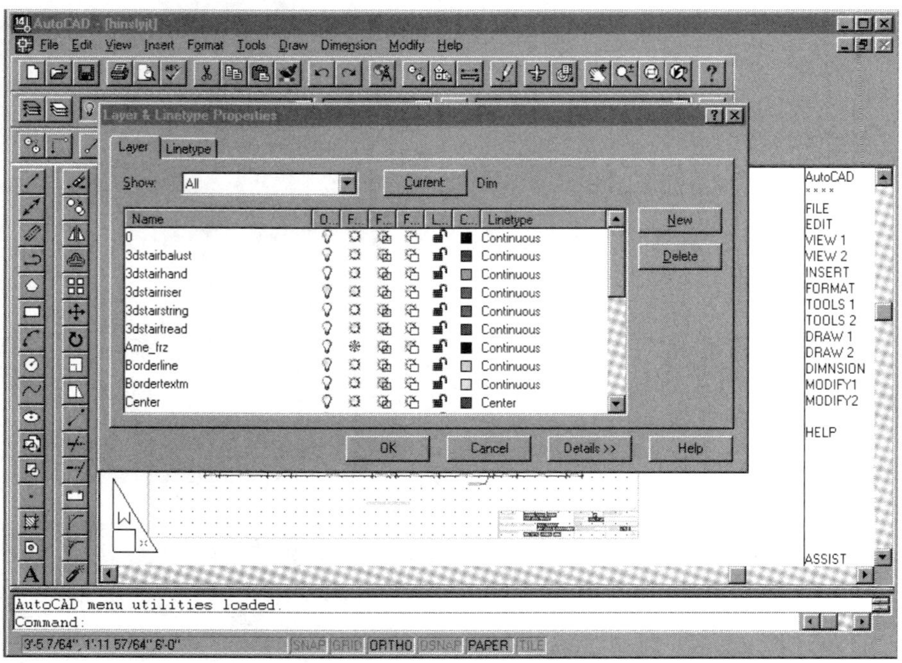

Figure 7–2
Layer and Linetype dialog box.

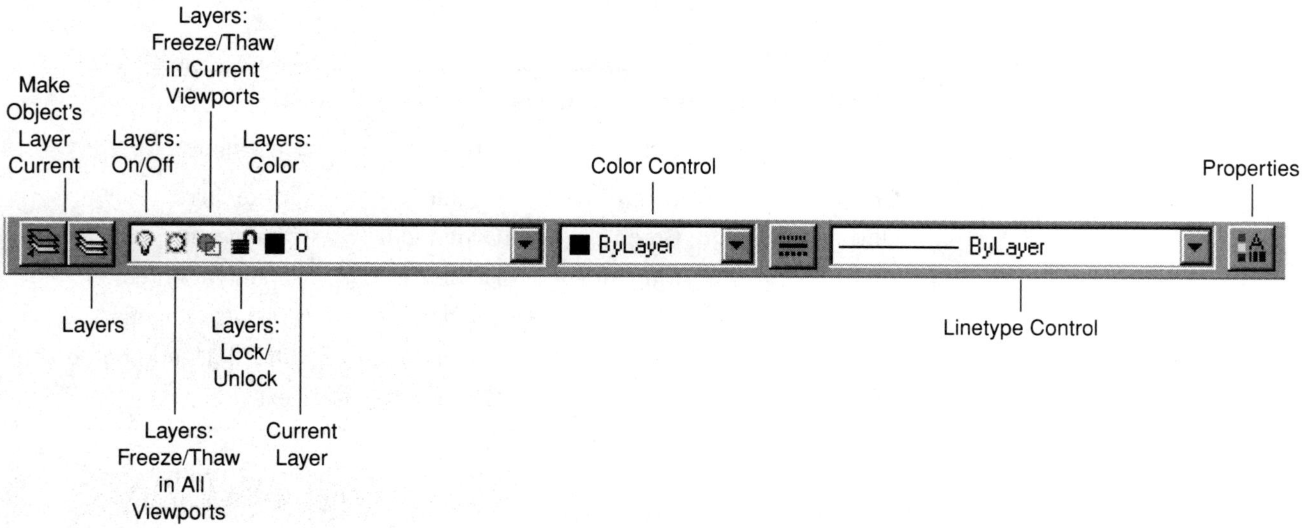

Figure 7–3
Object Properties toolbar.

Layers Freeze/Thaw in All Viewports	If the layer is frozen, the objects on that layer do not show. A layer frozen with this option will not be displayed in any viewport.
Layers: Freeze/Thaw in Current Viewport	Layer will not show in current viewport if it is frozen in that viewport.
Layers: Lock/Unlock	If a layer is locked, it will be displayed, but any objects located on that layer cannot be edited.
Layers: Color	Depicts the color assigned to that layer. All objects drawn on that layer will be displayed in the color assigned to the layer.
Color Control	Allows you to change how colors are assigned to a layer. Specific colors or specific objects can be assigned, which enables you to have multiple colors appear on a single layer.
Linetype	Displays the current linetype that is assigned to the current layer.
Linetype Control	Similar to color control. Linetypes can be singularly assigned to objects that are on the same layer.
Properties	If this option is selected, either an object must be selected or you must select an object. Once the object has been selected, a dialog box appears that lists the properties of the selected object.

Table 7–1

Standard Layer Names for a Manufacturing Drawing

LAYER NAME	COLOR	LINETYPE	DESCRIPTION
CEN	Cyan	Center	Centerlines
DIM	Green	Continuous	Dimensions
HID	Magenta	Hidden	Hidden features
OBJ	Black	Continuous	Solid object lines
TBK	Red	Continuous	Title block and borderlines
TXT	Green	Continuous	Text

As we mentioned previously, industry has tried to set standards or guidelines for layer names. Tables 7–1 through 7–6 provide an overview of different layers used based on these standards.

If there are several parts on a drawing, add the prefix **P** and a numerical value that indicates there are several parts, for example, P3-hat, which stands for part 3 hatch lines.

Table 7–2

Standard Layer Names for an Architectural Residential Drawing

LAYER NAME	COLOR	LINETYPE	DESCRIPTION
APP	White	Continuous	Appliances
CAB	Blue	Continuous	Cabinetry
DIM	Green	Continuous	Dimensions
DOR	Cyan	Continuous	Doors
ELC	Magenta	Continuous	Electrical
FIX	White	Continuous	Fixtures (plumbing)
FUR	Green	Continuous	Furniture
STR	Blue	Continuous	Stairs
TBK	Red	Continuous	Title block and border
WAL	Yellow	Continuous	Walls
WIN	Cyan	Continuous	Windows

Table 7–3

Standard Layer Names for an Architectural Commercial Drawing

Layer Name	Description
A00WALPN	Walls on a plan view
A00WALEL	Walls on an elevation view
A00WALSC	Walls on a sectional view
A00DORPN	Door symbols on a plan view
A00WINPN	Window symbols on a plan view
A00FIXON	Fixtures (plumbing) on a plan view
A00CABPN	Cabinetry on a plan view
A00DIMON	Dimensions on a plan view
A00TXTPN	Text on a plan view

Table 7–4

Standard Layer Names for a Mechanical Commercial Drawing

Layer Name	Description
M00ARHPN	Air-handling units on a plan view
M00SUPPN	Supply air on a plan view
M00RETPN	Return air on a plan view
M00VENPN	Ventilation on a plan view
M00CONON	Condensing system on a plan view
M00CTRPN	Controls on a plan view
M00DIMPN	Dimensions on a plan view
M00TXTPN	Text on a plan view

Table 7–5

Standard Layer Names for a Plumbing Commercial Drawing

Layer Name	Description
P00CWSPN	Cold-water supply on a plan view
P00DHWPN	Domestic hot water on a plan view
P00HWSPN	Hot-water supply on a plan view
P00WRPN	Hot-water return on a plan view
P00SANPN	Sanitary waste on a plan view
P00VENPN	Vents on a plan view
P00TEMPN	Tempered water on a plan view
P00STMPN	Storm drain on a plan view

TRY THIS

Add the standard layer names, linetypes, and colors to a drawing.

1. From the AutoCAD Start Up dialog box, select Use a Template.
2. Open your A-size border template.
3. Enter la at the command prompt.
4. Create the standard mechanical layer names with the correct colors and linetypes as indicated in Table 7–1.
5. To change the color of a layer, select the colored square of the corresponding layer.
6. To change the linetype, click on the linetype showing, and a linetype dialog box will appear. If the linetype is not listed, select Load, and a linetype dialog box will appear from which you can load the linetype you need.

Repeat the procedure for the B-size template that you created at the end of Chapter 2.

Architectural layers can be further defined by adding the prefix F to indicate floor level.

Numerous types of layers also are used in the construction industry. These include architectural, structural, mechanical, and landscape layers. Layer names are defined with a prefix letter to identify the discipline to which they are related. Disciplines include the following:

A for Architecture	S for Structural
M for Mechanical	P for Plumbing
F for Fire Protection	E for Electrical
C for Civil Engineering	L for Landscape

The layer name is then followed by a floor designation and a category designation (see Tables 7–3 through 7–6).

Table 7–6

Standard Layer Names for an Electrical Commercial Drawing

LAYER NAME	DESCRIPTION
E00PWRPN	Power on a plan view
E00HETPN	Heat on a plan view
E00LITPN	Lighting on a plan view
E00CGDPN	Ceiling grid on a plan view
E00COMPN	Communications on a plan view
E00CTRPN	Controls on a plan view
E00ALMPN	Alarm systems on a plan view

Third-party software add-ons to AutoCAD may also have specific layer name conventions that are used with particular applications.

DRAWING SCALES

Just as there are layer name conventions, so are there standard scale conventions. Standard scales that have been established include metric, engineer, and architect scales (see Table 7–7).

Scaling enables you to place drawing entities on different sizes of papers. Standard paper sizes are listed:

SIZE	ENGLISH MEASUREMENT	METRIC MEASUREMENT
A	8.5 × 11	256 × 196
B	11 × 17	394 × 251
C	17 × 22	525 × 396
D	22 × 34	829 × 524
E	34 × 44	1089 × 835

The actual paper surface area that can be used for plotting varies depending on the type of output device used. Each plotter or printer has physical devices that determines the amount of surface area that can be used for either plotting or printing. Check with the manufacturer to determine the largest parameters available for printing and/or plotting.

Table 7–7

METRIC	MECHANICAL ENGINEER	ARCHITECT
1:1	1″ = 1″	1″ = 1′
1:20	$\frac{1}{2}$″ = 1″	$\frac{3}{4}$″ = 1′
1:125	$\frac{1}{4}$″ = 1″	$\frac{1}{2}$″ = 1′
1:250	$\frac{1}{8}$″ = 1″	$\frac{3}{8}$″ = 1′
1:300		$\frac{1}{4}$″ = 1′
1:500		$\frac{3}{16}$″ = 1′
1:1000		$\frac{1}{8}$″ = 1′
1:8000		$\frac{3}{32}$″ = 1′

ACTIVITY 7-1

View the Tutorial on Managing Layers and Linetypes

This activity was developed by AutoDesk to teach you how to manage layers.

ACTIVITY STEPS

1. Start AutoCAD R14.
2. Select Start from Scratch in the Start Up dialog box.
3. Select the What's New option from the Help pull-down menu.
4. At the main menu, select Managing Layers and Linetypes.
5. View the short tutorial, which will run automatically.

ACTIVITY 7-2

Create New Layers on a Template Drawing

This activity was designed to give you practice in adding layer names and assigning linetypes and color to template drawings.

ACTIVITY STEPS

1. Start AutoCAD R14.
2. Select Use a Template in the Start Up dialog box.
3. Select Archeng.dwt (see Figure 7–4). This template is for architectural drawings that are to be printed/plotted on 36″ × 24″ paper.
4. Type la at the command prompt.
5. Two layers, 0 and Title_block, should show up in the Layers & Linetype Properties dialog box. Change the color to red for the Title_block layer.
6. Select New to create new layers.
7. Refer to Table 7–2 for layer names, colors, and linetypes. Add the layers with the associated linetypes and colors as listed in Table 7–2.
8. Save the file using a different name.

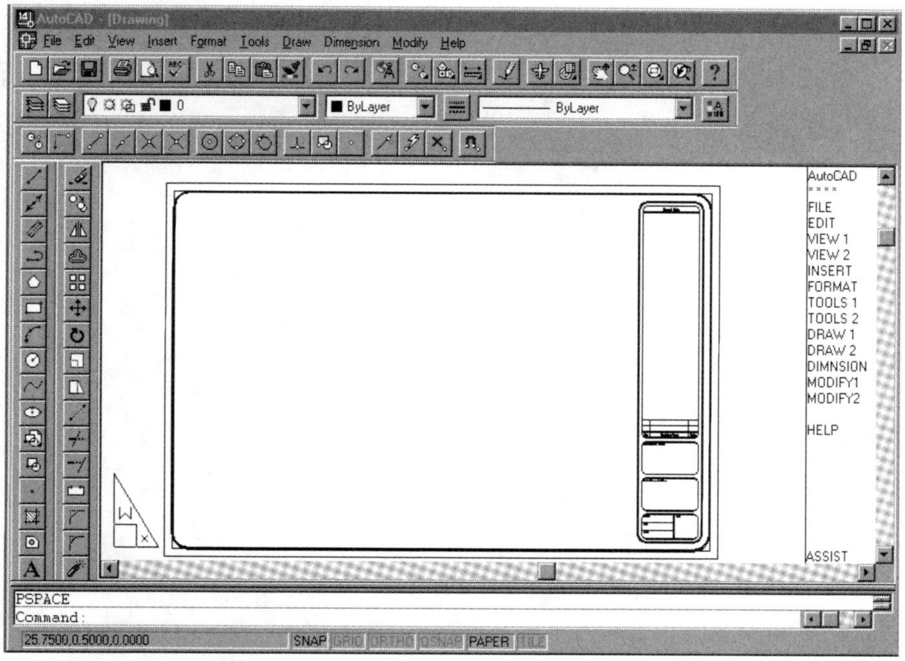

Figure 7–4
Archeng.dwt.

CHAPTER

8

Dimension Variables

AFTER READING THIS CHAPTER, YOU WILL BE ABLE TO:

- Understand the syntax used with setting dimension variables.
- Use dimension commands to correctly place dimensions on a drawing.

KEY CONCEPTS

Dimension drawing commands (Linear, Aligned, Ordinate, Radius, Diameter, Angular, Baseline, Continue, Leader, Tolerance, and Center Mark)

Dimension editing commands (Dimedit and Dimtedit)

Dimension line

Dimension style commands

Dimension text

Dimension utility commands (dimension variables)

Extension line

ELEMENTS OF A DIMENSION

The horizontal line that is broken by the text is called the **dimension line**.

Extension lines are located at the end of dimension lines.

Before discussing dimensions, let's look at what makes up a dimension. There are three basic parts: an **extension line**, a **dimension line**, and **dimension text**. In Figure 8–1 the horizontal line that is broken by the text is called the **dimension line**. Dimension lines are terminated by extension lines. Dimension lines typically have an arrowhead, tick mark, or some other symbol that designates the termination point of the line. The vertical lines in Figure 8–1 represent extension lines. These are the boundary lines of the dimension. The dimension text appears with the dimension line. The default setting for the dimension text is to appear at the middle point of the dimension line, but it can be repositioned at different points along the line. AutoCAD does dimensioning semiautomatically. It will construct the dimension lines and measure the distances for you.

To begin dimensioning, select the Dimension pull-down menu or select DIMNSION from the screen menu (see Figure 8–2), or enter DIM at the command prompt. Dimension commands also can be started from the Dimension toolbar (see Figure 8–3).

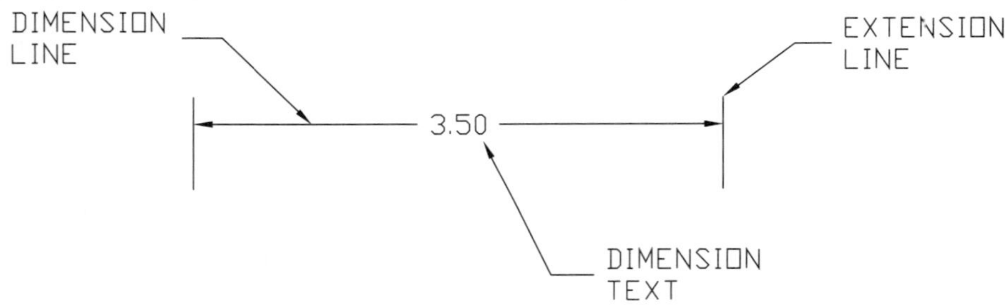

Figure 8–1
Dimension elements.

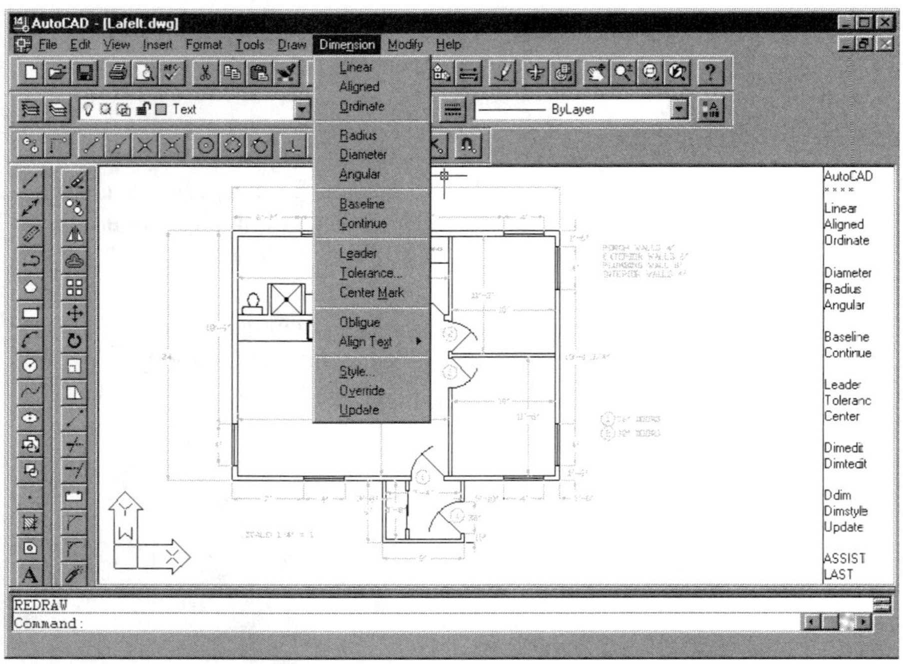

Figure 8–2
Dimension pull-down menu.

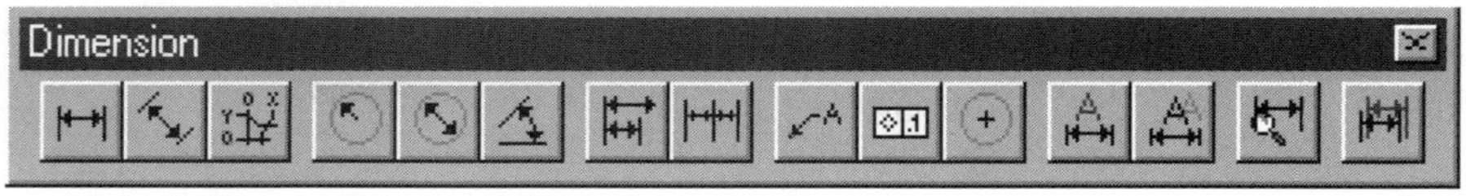

Figure 8–3
Dimension toolbar.

AutoCAD dimensioning commands can be grouped into four basic types: dimension drawing commands, dimension editing commands, dimension utility commands, and dimension style commands (*Using AutoCAD 14*, Auto-Desk Press 1997).

DIMENSION DRAWING COMMANDS

Dimension drawing commands are used to create various types of dimensions. The following table lists the dimension drawing commands.

Dimension Drawing Commands

Linear	Draws horizontal, vertical, or rotated dimensions.
Aligned	Creates a dimension parallel to an object or extension line origins you pick.
Ordinate	Dimensions the X or Y coordinate from a specified point.
Radius	Creates a dimension that depicts the radius of an arc or circle.
Diameter	Dimensions the diameter of a circle.
Angular	Creates a dimension between two nonparallel lines.
Baseline	Continues a dimension in reference to the first extension line.
Continue	Continues a dimension from the second extension line of the selected dimension.
Leader	Attaches text to a line and arrowhead.
Tolerance	Allows you to select a tolerance symbol to display with the dimension.
Center Mark	Creates a center mark and/or centerlines at the center point of an arc or circle.

TRY THIS

Dimension a rectangle.

1. Open AutoCAD.
2. From the Start Up dialog box, select Use a Template. Select the A-size template you created in Chapter 2.
3. Make sure to switch to model space to create the rectangle and the dimensions.
4. Select the Rectangle icon from the Draw toolbar.
5. Enter 3,4 as the start point and 7,6 as the other corner.
6. A rectangle should show in the drawing editor.
7. From the screen menu, select DIMNSION and then select Linear.

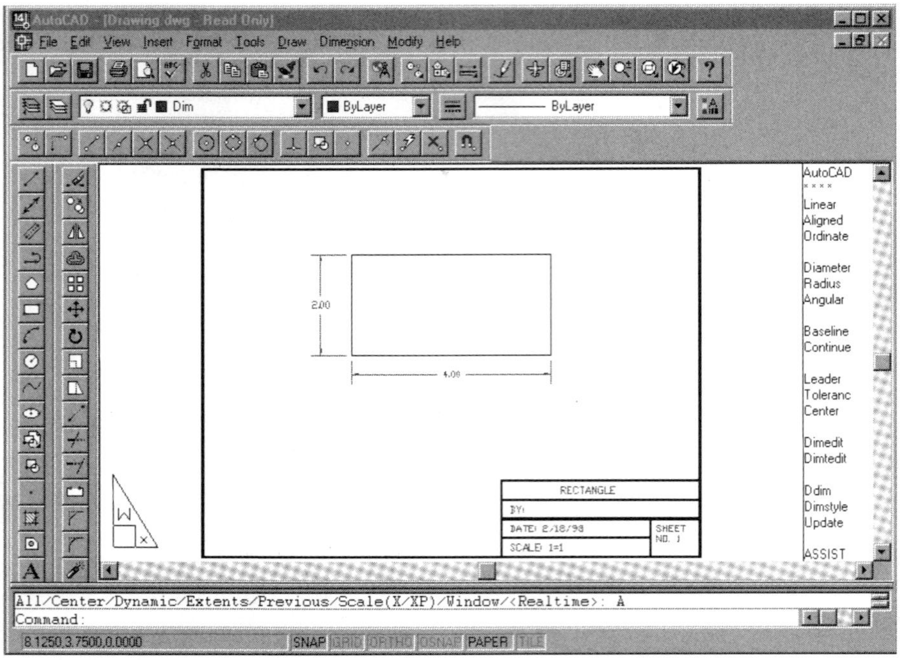

Figure 8–4
Dimensioned rectangle.

8. Create the vertical dimension. Use object snap Endpoint to locate the starting and ending points of the dimension.
9. Repeat Step 8 and create the horizontal dimension.

The dimensioned rectangle should look similar to Figure 8–4.

Dimensioning Arcs and Circles

Radius dimensions are used with arcs and circles, and diameter dimensions are used with circles. Common methods for dimensioning an arc or a circle are shown in Figure 8–5.

Try This

Dimension two circles using the diameter dimensioning option.

1. Start AutoCAD.
2. Select Start from Scratch in the Start Up dialog box.
3. From the Draw pull-down menu, select Circle.
4. Draw two circles, one 5″ in diameter and the other 1″ in diameter.
5. Dimension the 5″ circle with the Diameter option in the Dim menu.

The resulting drawings should be similar to those in Figure 8–6.

If your dimensions do not appear exactly as seen in Figure 8–6, you may need to change some of your dimension variables.

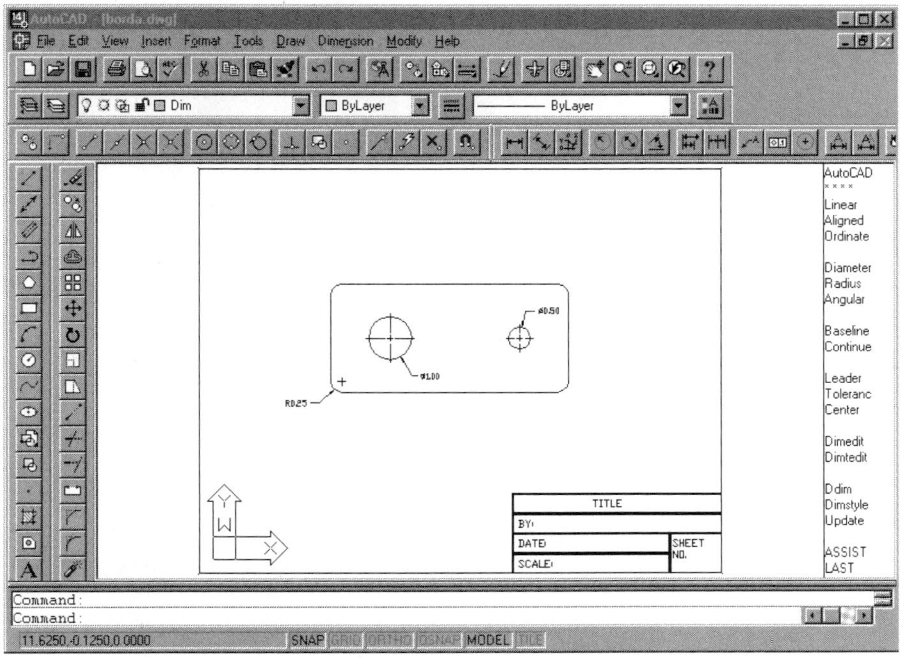

Figure 8–5
Dimensioned arc and circles.

Dimensioning Angles

The Angular dimensioning option is used to dimension angles. There are four ways (see Figure 8–7) to specify angular dimensions:

- Select two nonparallel lines.
- Select an arc.
- Select a circle.
- Select three points.

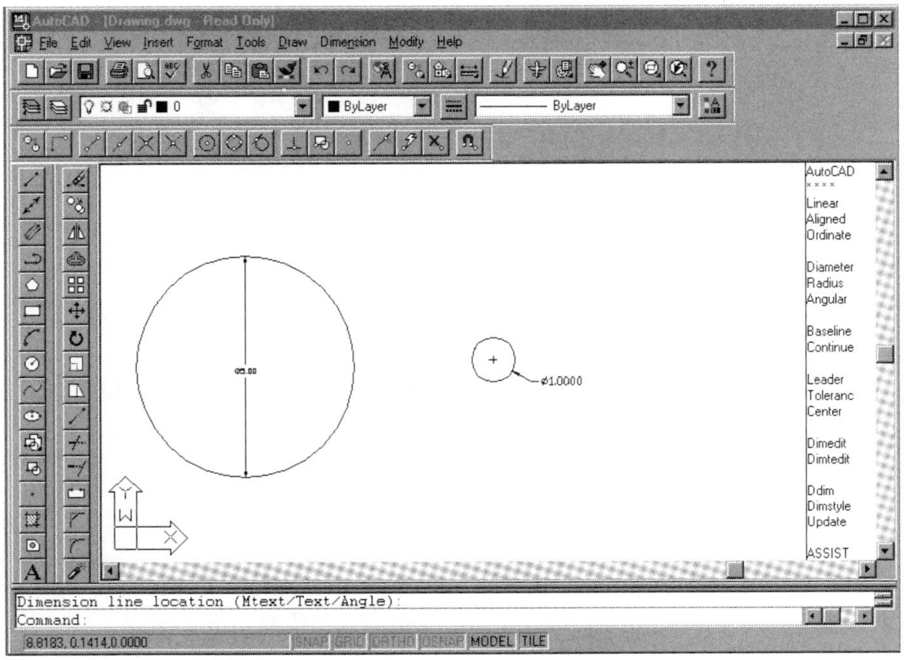

Figure 8–6
Two examples of dimensioned circles.

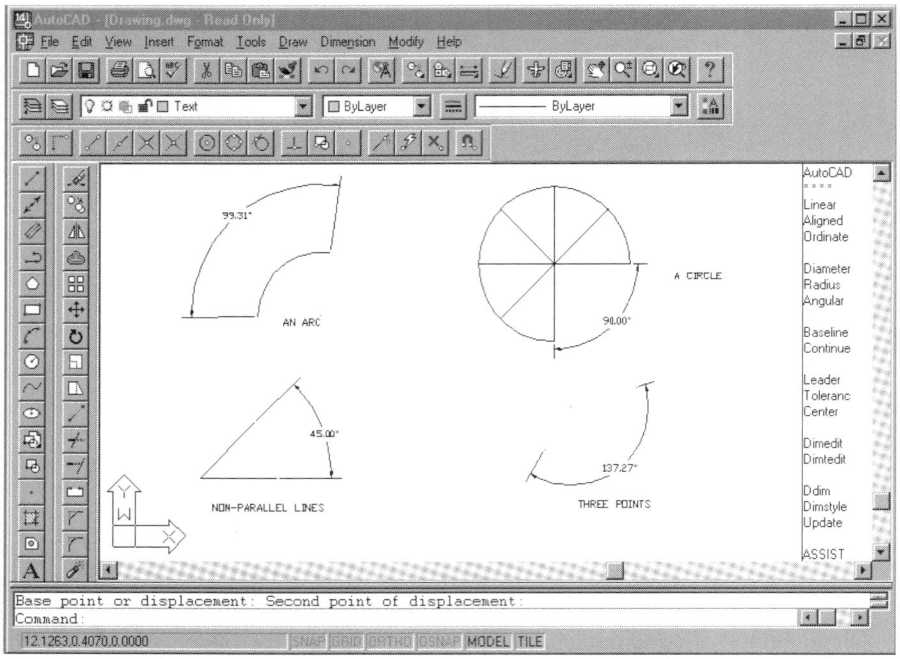

Figure 8–7
Four methods of angular dimensioning.

TRY THIS

Use the angular dimension command to dimension two objects.

1. Open AutoCAD.
2. Select the Start from Scratch option from the Start Up dialog box.
3. Select the Line icon from the Draw toolbar to draw a line.
4. Draw one horizontal line from point 3,3 that is 3 units long.
5. Draw one diagonal line from point 3,3 that is 3 units long and forms a 120° angle with the horizontal line (3<120).
6. Use the Angular dimension variable to dimension the angle.
7. Select the Arc icon from the Draw toolbar. Draw an arc (SEA) that is 75°.
8. Dimension the arc.

Baseline and Continue Dimension Commands

When you are doing linear dimensions, it is sometimes easier to refer to previous dimensions rather than to choose reference points that have been used by prior dimensions. AutoCAD includes two dimension options that allow you to use previous dimensions, namely, **Baseline** and **Continue**. The Baseline dimension command creates continuous dimensions from the first extension line after you specify an initial dimension (AutoDesk Press 1997, pp. 15–17). Figure 8–8 shows a sample of baseline dimensions. The dimen-

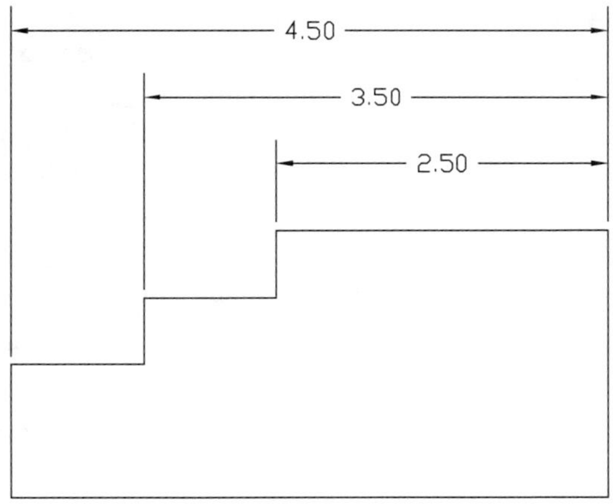

Figure 8–8
Baseline dimensions.

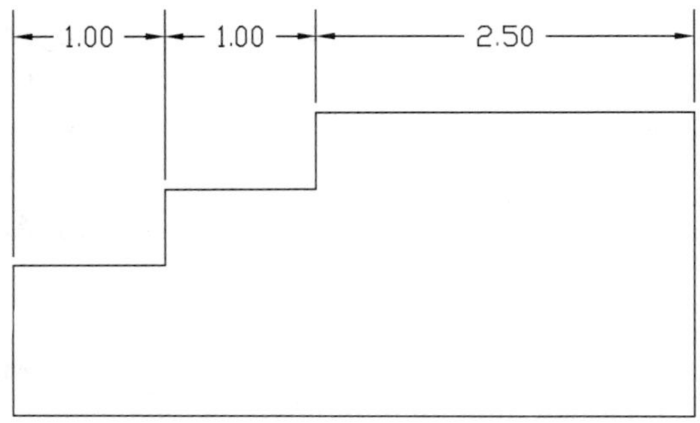

Figure 8–9
Continued dimension.

sion closest to the object (2.50) was the first dimension. All the other dimensions were measured from the *first* extension line of that dimension.

A continued dimension (see Figure 8-9) is different from a baseline dimension in that all measurements are taken from the *second* extension line of the dimension. The continued dimension will usually be collinear with the original dimension.

Center Marks

Center marks can be automatically generated with the **dimcen** command. Dimcen controls the size of the center mark and how it will look. If you enter a negative number for the dimcen value, centerlines along with the center mark will appear. If you enter a positive value, only the center mark will appear. In order to have the center mark appear with a circle or radius, you must set the dimcen variable to the desired value. Use the following sequence to set the size of the center mark:

1. Enter dim at the command prompt.
2. Enter dimcen at the command prompt.
3. Enter a numerical value at the Current value: prompt.
4. At the Dim: command prompt type cen and select the arc or circle in which you want to create the center mark with or without the centerlines.

TRY THIS

Create a center mark in one circle. Create a center mark with centerlines in a second circle .

1. Start AutoCAD.
2. Select Start from Scratch at the Start Up dialog box.
3. Select the Circle icon from the Draw toolbar.
4. Pick any point as the center point.
5. Enter 1.5 as the radius.
6. Copy the first circle and move the second one so that it does not intersect the first circle.
7. At the command prompt, enter dim.
8. At the Dim: prompt, enter dimcen. Type in a value of 0.0625. This will generate a 0.125″ center mark.
9. At the Dim: prompt, enter cen. Pick one of the circles. A 0.125″ center mark should appear.
10. At the Dim: prompt, enter dimcen. Type in a value of −0.0625. This will generate a 0.125″ center mark complete with centerlines.
11. At the Dim: prompt, enter cen. Pick the other circle. A center mark with centerlines should appear.

DIMENSION EDITING COMMANDS

There are two dimension edit commands in AutoCAD: **Dimedit** and **Dimtedit**. The Dimedit command sets the dimension text to its default position, changes existing text, and forces extension lines to a specified angle. Dimedit options include the following:

H	Home text position.
N	New text position.
R	Rotate text.
O	Set text at an oblique angle.

Dimtedit is used to change text placement as well as text orientation. Dimtedit options include the following:

L	Move text to the left.
R	Move text to the right.
H	Home text position.
A	Angle text.

DIMENSION UTILITY COMMANDS

There are numerous dimension variables that you can set to help you dimension. Sometimes when doing a drawing it is necessary to conform to dimension standards. Knowing dimension variables and how to set them is critical to having a drawing look and be correct. Several of the dimension variables have settings of either ON or OFF, whereas for others you must enter a numerical value. The following are some of the dimension variables that you must check before beginning to draw:

DIMASO	Associative dimension variable. If DIMASO is on, and the dimension changes, each part of the dimension will automatically be updated.
DIMASZ	Indicates the size of the arrowheads.
DIMDEC	Indicates the number of decimal places.
DIMEXE	Determines the distance the extension line will extend past the dimension line.
DIMEXO	Determines the extension line origin offset between where the dimension was selected to start and where the extension line actually begins.
DIMGAP	Sets the distance between the text and the end of the dimension line closest to the text.
DIMSCALE	Sets a universal scale factor for all dimension variables. If you were drawing at a $\frac{1}{4}''$ = 1′ scale, the dimscale factor would be 48. This value would automatically scale every dimension variable by a factor of 48.
DIMTXT	Determines the size of the text used in dimensioning.
DIMTSZ	If this variable has a value greater than zero, it displays a tick mark (/) instead of an arrowhead. For instance, if you enter a value of .0625, a tick mark that measured 0.125 will appear at the end of the dimension line.
DIMTXTSTY	Lets you set the text style that you want to use for dimensioning.
DIMUNIT	This value corresponds to the five options (Decimal, Engineering, Architectural, Fractional, or Scientific) in the Advanced or Quick Setup options. The dimension displayed corresponds to the number selected. For example, for architectural dimensions, this value is 3.

To view the dimension variable settings, type **Status** at the dim command prompt. A text box will appear with a listing of all the dim variables. If it is necessary to change a dimension variable, enter the variable name at the command prompt. Any options associated with that variable will then be displayed.

TRY THIS

Change the following dimension variables.

1. Start AutoCAD.
2. Select Start from Scratch at the Start Up dialog box.
3. From the Draw pull-down menu, select Rectangle.
4. Create a rectangle that measures 3 × 4.
5. At the command prompt, enter dim.
6. At the Dim: prompt, enter Status.
7. Follow the prompts on the text display screen. There should be three pages of dimension variables. At the end of the third page, the Dim: prompt should be displayed.
8. At the Dim: prompt in the text display screen, enter the following variables (you can change only one variable at a time). After entering the variable press the <Enter> key in order to type in a value.

Dimasz = 0.125	Dimexe = 0.125
Dimexo = 0.125	Dimgap = 0.0625
Dimtxt = 0.125	Dimdec = 2

9. Check to be sure Dimaso is on.
10. Close the dimension text window.
11. Dimension the rectangle.

DIMENSION STYLE COMMANDS

If you wish to create a customized dimension style, you can do so through the Dimension Styles dialog box. At the command prompt, enter ddim, or go to the Dimension pull-down menu and select Style. The Dimension Styles dialog box should appear (see Figure 8–10). This dialog box controls almost all the dimension variables that you can set. After you customize the settings, you can save them by giving them a name. Anytime that you want to use these settings simply select the style name under which you saved the settings.

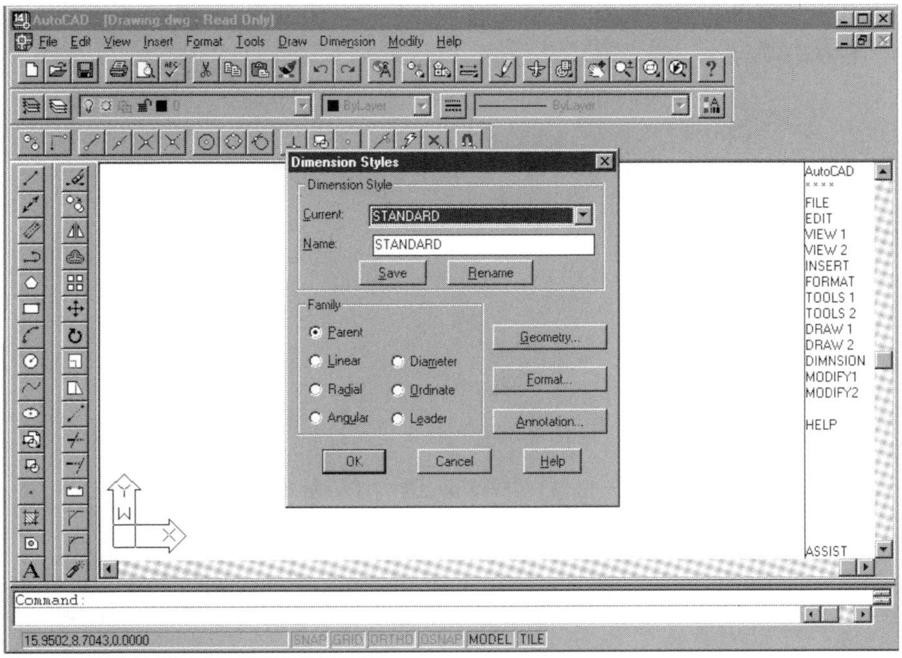

Figure 8–10
Dimension Styles dialog box.

Activity 8–1

Draw Bolt Hole Circles

Plotter paper size:	A	
Suggested settings:	Grid	0.50″
	Snap	0.125″
	Layers (7)	**0** (default border)
		Cen, Linetype center, Color: cyan
		Dim, Linetype continuous, Color: green
		Hid, Linetype hidden, Color: magenta
		Obj, Linetype continuous, Color: black
		Tbk, Linetype continuous, Color: red
		Txt, Linetype continuous, Color: green

Hints:

1. Open your border template file for an A-size drawing. After it has loaded, use the SAVEAS command to rename the drawing file ACT8-1. Use Figure 8–11 on p. 137 as the model for the drawing.
2. Make sure you are in model space before you begin drawing the objects.
3. Be sure to check layer settings before you begin to draw or enter text.
4. Use the object snap commands to create the entities.

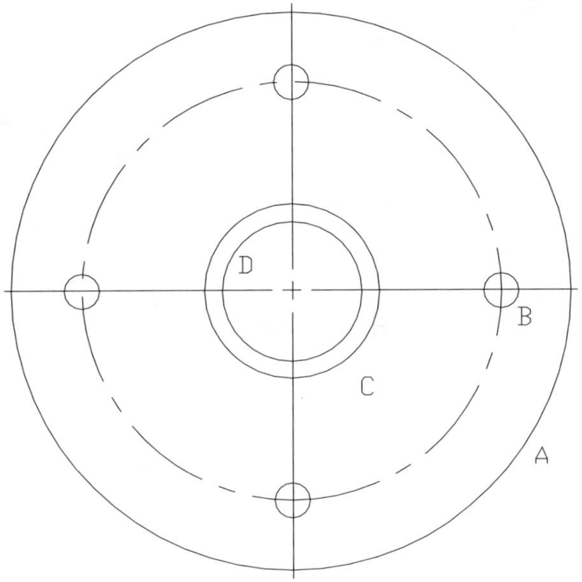

A	B	C	D
4.00	.25	1.25	1.00

BOLT HOLE CIRCLES

BY:

DATE: 2/16/98

SCALE: 1=1

SHEET NO. 1

Figure 8–11
Activity 8–1

ACTIVITY 8–2

Draw a Flange Bushing

Plotter paper size: B
Suggested settings: Grid 0.50″
Snap 0.125″
Layers (7) **0** (default border)
Cen, Linetype center, Color: cyan
Dim, Linetype continuous, Color: green
Hid, Linetype hidden, Color: magenta
Obj, Linetype continuous, Color: black
Tbk, Linetype continuous, Color: red
Txt, Linetype continuous, Color: green

Hints:

1. Open your border template file for a B-size drawing. After it has loaded, use the SAVEAS command to rename the drawing file ACT8-2. Use Figure 8–12 on p. 139 as the model for the drawing.
2. Make sure you are in model space before you begin drawing the objects.
3. Be sure to check layer settings before you begin to draw or enter text.
4. Use the object snap commands to create the entities.

ACTIVITY 8–3

Draw a Short Shaft

Plotter paper size: B
Suggested settings: Grid 0.50″
Snap 0.125″
Layers (7) **0** (default border)
Cen, Linetype center, Color: cyan
Dim, Linetype continuous, Color: green
Hid, Linetype hidden, Color: magenta
Obj, Linetype continuous, Color: black
Tbk, Linetype continuous, Color: red
Txt, Linetype continuous, Color: green

Hints:

1. Open your border template file for a B-size drawing. After it has loaded, use the SAVEAS command to rename the drawing file ACT8-3. Use Figure 8–13 on p. 140 as the model for the drawing.
2. Make sure you are in model space before you begin drawing the objects.

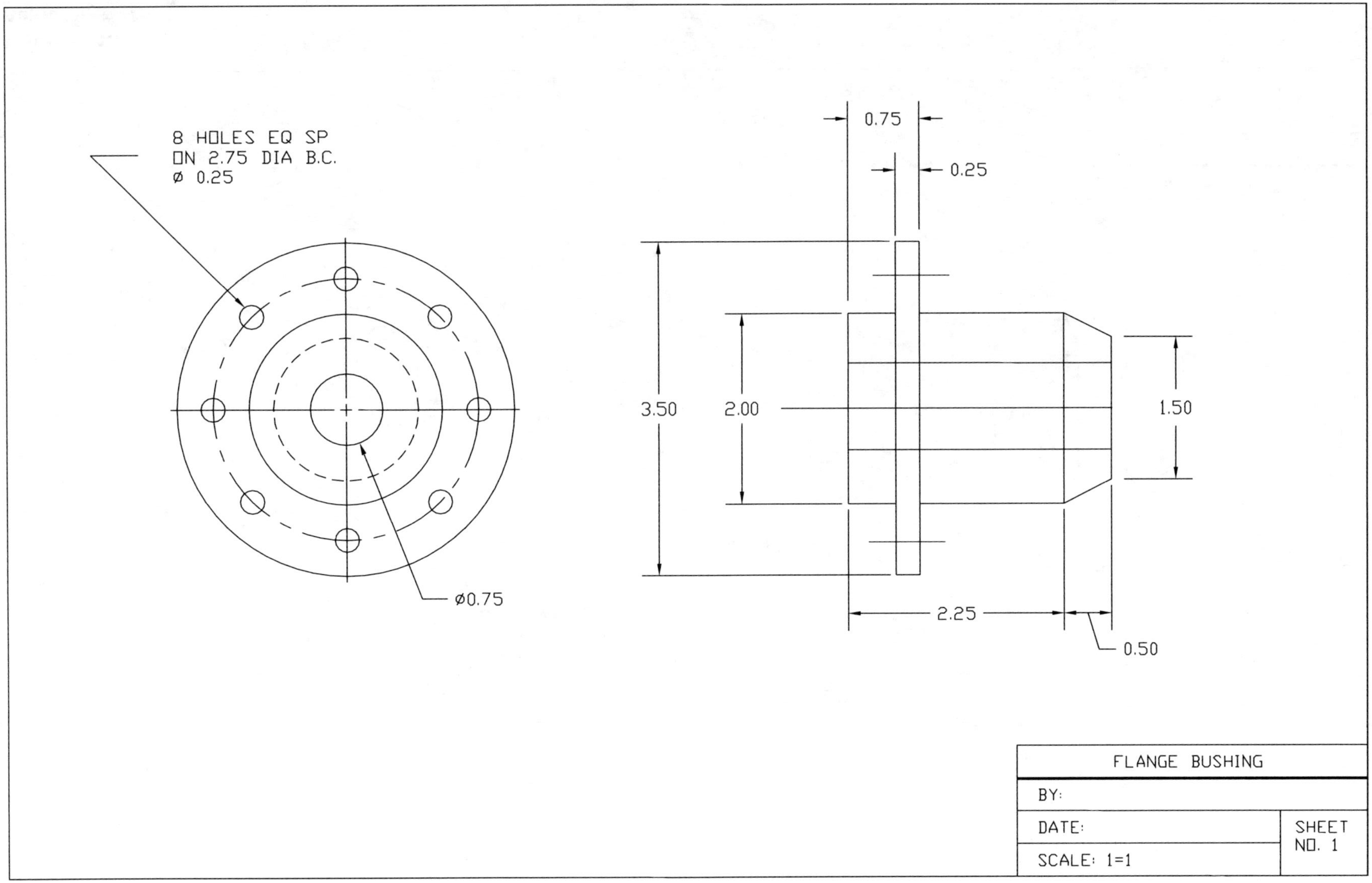

Figure 8–12
Activity 8–2

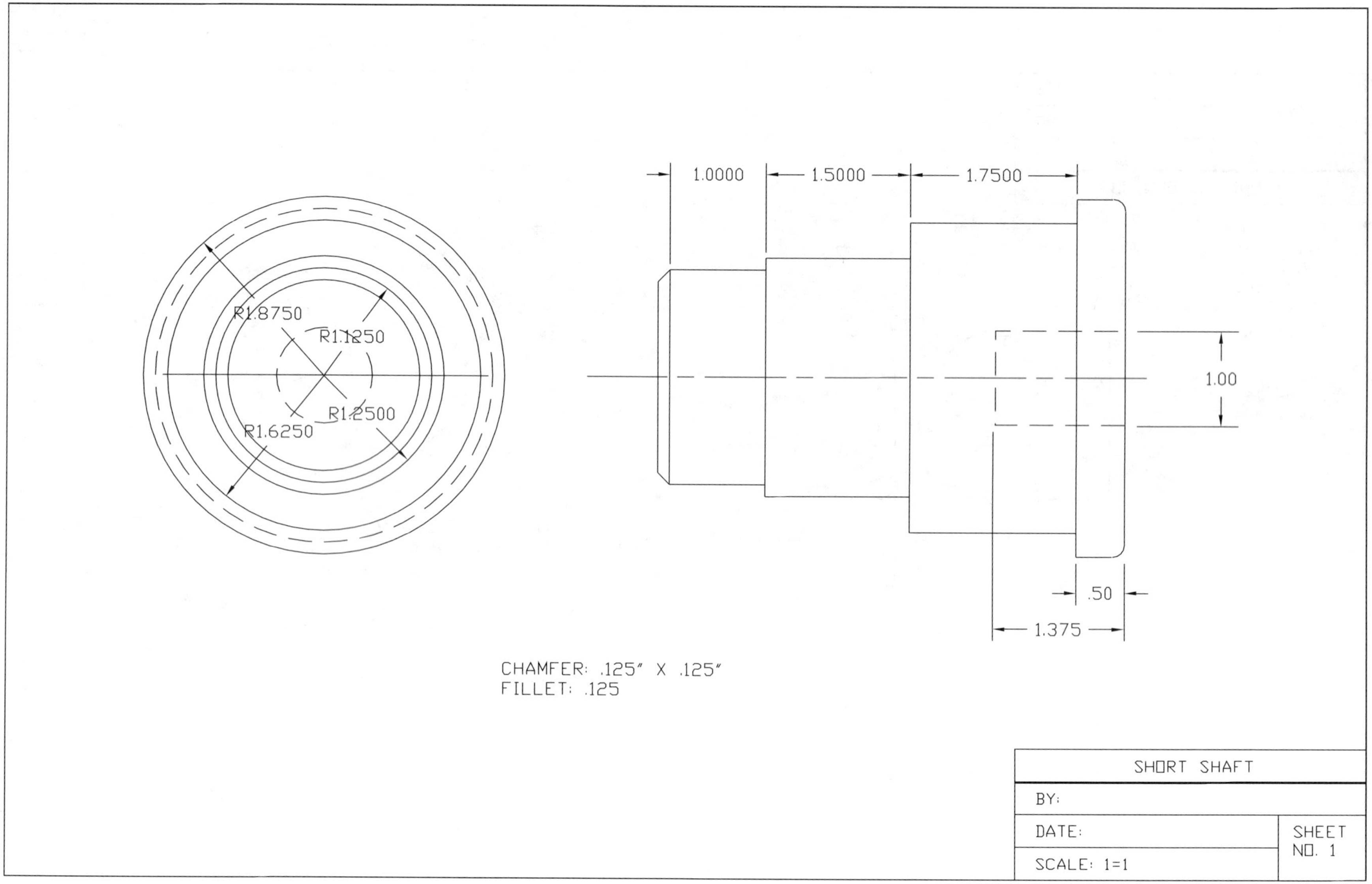

Figure 8–13
Activity 8–3

3. Be sure to check layer settings before you begin to draw or enter text.
4. Use the object snap commands to create the entities and place the dimensions.

ACTIVITY 8–4

Draw a Grate

Plotter paper size:	B	
Suggested settings:	Grid	0.50″
	Snap	0.125″
	Layers (7)	**0** (default border)
		Cen, Linetype center, Color: cyan
		Dim, Linetype continuous, Color: green
		Hid, Linetype hidden, Color: magenta
		Obj, Linetype continuous, Color: black
		Tbk, Linetype continuous, Color: red
		Txt, Linetype continuous, Color: green

Hints:

1. Open your border template file for a B-size drawing. After it has loaded, use the SAVEAS command to rename the drawing file ACT8-4. Use Figure 8–14 on p. 142 as the model for the drawing.
2. Make sure you are in model space before you begin drawing the objects.
3. Be sure to check layer settings before you begin to draw or enter text.
4. Use the object snap commands to create the entities and locate the dimensions.

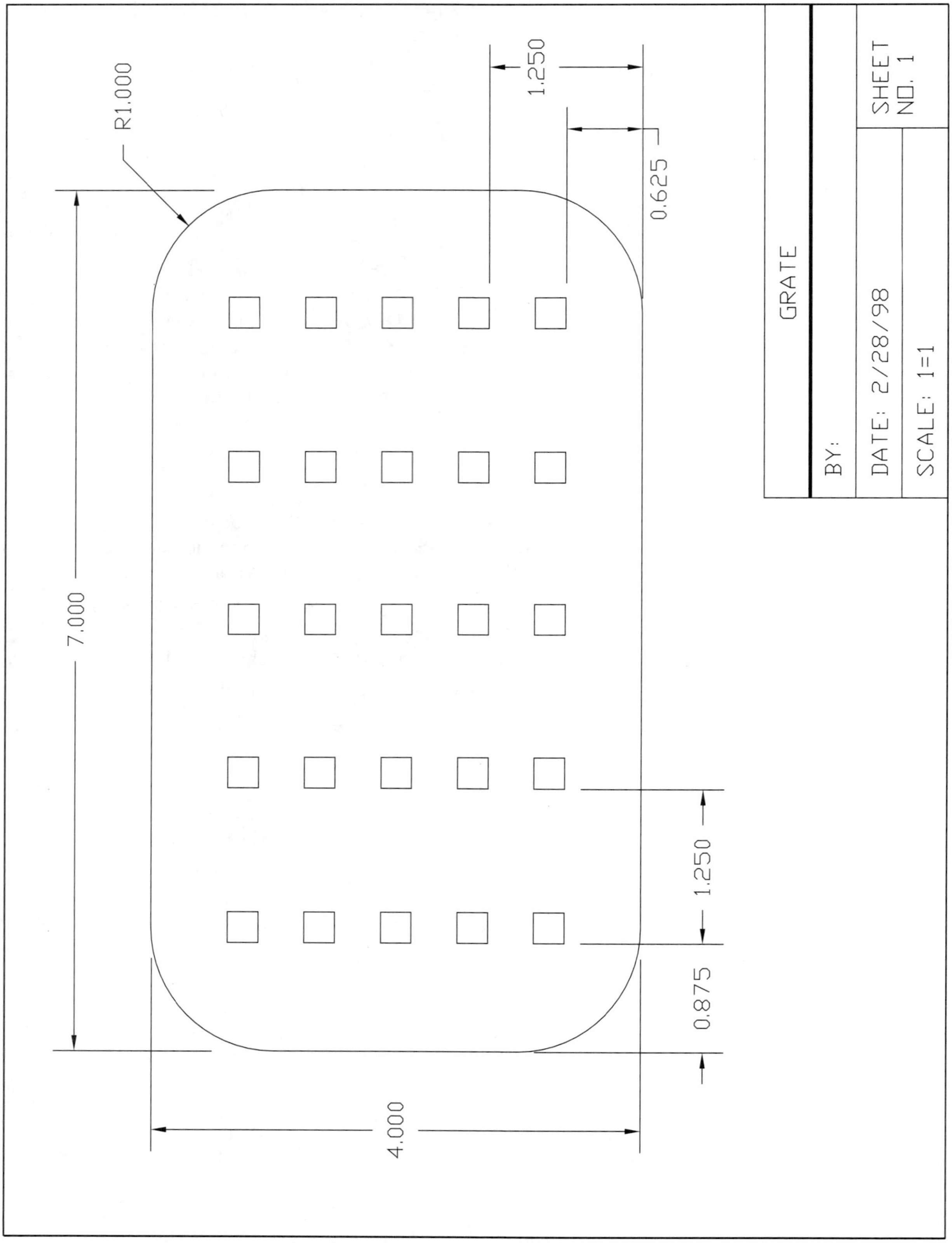

Figure 8–14
Activity 8–4

CHAPTER

9

Printer/Plotter Configuration

AFTER READING THIS CHAPTER, YOU WILL BE ABLE TO:

- Configure a printer or plotter in order to print or plot a drawing.

Before printing or plotting a drawing, you must be sure that the printer or plotter has been configured. Each printer/plotter configuration contains information such as the device name, device model number, output port, and other specific printer/plotter driver settings. A plotter configuration file can also contain information on paper size, orientation, plot scale factors, pen parameters, plot origin, and plot rotation.

To execute the print/plot command, you can use one of four methods: you can click on the printer icon in the Standard toolbar, select Print from the File pull-down menu, type print or plot at the command prompt, or select Plot in the File directory in the screen menu (see Figure 9–1).

Once the plot command has been executed, you will be presented with a Print/Plot Configuration dialog box in which you need to set certain options. You need to remember that the settings in this dialog box can change, because each individual who uses the plotter may have different print/plot requirements from yours. Each time you use the plotter, you must check the following settings in the Print/Plot Configuration dialog box:

- The **Device and Default Selection** allows you to pick the output device on which to print or plot the drawing (see Figure 9–2).
- **Pen Assignments** lets you assign a pen to a certain color, determine the pen speed, and set the line width as well as the linetype. Colors usually differentiate layers that have specific characteristics you want to print or plot. Figure 9–3 shows the listings in the Pen Assignments dialog box.

TRY THIS

Check the default printer.

1. Open AutoCAD.
2. Select Start from Scratch.

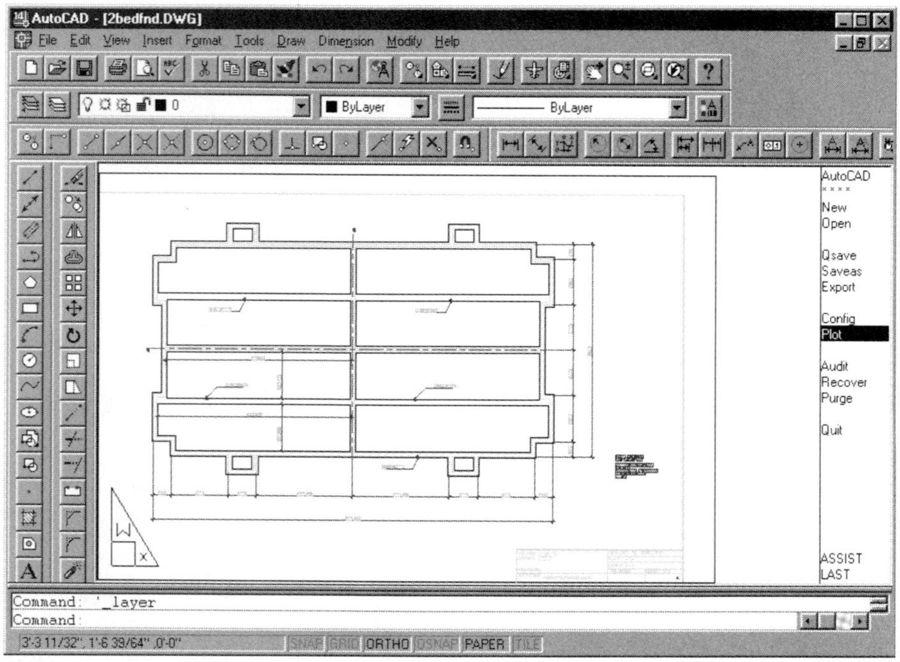

Figure 9–1
Screen menu Plot command.

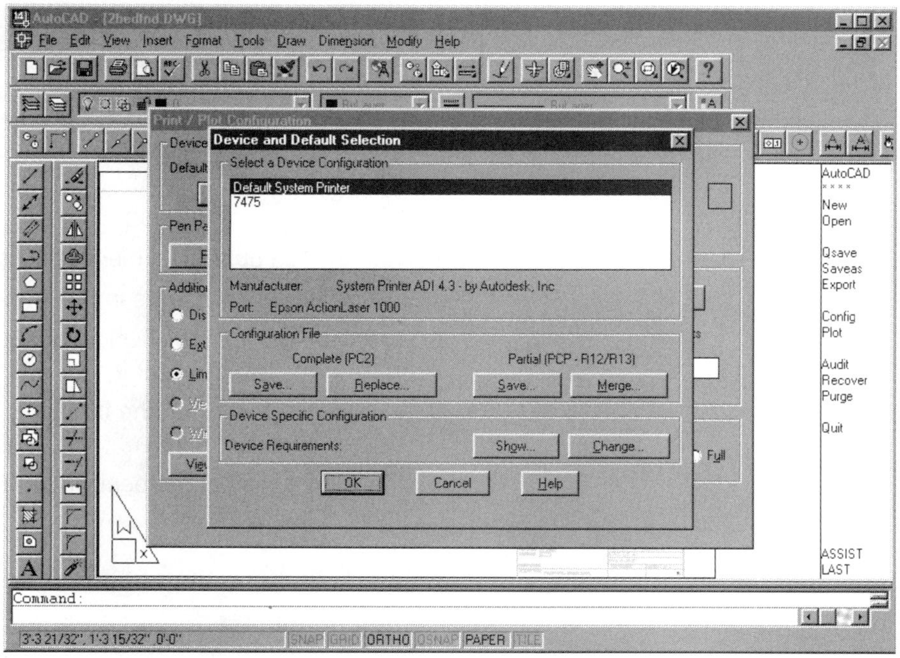

Figure 9–2
Device and Default Selection dialog box.

3. From the File pull-down menu, select Print.
4. Select the Default System Printer in the Print/Plot Configuration dialog box.
5. Identify the printer/plotter options available.

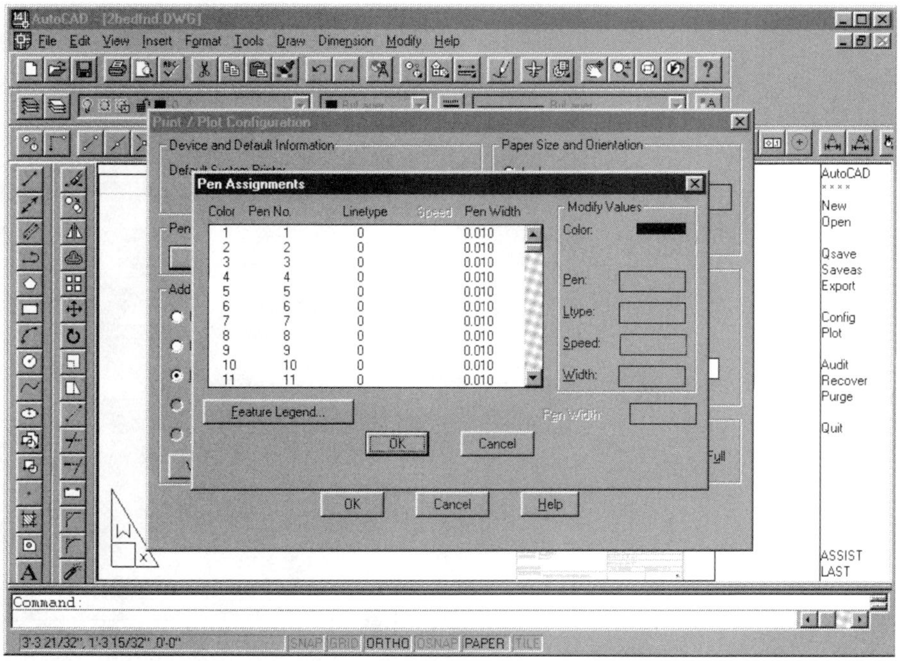

Figure 9–3
Pen Assignments dialog box.

TRY THIS

Check pen settings.

1. Open AutoCAD.
2. Select Start from Scratch.
3. From the File pull-down menu, select Print.
4. Select Pen Assignments in the Print/Plot Configuration dialog box.
5. Select Pen No. 1 and check the assigned color. It should be red. Click on Pen No. 1 to deselect it.
6. Repeat the process for the first seven pens to check the color assigned to each number.
7. Check the speed of the pens. In older plotters, faster pen speed often meant a poorer plot.

- **Optimization** controls plotter pen efficiency by controlling line retracing.
- Included in the **Additional Parameters** section of the Print/Plot Configuration dialog box are the options **Display**, **Extents**, **Limits**, **View**, and **Window**. These determine what portion of the drawing you want plotted (see Figure 9–4). If you choose Display, only those objects showing in the display area are plotted. The Extents option plots all drawing entities. The Limits option plots only those objects in the area defined by Limits. If you select View, you will plot a saved view. If you select Window, you will define an area you want plotted with a window.

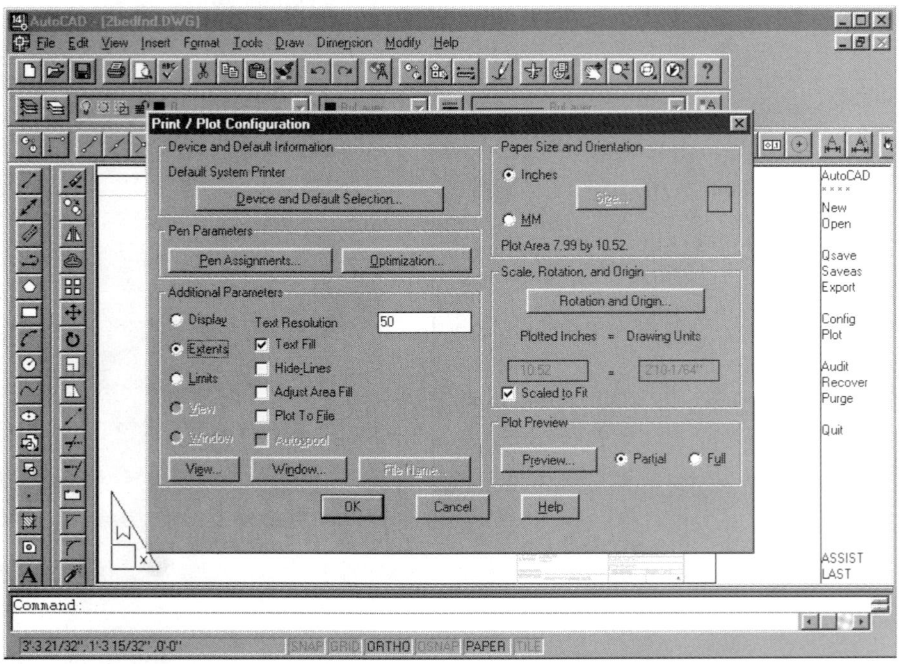

Figure 9–4
Print/Plot Configuration dialog box.

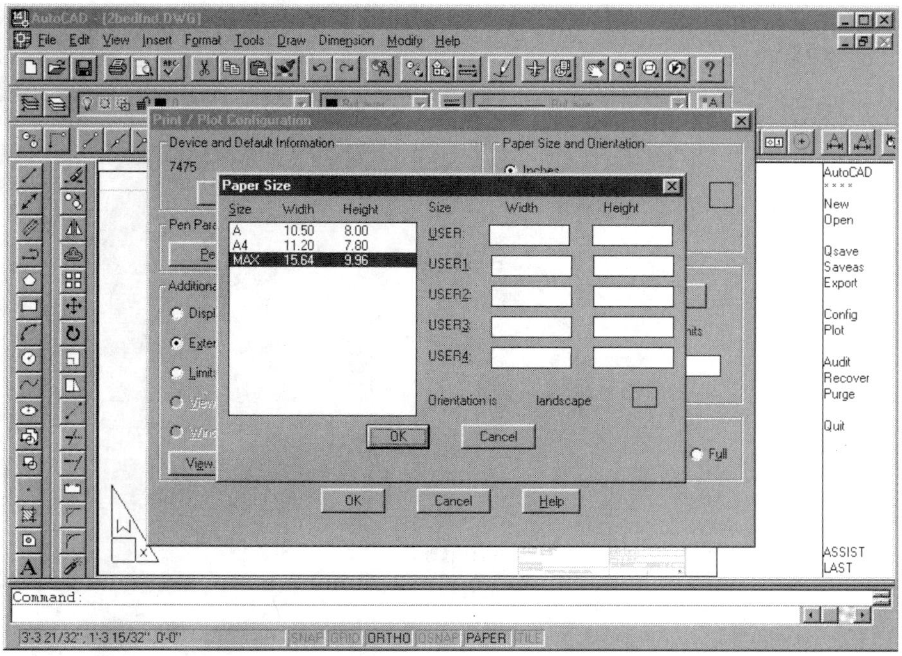

Figure 9–5
Paper Size option.

- **Paper Size** is either in inches or in millimeters (mm). If the default system printer is selected, standard default sizes are listed in the Paper Size dialog box. You can also create custom sizes (see Figure 9–5). Orientation is determined by the default setting of the printer.
- **Rotation and Origin** refer to positioning the drawing on the paper.
- If objects are drawn full size, either they may be fitted to a piece of paper, or a scale value may be entered. Most drawings are plotted at a precise scale.
- **Preview** has two options, **Partial** and **Full**. Preview allows you to see how the drawing will be arranged on the piece of paper after you have made your settings. The Partial option shows an outline view of the drawing on the paper (see Figure 9–6). The Full option shows the actual position of the drawing on the paper based on the settings you have selected (see Figure 9–7).

Other options in the Print/Plot Configuration dialog box that can be selected include the following:

- Text Fill makes letters solid in color.
- Hide Lines hides lines in the background of a solid object that are covered by any part of the object.
- Adjust Area Fill is based upon pen width. You can enter a numerical value to guarantee that all filled areas will be drawn a certain width.
- Plot to File creates a file that can be plotted at a later time without using AutoCAD.

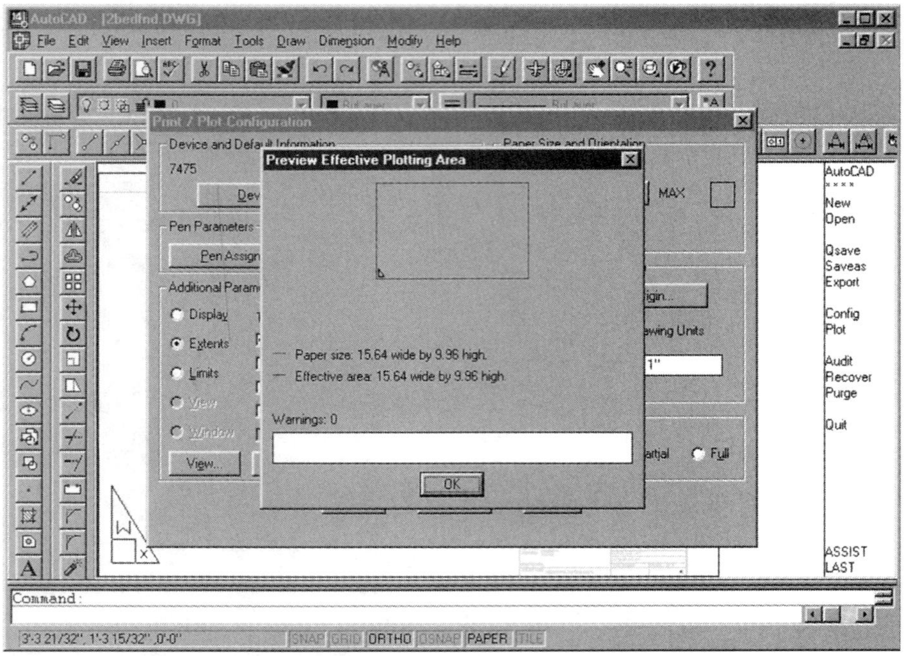

Figure 9–6
Partial preview option.

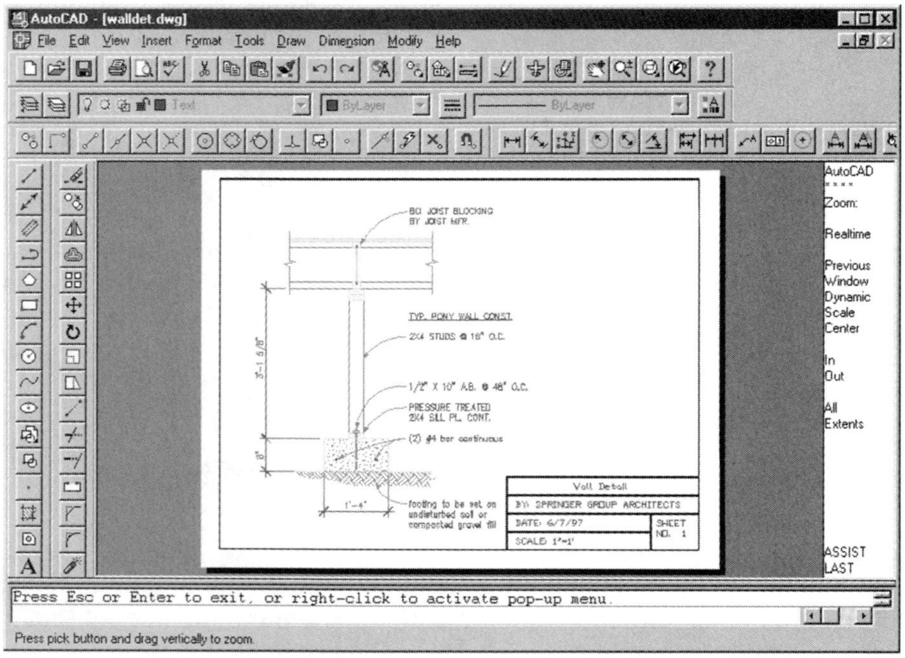

Figure 9–7
Full preview option.

Chapter 9 ■ Activities

Activity 9–1

Plot the Entities Drawing

From the Chapter 2 activities, open the Entities drawing. Select Print from the File pull-down menu. Set the necessary plot parameters based on the available output device attached to your computer or network.

- Check Device to determine if the appropriate printer/plotter has been selected.
- Check Pen Assignments.
- Determine whether you want to plot Display, Extents, Limits, View or Window.
- Make sure Inches is selected, and check for correct paper size.
- Set Rotation to 0, and set the X and Y origin offsets to 0.
- Plot the drawing full scale, 1=1.
- Do a Full preview of the drawing to check its location on paper.
- Make any adjustments necessary.

It should fit on an A-size sheet of paper.

Activity 9–2

Plot the Shim Drawing

Repeat Activity 9–1, only plot the Shim drawing that was also created at the end of Chapter 2.

Activity 9–3

Plot the Object Snaps Drawing

Plot the Object Snaps drawing that was created at the end of Chapter 5.

ACTIVITY 9–4

Plot the Drawings from the Chapter 6 Activities

Plot the drawings from Activities 6–1 through 6–4 at the end of Chapter 6.

ACTIVITY 9–5

Plot the Drawings from the Chapter 8 Activities

Plot the drawings from Activities 8–1 through 8–4 at the end of Chapter 8.

CHAPTER

10

System Dimension Variables

AFTER READING THIS CHAPTER, YOU WILL BE ABLE TO:

- Understand better the system dimension variables and how drawing entities are affected by drawing scales.

KEY CONCEPTS

Dimension system variables

Dimscale

Limits

Ltscale

Zoomxp

ESTABLISHING DRAWING LIMITS

The **drawing limits** are two-dimensional (X,Y) points in the world coordinate system that represent a lower-left corner of the drawing area and an upper-right corner of the drawing area. Drawing limits also determine the area of the drawing that can display grid dots.

Before you begin any drawing, it is important to establish certain drawing parameters. Determining the **drawing limits** is one of the most important parameters to establish before starting any drawing activity. The relationship between the drawing limits set in model space and the paper size established in paper space is critical for printing or plotting a drawing to scale. Because drawing entities are typically drawn full scale in AutoCAD it is necessary to correctly scale a drawing created in model space to the paper size set in paper space. When drawings are scaled, certain drawing entities are affected. Architectural drawing activities will be used to illustrate the various topics discussed in this chapter. If you were going to plot or print a drawing on B-size paper (17″ × 11″) you would first have to account for the mechanical limits of the printer/plotter to establish the actual plot area of the sheet of paper.

For example, let's say that you have determined that you will create a drawing using $\frac{1}{4}''$ = 1′ as the scale. If you are going to output this drawing on B-size paper, the drawing limits will be 62′ × 40′ (15.5 × 10). These limits were determined by multiplying the size of the sheet of paper (15.5 × 10) by 4, taking into account the printer/plotter requirements.

If you had selected $\frac{1}{8}''$ = 1′ as the drawing scale, then the model space drawing limits would have been 124′ × 80′ for B-size paper. In order to select the correct drawing scale, it is necessary to have some understanding of the size of the drawing area needed to create the drawing entities.

TRY THIS

Calculate the appropriate limits for the following drawing scales.

1. $\frac{1}{16}''$ = 1′ for a drawing to be plotted on B-size paper (15.5 × 10).
2. $\frac{1}{8}''$= 1″ for a drawing to be plotted on A-size paper (10 × 7.7).
3. $\frac{1}{8}''$ = 1′ for a drawing to be plotted on B-size paper (15.5 × 10).

SETTING DIMENSION SYSTEM VARIABLES

Drawing scales also affect the settings of the dimension system variables, which control the appearance of dimensions. You can set dimension system variables on the command line or through the Dimension Styles (DDIM) dialog box (see Figure 10–1). You can also enter DDIM at the command prompt line or select Style from the Dimension pull-down menu. The DDIM dialog box will appear on screen.

Dimension system variables must be set to account for any scale factor used to create a drawing, and certain standards for dimension variables

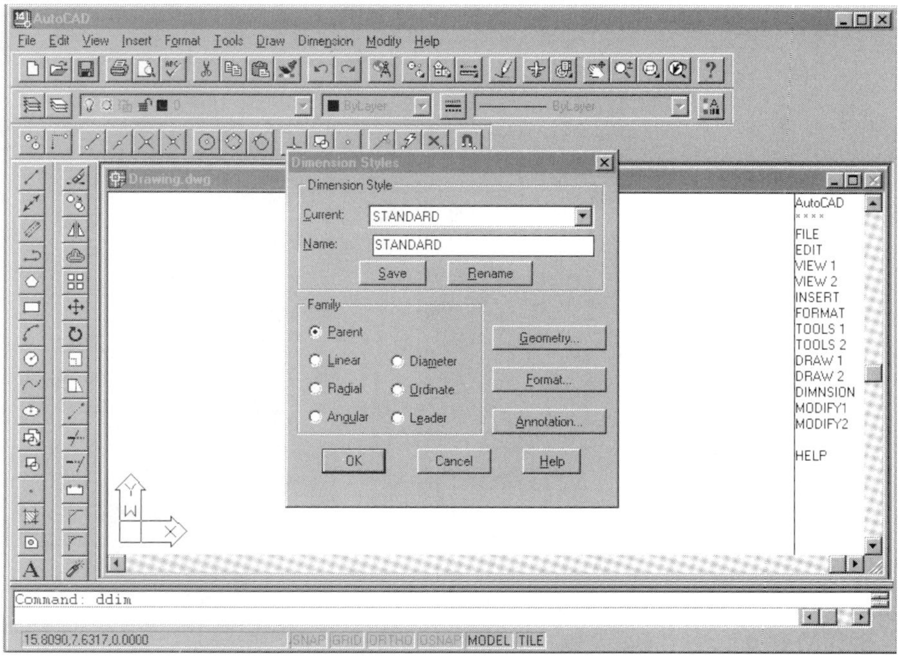

Figure 10–1
Dimension Styles dialog box.

need to be followed when creating a drawing. For instance, a typical text height on a drawing is $\frac{1}{8}$″ (0.125) tall. Table 10–1 lists the relationships between text size and drawing scale. You would set the same scale factor values to generate dimension arrowheads or tick marks that would print or plot at $\frac{1}{8}$″ (0.125).

To set the size of the most commonly used variables, select Geometry in the DDIM dialog box. The dialog box (see Figure 10–2) that appears allows you to set the following dimension system variables: arrowhead size (dimasz), type of arrowhead, dimension line offset (dimexo), dimension line extension (dimexe), center mark size (dimcen), dimscale, suppression (turning off) of the first or second dimension line, and suppression of the first or second extension line. You can also set the color of selected dimension system variables.

Table 10–1

Correlating Scale Factors with Text Size

SCALE	SCALE FACTOR	TO PLOT TEXT SIZE AT...	SET DRAWING TEXT SIZE TO...
$\frac{1}{8}$″ = 1′-0″	96	$\frac{1}{8}$″	12″
$\frac{3}{16}$″ = 1′-0″	64	$\frac{1}{8}$″	8″
$\frac{1}{4}$″ = 1′-0″	48	$\frac{1}{8}$″	6″
$\frac{3}{8}$″ = 1′-0″	32	$\frac{1}{8}$″	4″
$\frac{1}{2}$″ = 1′-0″	24	$\frac{1}{8}$″	3″
$\frac{3}{4}$″ = 1′-0″	16	$\frac{1}{8}$″	2″
1″ = 1′-0″	12	$\frac{1}{8}$″	1.5″
$1\frac{1}{2}$″ = 1′-0″	8	$\frac{1}{8}$″	1.0″

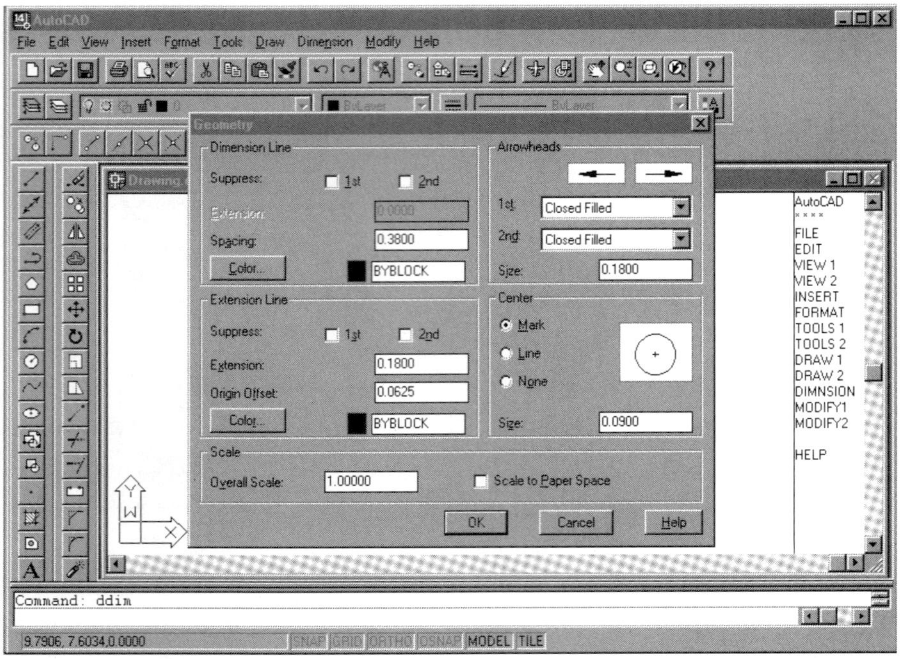

Figure 10–2
DDIM Geometry dialog box.

TRY THIS

Set the following dimension system variables in the DDIM Geometry dialog box.

1. From the Dimension pull-down menu, select Style.
2. Choose Geometry to open the Geometry dialog box.
3. Set the arrowhead size to 0.125.
4. Set the Extension to 0.125.
5. Select Line in the Center option, and change the size to 0.0625.
6. Choose OK to exit the Geometry dialog box.
7. Choose OK to exit the DDIM dialog box.

Another option in the DDIM dialog box is **Format**. When you select the Format option, a dialog box appears that allows you to make settings that affect the way horizontal and vertical dimensions appear on the screen (see Figure 10–3).

The third option in the DDIM dialog box is **Annotation**. This option allows you to set text-related factors associated with dimensioning, such as type of units (dimunit), number of decimal places to be shown (dimdec), tolerances, text height (dimtxt), text style (dimstyle), and the gap between the text and the dimension lines (dimgap) (see Figure 10–4).

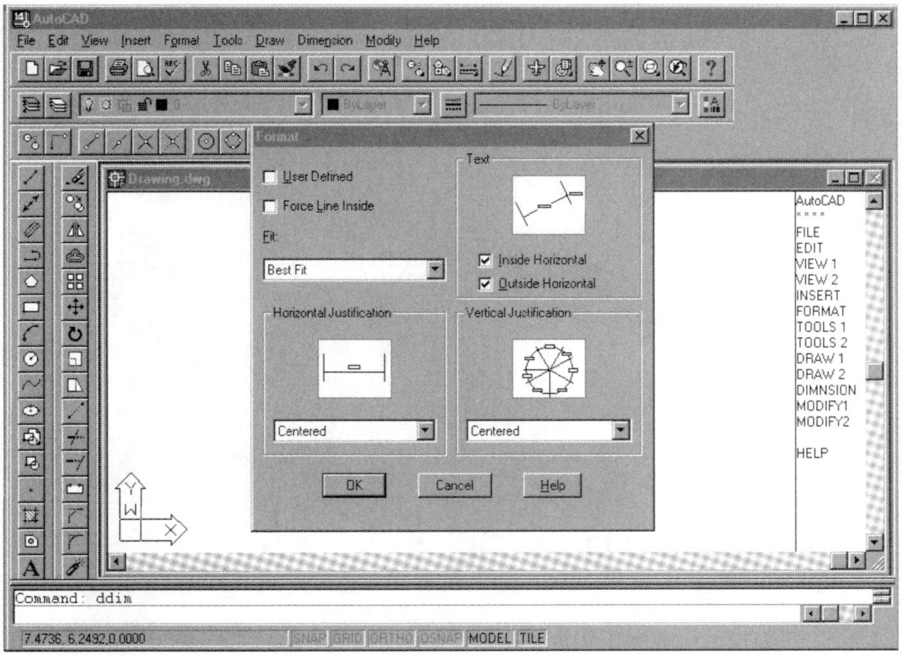

Figure 10–3
DDIM Format dialog box.

TRY THIS

Set the following dimension system variables in the DDIM Annotation dialog box.

1. From the Dimension pull-down menu, select Style.
2. Choose <u>A</u>nnotation to open the Annotation dialog box.
3. Change the units to Architectural.
4. Change the Text height to 0.125.

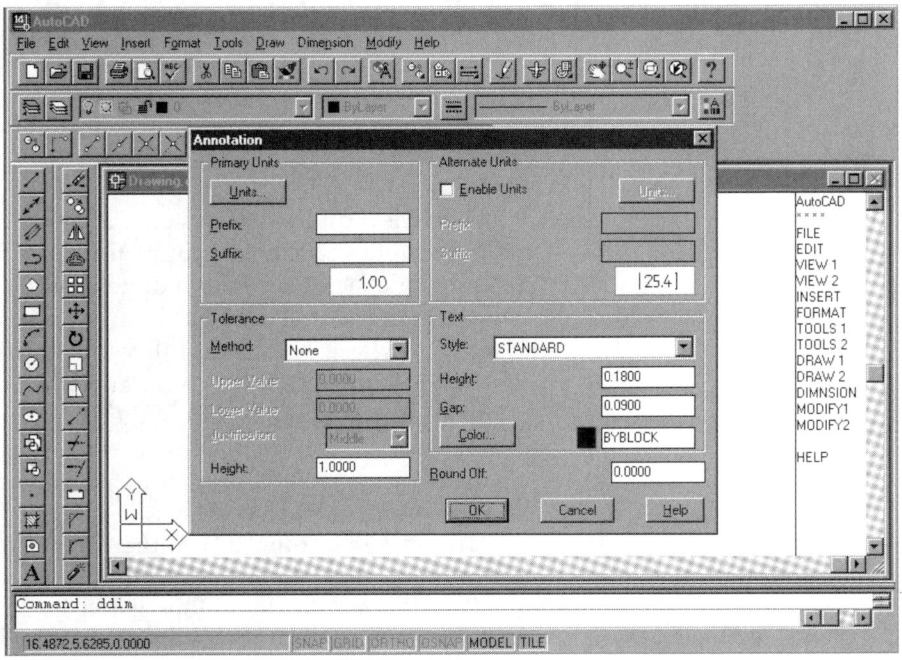

Figure 10–4
DDIM Annotation dialog box.

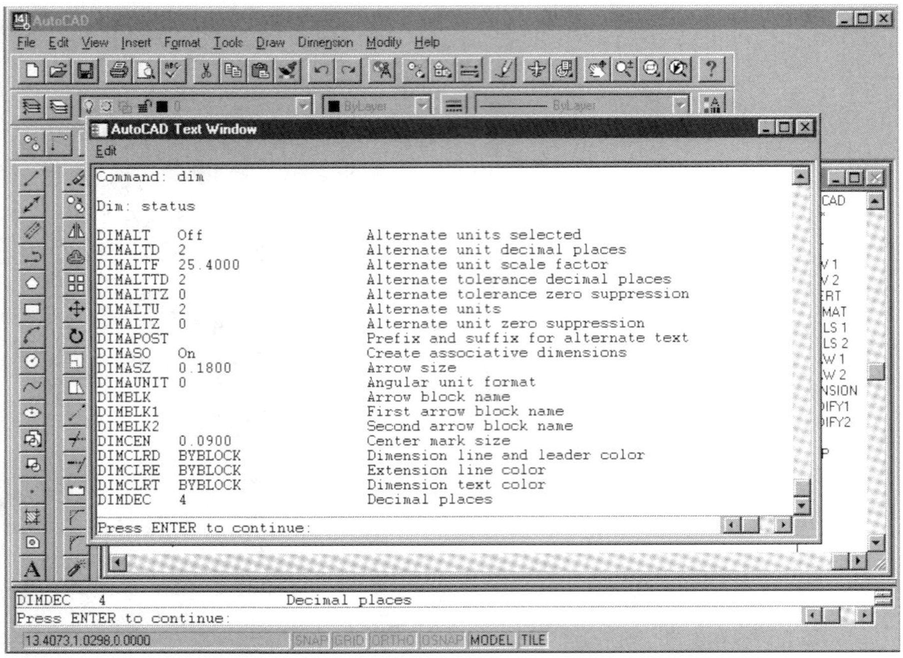

Figure 10–5
Text window listing all the dimension system variables and their settings.

5. Change the Text color to green.
6. Choose OK to exit the Annotation dialog box.
7. Choose OK to exit the DDIM dialog box.

One way to check all the dimension system variables in a text dialog box is to type dim at the command prompt and then type status. A listing of the dimension system variables and their settings will be listed in a text dialog box (see Figure 10–5). You can also enter the acronym of each dimension system variable at the command prompt to determine its existing setting.

Dimscale

Dimscale is a dimension system variable that can be used to adjust dimension variable values to account for the drawing scale. Dimscale sets the overall scale factor applied to dimensioning variables that specify sizes, distances, or offsets. AutoCAD computes a scale factor that translates text sizes, arrowhead sizes, and other scaled distances to plot at their face values. The AutoCAD Help command for Dimscale (see Figure 10–6) gives more information about setting the Dimscale system variable.

If the dimension variables are set to reflect a 1:1 ratio, then the Dimscale dimension variable can be set to correspond to the drawing scale. The default setting for Dimscale is 1.

If you were going to use the dimension system variable settings displayed in Table 10–2 in a drawing, and if you had selected a drawing scale of $\frac{1}{4}''$ = 1′, each of the values listed in the second column of Table 10–2 would also have to be adjusted to reflect the drawing scale. The third col-

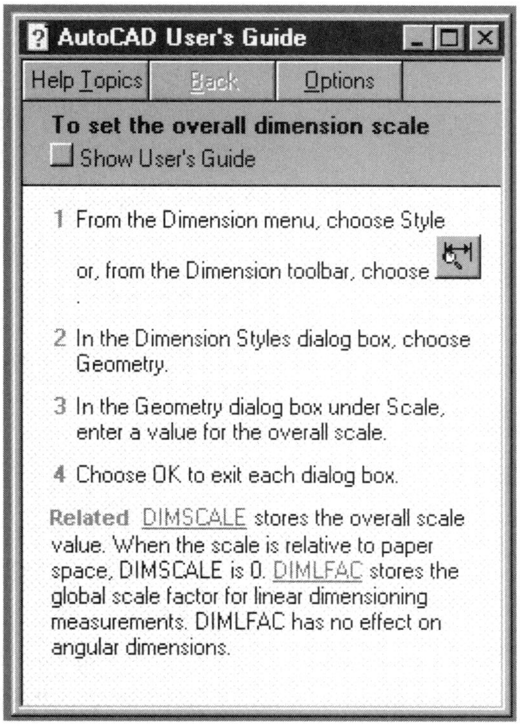

Figure 10–6
Setting the Dimscale system variable.

Table 10-2

DIMENSION VARIABLE	VALUE	ADJUSTED VALUE
Dimtxt (text height)	0.125	6″
Dimgap (distance between dimension line and text)	0.125	6″
Dimexe (extension above dimension line)	0.125	6″
Dimexo (extension line origin offset)	0.0625	3″
Dimtsz (tick mark)	0.0625	3″

umn of the table lists the new values based on the drawing scale of $\frac{1}{4}'' = 1'$. Each of the individual values would have to be adjusted in order to plot to the correct size.

A drawing scale of $\frac{1}{4}'' = 1'$ translates to a Dimscale setting of 48 (the same ratio as $\frac{1}{4}'' = 12''$, or 4×12). Keep in mind that the unit designation must be the same for both values; you can't multiply inches by feet.

Setting Ltscale Values

Linetypes other than a solid continuous line consist of a repeating pattern of dashes, dots, and blank spaces. The length of dashes, dots, and the gaps between the dashes should not be over- or underexaggerated on a drawing. The smaller the scale, the more repetitions that occur for each drawing unit.

Scaling can also affect the appearance of lines. To compensate for scaling, you use the **Ltscale** command to change the appearance of lines. Ltscale stands for linetype scale. Just as text is affected by the scale of a drawing, so are linetypes. The default ltscale is 1.0. Follow the listed steps to set the ltscale.

1. From the Format pull-down menu, select Linetype.
2. From the Layer & Linetype Properties dialog box, select the Linetype tab.
3. Select Details.
4. In the Details section of the dialog box, enter the values for the global scale factor and the current object scale. The global scale factor affects the scale factor for all new and existing linetypes. The current object scale changes the linetype scale of any subsequently drawn objects relative to the global scale.
5. Select paper space for scaling to make the scaling current for paper space linetype scaling.

You may have to adjust the ltscale several times before the lines are correct. Be sure to view the drawing entities in paper space after you have changed the ltscale to see how the lines are represented.

TRY THIS

Use the LTSCALE command to change the appearance of lines.

1. Open a new drawing.
2. Change the units to Architectural.
3. In model space set the limits to 80′, 62′.
4. Zoom All to view the area defined by your limits setting.
5. Set your grid to a value of 4′.
6. Open the Layer dialog box and click on the Linetype tab.
7. Load the Centerline linetype.
8. Click on the Layer tab and create a new layer called Centerline.
9. Assign the Centerline linetype to the Centerline layer.
10. Set the Centerline layer as the current layer.
11. Choose OK.
12. Draw a horizontal line of any length.
13. Depending on the length of the line it may appear as a solid line.
14. At the command prompt, type LTSCALE.
15. Enter the value 96 and press <Enter>.

The line should change in appearance to short and long dashes.

Selecting the Zoomxp Value

In order to plot a drawing that has different model space and paper space limits, it is necessary to properly scale the view in model space before going to paper space to plot the drawing. This scale factor represents the ratio between the size of the drawing and the actual size of the drawing displayed in the paper space viewport(s). The **zoomxp** command is used to do this. In order to properly scale a drawing from model space to paper space, use the following steps:

1. Make sure that you are in model space.
2. From the View pull-down menu select Zoom, then select Scale.
3. Enter the scale factor followed by xp.

It is a good idea to do a Zoom All before doing a Zoom xp. If you had created a drawing that used a drawing scale of $\frac{1}{8}''=1'$, then the zoomxp value would be $\frac{1}{96}$.

Chapter 10 ■ Activities

Activity 10–1

Draw a Bike Rack

Plotter paper size: B		
Suggested settings:	Grid	2′
	Snap	3″
	Layers (7)	**0** (default border) **Hatch**, Linetype continuous, Color: cyan **Object (obj)**, Linetype continuous, Color: black **Hidden (hid)**, Linetype continuous, Color: magenta **Tbk (title block)**, Linetype continuous, Color: red **Txt (text)**, Linetype continuous, Color: green **Dim (dimensions)**, Linetype continuous, Color: green
	Units	Architectural
	Model space limits	31′, 20′

Hints:

1. Open the B-size drawing template that you created in Chapter 2. After it has completed loading, use the SAVEAS command to rename the drawing file ACT10-1.
2. Change the units to Architectural.
3. Set the model space limits to 31′, 20′.
4. Set the grid to 2′.
5. In model space execute a Zoom All (a).
6. Create the bike rack drawing in Figure 10–7 on p. 161.
7. Include all hatches and dimensions shown in the figure.
8. After completing the drawing, be sure to do a Zoom All (a) and then a Zoomxp of $\frac{1}{24}$.
9. Switch to paper space to print or plot the drawing.

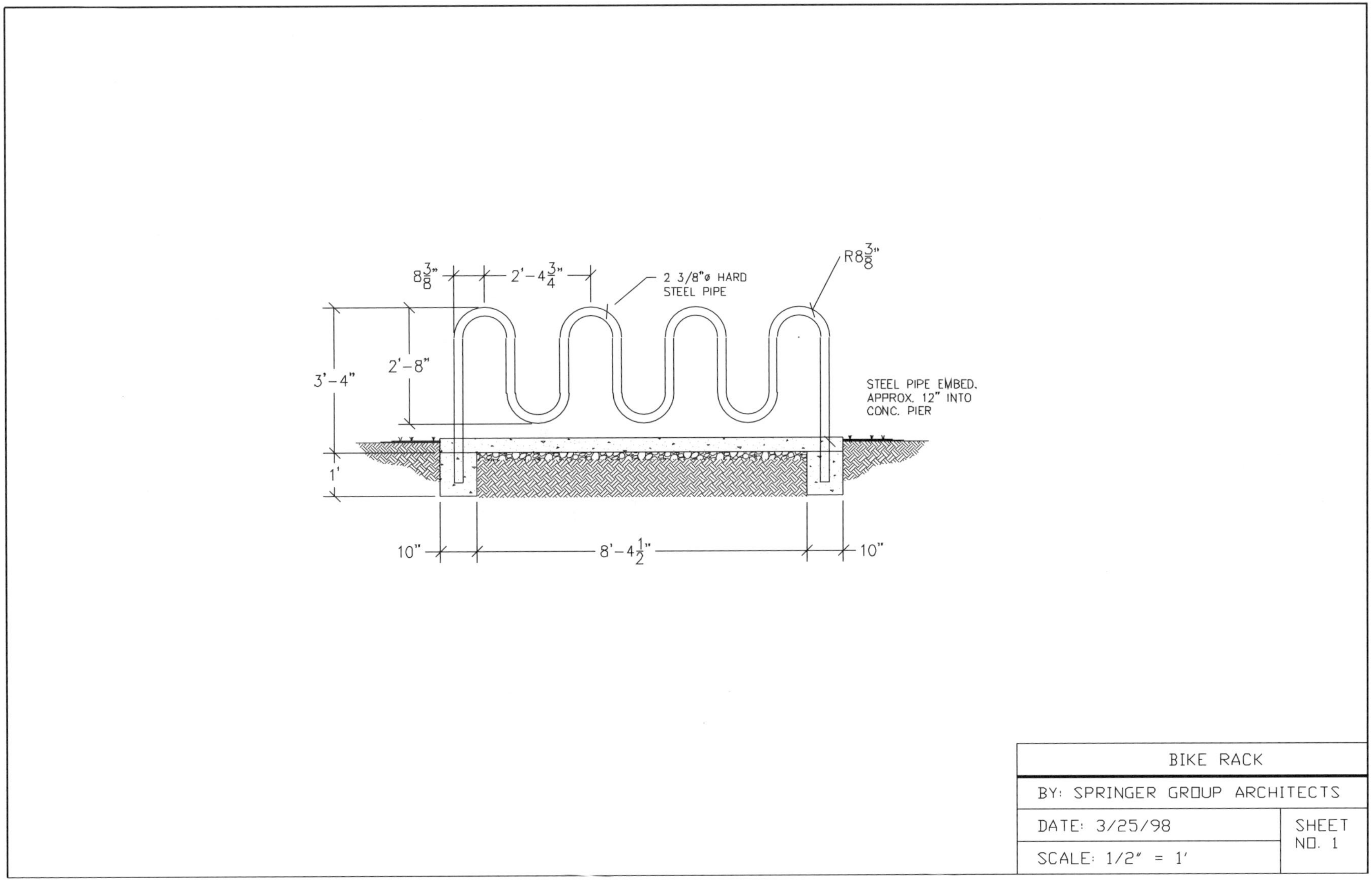

Figure 10–7
Activity 10–1

ACTIVITY 10–2

Draw a Curb Detail

Plotter paper size: B

Suggested settings:	Grid	6″
	Snap	3″
	Layers (7)	**0** (default border) **Hatch**, Linetype continuous, Color: cyan **Object (obj)**, Linetype continuous, Color: black **Hidden (hid)**, Linetype continuous, Color: magenta **Tbk (title block)**, Linetype continuous, Color: red **Txt (text)**, Linetype continuous, Color: green **Dim (dimensions)**, Linetype continuous, Color: green
	Units	Architectural
	Model space limits	124″, 80″

Hints:

1. Open the B-size drawing template that you created in Chapter 2. After it has completed loading, use the SAVEAS command to rename the drawing file ACT10-2.
2. Change the units to Architectural.
3. Set the model space limits to 124″, 80″.
4. Set the grid to 6″.
5. In model space execute a Zoom, then All (a).
6. Create the curb detail drawing in Figure 10–8 on p. 163.
7. Include all hatches and dimensions shown in the figure.
8. After completing the drawing be sure to do a Zoom, then All (a) and then a Zoomxp of $\frac{1}{8}$.
9. Switch to paper space to print or plot the drawing.

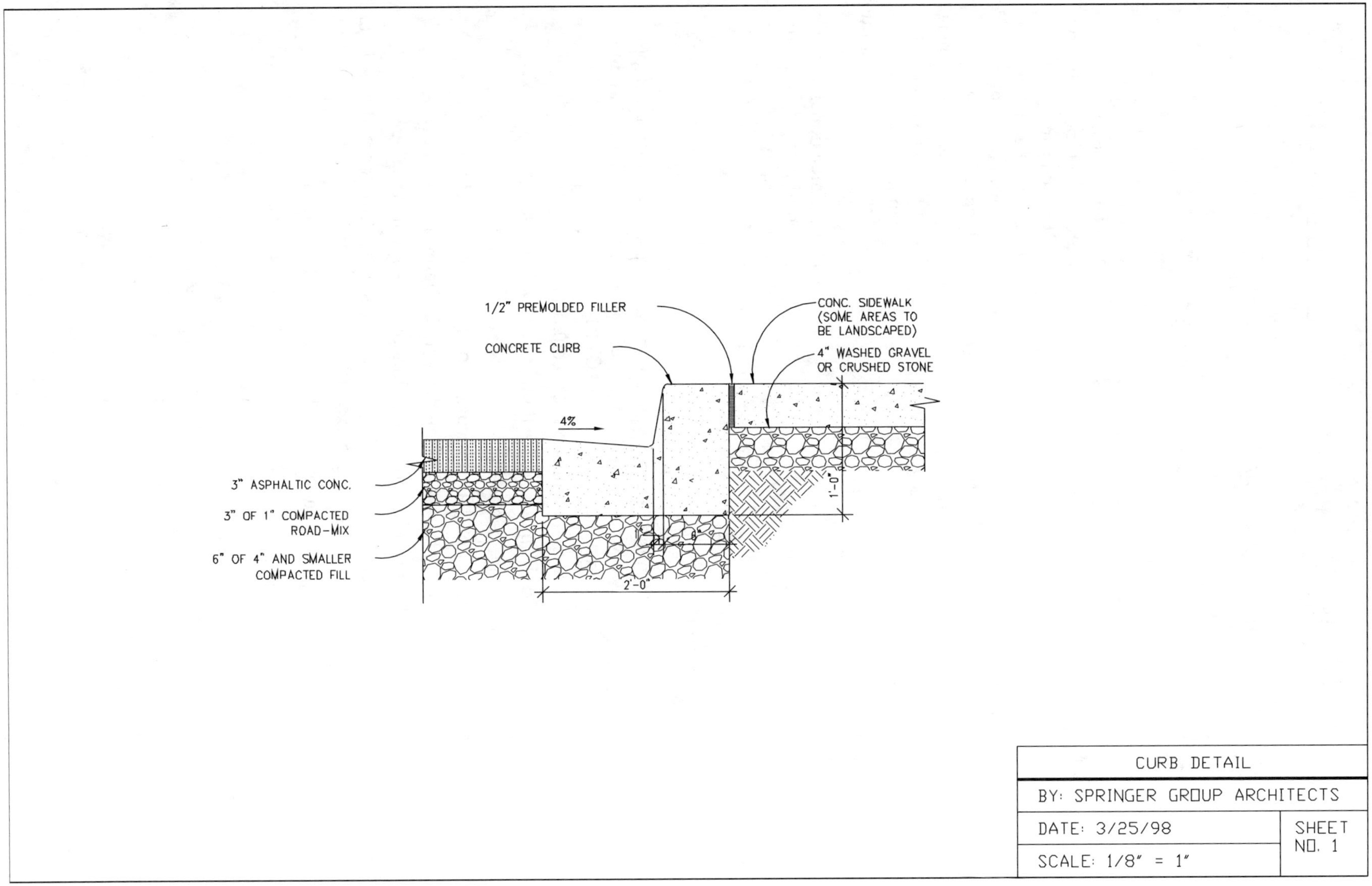

Figure 10–8
Activity 10–2

ACTIVITY 10-3

Draw a Wall Detail

Plotter paper size: A

Suggested settings:	Grid	6″
	Snap	3″
	Layers (7)	**0** (default border) **Hatch**, Linetype continuous, Color: cyan **Object (obj)**, Linetype continuous, Color: black **Hidden (hid)**, Linetype continuous, Color: magenta **Tbk (title block)**, Linetype continuous, Color: red **Txt (text)**, Linetype continuous, Color: green **Dim (dimensions)**, Linetype continuous, Color: green
	Units	Architectural
	Model space limits	10′, 7.7′

Hints:

1. Open the A-size drawing template that you created in Chapter 2. After it has completed loading, use the SAVEAS command to rename the drawing file ACT10-3.
2. Change the units to Architectural.
3. Set the model space limits to 10′, 7.7′.
4. Set the grid to 6″.
5. In model space execute a Zoom, then select All (a).
6. Create the wall detail drawing in Figure 10–9 on p. 165.
7. Include all hatches and dimensions shown in the figure.
8. After completing the drawing be sure to do a Zoom, then select All (a) and then a Zoomxp of $\frac{1}{12}$.
9. Switch to paper space to print or plot the drawing.

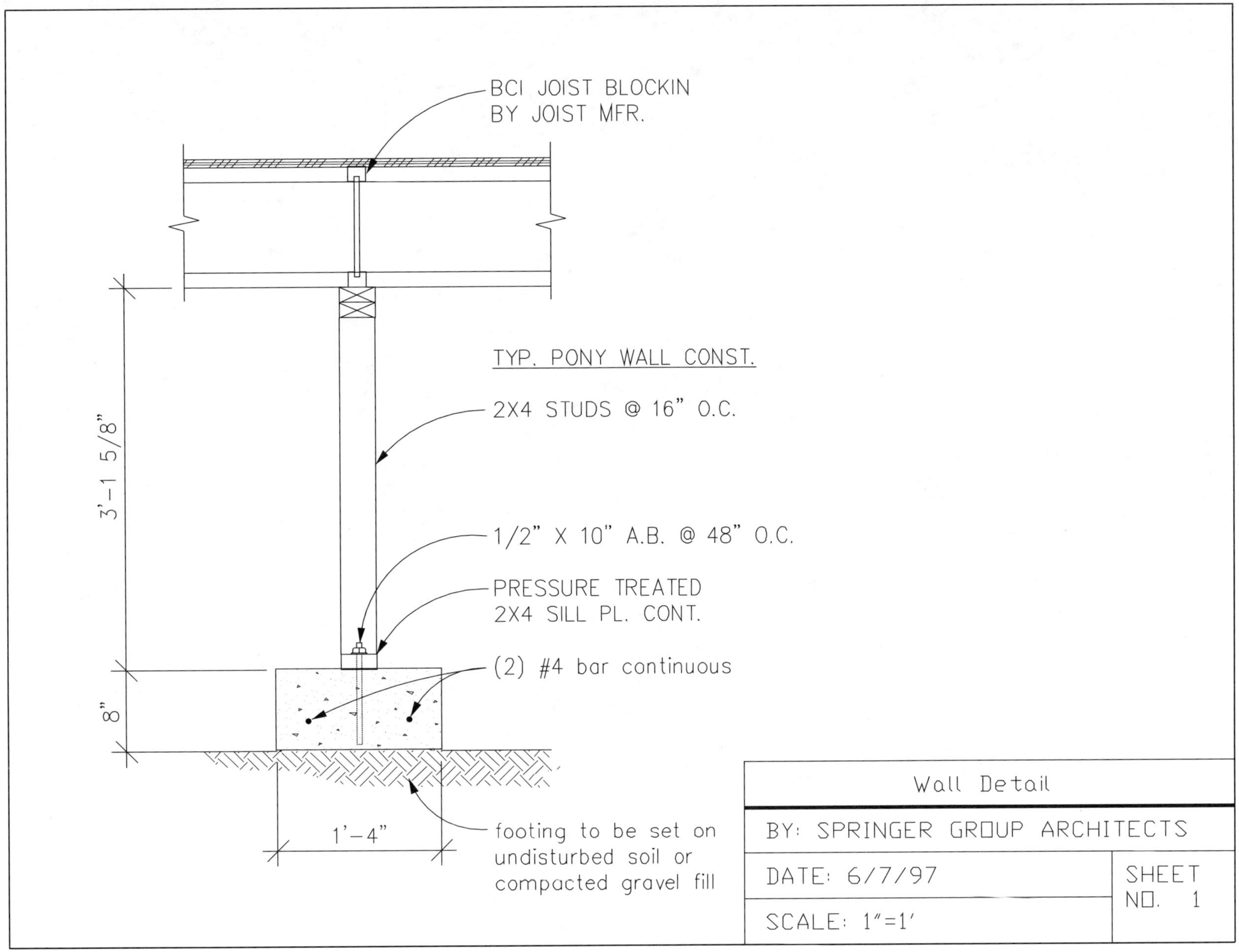

Figure 10–9
Activity 10–3

CHAPTER

11

More Drawing Aids

AFTER READING THIS CHAPTER, YOU WILL BE ABLE TO:

- Work more efficiently with drawings.

KEY CONCEPTS

- Area
- Block
- Change and DDchprop
- Dist
- List

BLOCK

A **block** is a collection of objects you can group together to form a single object, or a block definition.

If you are going to use drawing objects repetitively, it is useful to create a library of symbols that can be inserted into any drawing. Typically these libraries are composed of drawing objects known as **blocks**. A block is a collection of objects that are grouped together to form a single object. A block can be saved with a current drawing, or a block can be inserted into a different drawing.

There are three commands associated with blocks: **Block**, **Bmake**, and **Wblock**. The Block command is entered at the command prompt line. You will have to draw those objects that you want included in a block prior to executing the Block command. When the Block command is executed, you will be asked for a block name and then a block insertion point. The insertion point is a reference point for placing the newly created block in a drawing. After entering the insertion point, you select those objects that will be included in the block (see Figure 11–1).

Once the desired objects have been selected, they will disappear from the screen. However, they are still in the database of the drawing. Multiple blocks can exist in the same drawing.

TRY THIS

Create a block.

1. Open AutoCAD and select Start from Scratch.
2. Draw a six-sided polygon that is inscribed within a 1″-radius circle.
3. Enter Block.

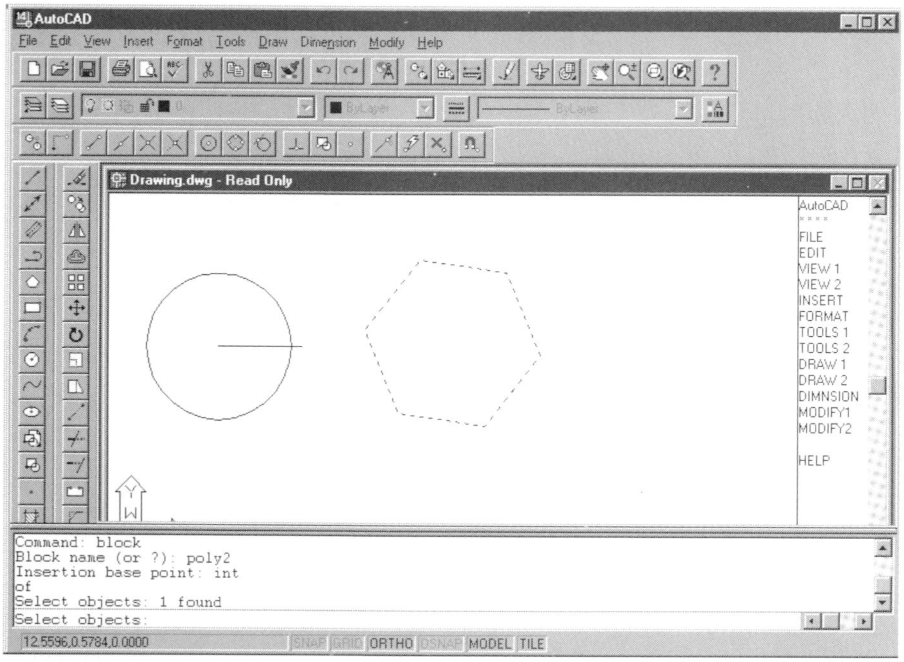

Figure 11–1
Defining block parameters.

4. Enter Polygon as the name for the block.
5. Pick near the center of the polygon as the reference point for insertion of the block.
6. Select any line of the block and press <Enter>.
7. Save the drawing as Block1 and exit.

The six-sided polygon should have disappeared from the screen.

The Bmake command can also be used to create blocks. However, objects that are selected for the block do not disappear from the screen after object selection has been completed. You can find the Bmake option in the Draw pull-down menu, or you can type bmake at the command prompt. When the Bmake command is shorted, the dialog box shown in Figure 11–2 will appear.

TRY THIS

Create a block.

1. Open AutoCAD and select Start from Scratch.
2. Draw an eight-sided polygon that is inscribed within a 1.5″-radius circle.
3. From the Draw pull-down menu select Block, and then Make (or type bmake at the command prompt).
4. Enter Poly8 as the name for the block.

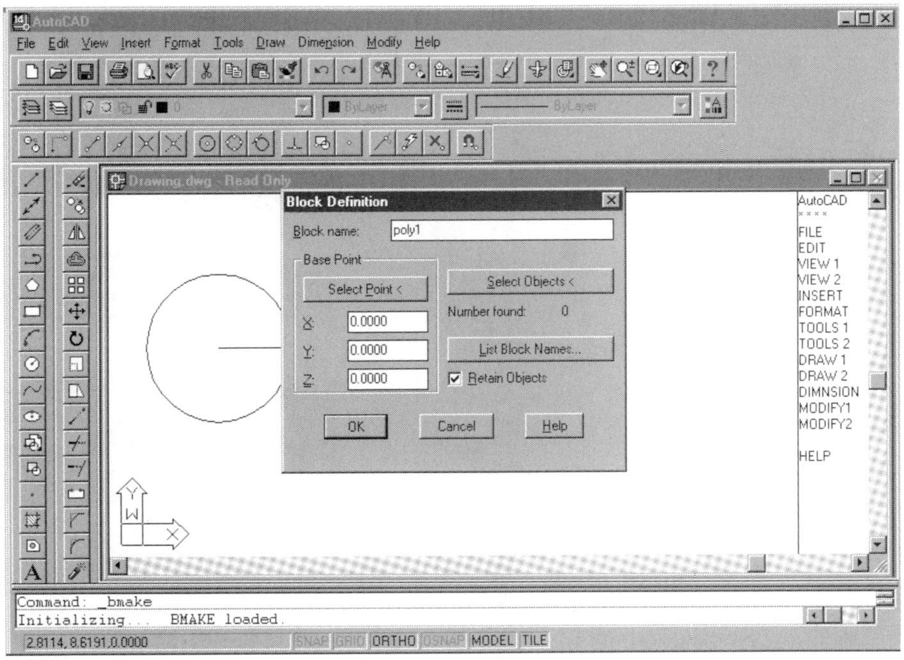

Figure 11–2
Block Definition dialog box.

5. Pick near the center of the polygon as the reference point for insertion of the block.
6. Select any line of the block and press <Enter>.
7. Save the drawing as Block2 and exit.

The eight-sided polygon should still be displayed on the screen.

The blocks created from the Block and Bmake commands can be inserted only into the drawing from which they originated.

If you wish to insert a block into another drawing, use the **Wblock** command. The Create Drawing File dialog box appears when the Wblock command is executed (see Figure 11–3), and a new drawing file is created. You must provide a name for the drawing file as well as the name of the block that you wish to use.

TRY THIS

Create a new drawing file with the Wblock command.

1. Open AutoCAD and select Open a Drawing.
2. Open the drawing from Activity 2-3 (Entities).
3. From the Draw pull-down menu select Block, and then Make (or type bmake at the command prompt).
4. Enter Donut as the name for the block.
5. Select the donut as the object that will define the block.
6. Select any edge of the donut and press Enter.

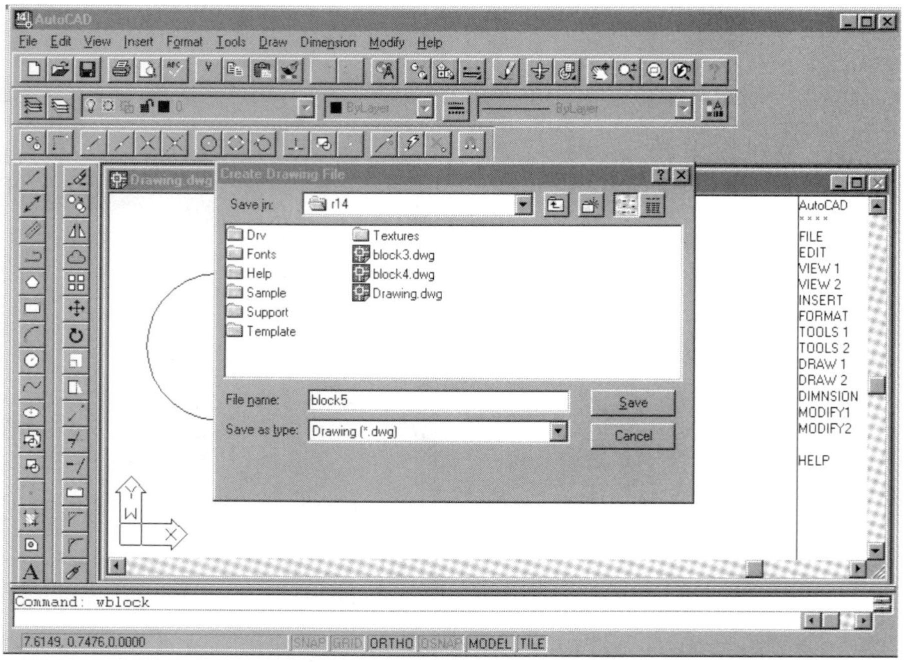

Figure 11–3
Creating a new drawing file with the Wblock command.

7. Type wblock at the command prompt.
8. Type Donut as the drawing file name.
9. Type Donut as the block name. Press <Enter>.
10. Exit the program.

A new drawing file called Donut should have been created.

The **Explode** command when used for exploding blocks separates those elements making up the block.

Blocks can be scaled and rotated on the X axis, Y axis or proportionately. If you want to edit a block, you must **Explode** it. To explode a block, from the Modify pull-down menu select Explode, or at the command prompt type Explode. At the Select Object: prompt Pick the object to explode.

If a block is exploded, all objects that were grouped together to form a block are separated and take on their individual characteristics. If a block is redefined in a drawing, all references to that block are updated in the drawing.

The command used to place a block in a drawing is Insert. This command is a submenu option in the Insert pull-down menu, or you can type insert at the command prompt. If you use the Insert command from the pull-down menu, a dialog box will appear (see Figure 11–4). When you start this command, you will be asked for a block name, an insertion point, and a scale factor.

TRY THIS

Inserting a block.

1. Open AutoCAD and select Open a Drawing.
2. Open drawing Block1.

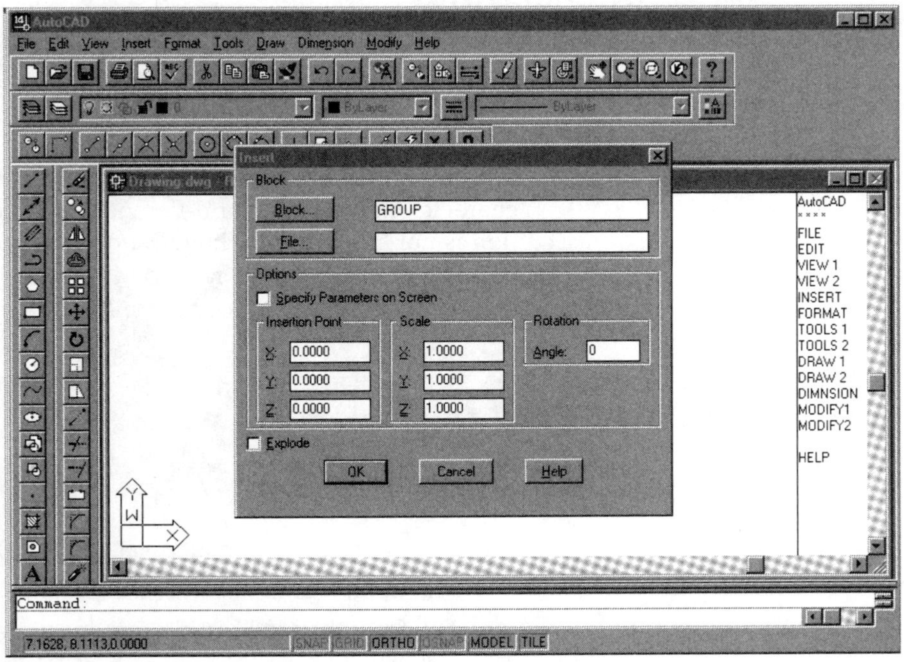

Figure 11–4
Insert dialog box.

3. From the Insert pull-down menu, select Block.
4. Enter Polygon as the name for the block.
5. Select a point in the drawing to place the new polygon.
6. Press <Enter> three times to accept the default X,Y scale factor and rotation.
7. Repeat Steps 1–6 for Block2 using the assigned name of the block.
8. Exit the program.

TRY THIS

Inserting a file saved as a Wblock.

1. Open AutoCAD and select Start from Scratch.
2. From the Insert pull-down menu, select Block.
3. Enter Donut as the name for the block.
4. Randomly pick a point to place the donut.
5. Press <Enter> three times to accept the default X,Y scale factor and the default rotation.
6. Exit the program.

CHANGING OBJECT PROPERTIES

While drawing you may inadvertently create objects on the wrong layer, or after you have drawn them you may want to change the color, linetype, ltscale, elevation, thickness, or layer. Rather than redrawing the objects, you can use either the Change or DDchprop command to change certain object characteristics. The major differences between the commands are that elevation is not an option in the DDchprop dialog box (see Figure 11–5), and the Change command does not use a dialog box. Instead, you type options at the command prompt (see Figure 11–6).

TRY THIS

Change object properties.

1. Start AutoCAD and select Open a Drawing.
2. Open drawing file ACT6-2 (slider bracket).
3. From the Modify pull-down menu, select Properties.

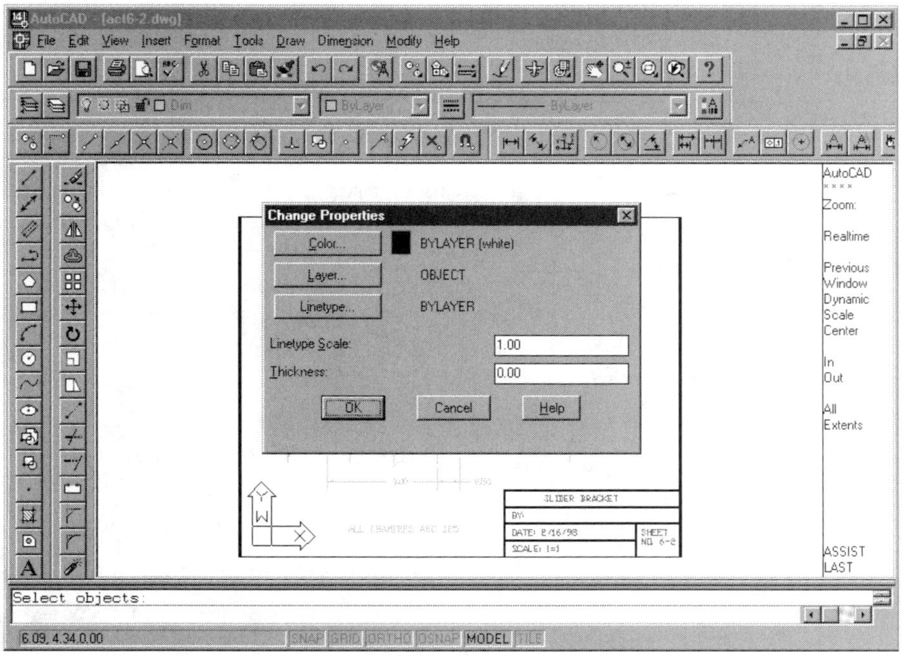

Figure 11–5
DDchprop dialog box.

4. Select any solid line of the object, and press <Enter>.
5. The Properties dialog box should appear.
6. Change the Layer to Dim.
7. The object should have changed color to green, since that was the color assigned to the Dim layer.
8. Repeat the command again, and practice changing linetypes and colors.
9. Exit the program without saving the changes.

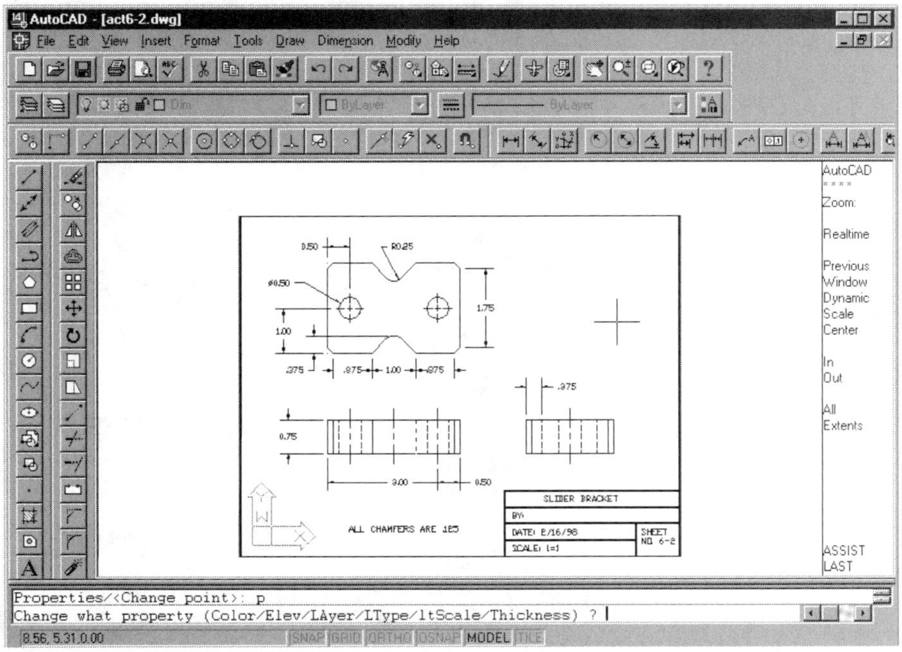

Figure 11–6
CHPROP command.

DIST

In addition to changing object properties, often it is necessary to check certain object properties while drawing. AutoCAD R14 includes commands that give you the ability to do this. If you need to measure the length of a line, for example, you can use the **Dist** (distance) command. You can start the Dist command from the Inquiry flyout on the Standard toolbar (see Figure 11–7), or you can type dist at the command prompt. The command sequence is as follows:

Command: dist
First point: Specify a point (1).
Second point: Specify a point (2).
Distance = calculated distance
Angle in XY plane = angle Angle from XY plane = angle
Delta X = change in X, Delta Y = change in Y, Delta Z = change in Z

Figure 11-8 shows how the Dist command might be used to measure a horizontal line. In this example the Osnap end command was used to select the endpoints of the lines.

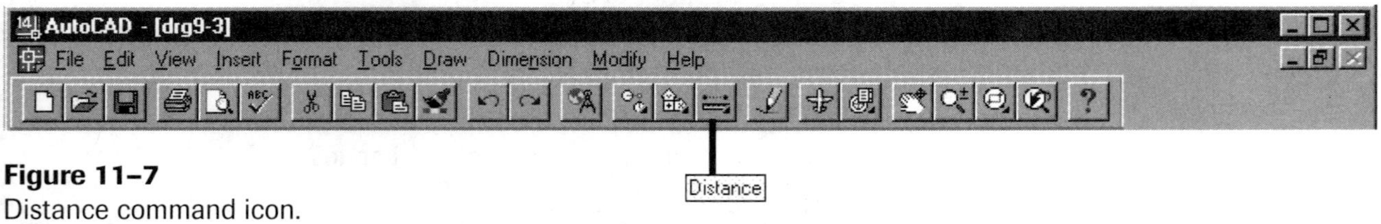

Figure 11–7
Distance command icon.

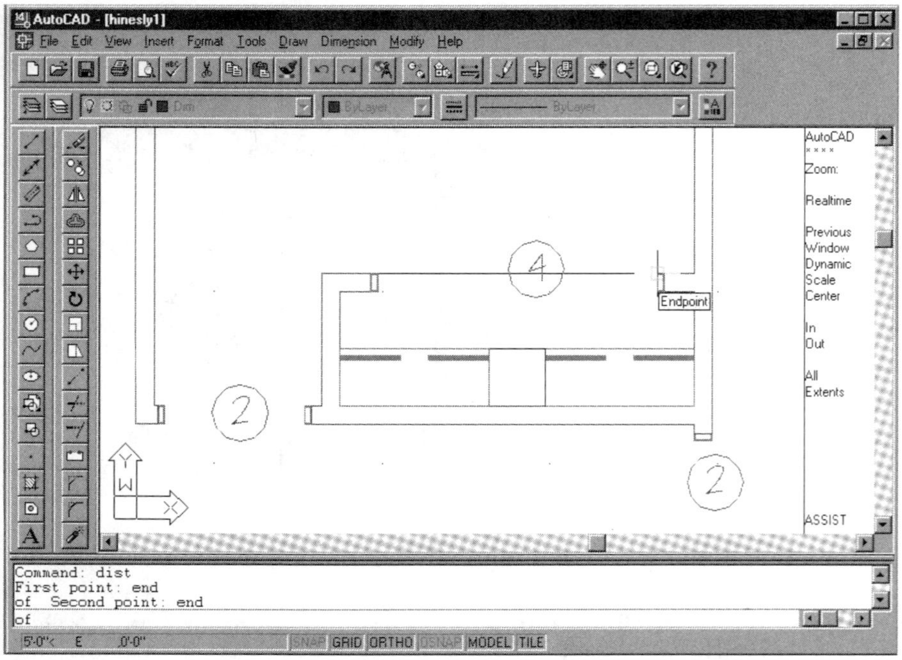

Figure 11–8
Dist command.

TRY THIS

Measure lines using the Dist command.

1. Open AutoCAD and select Start from Scratch.
2. Draw horizontal lines of varying lengths.
3. Use the dist command to measure the lines.
4. Exit the drawing without saving it.

AREA

Another object property that can be measured is area. The **Area** command will calculate the area and outside circumference of an enclosed polygon. You can select the Area command from the Tools menu Inquiry option or you may type Area at the command prompt. Area command options include the following selections.

<First point> / Object / Add / Subtract:

In Figure 11–9 the area of the concrete slab was calculated. Readings were given in both square inches and square feet. The perimeter of the rectangle was also calculated.

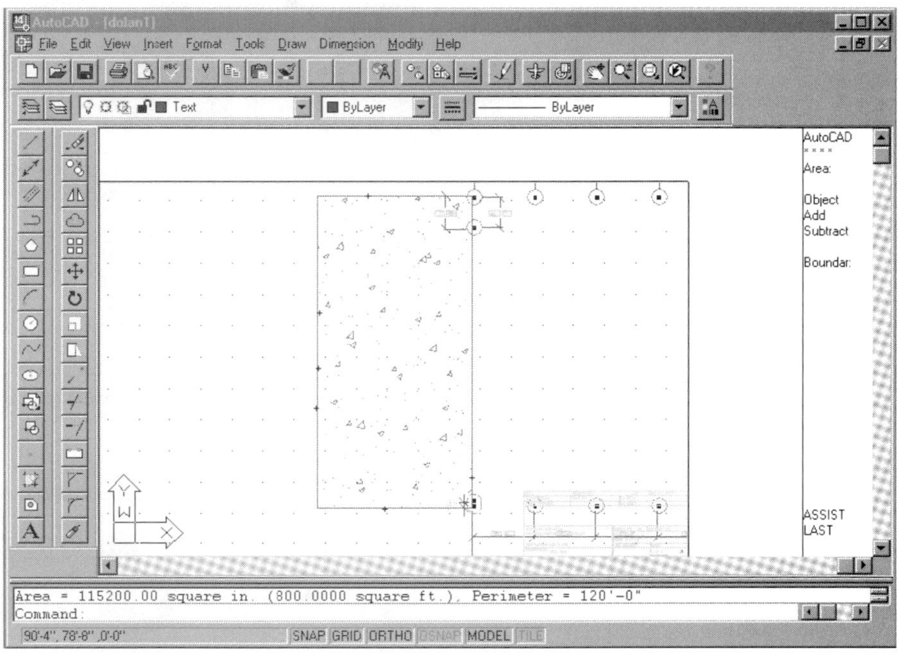

Figure 11–9
Area command.

TRY THIS

Calculate the area of a polygon.

1. Open AutoCAD and select Start from Scratch.
2. Draw polygons of varying sizes.
3. Use the Area command to calculate the area of the polygons.
4. Exit the drawing without saving it.

LIST

Another command used to check object properties is **List**. The List command describes the object type, object layer, and X,Y,Z position relative to the current UCS and whether the object is in model space or paper space. The List command may be selected from the Tools pull-down menu under Inquiry or List may be typed at the command line. After starting the command, you will select an object. Once the object has been selected a dialog box will appear that lists the object properties (see Figure 11-10). The List command is often used to determine the properties of a certain object.

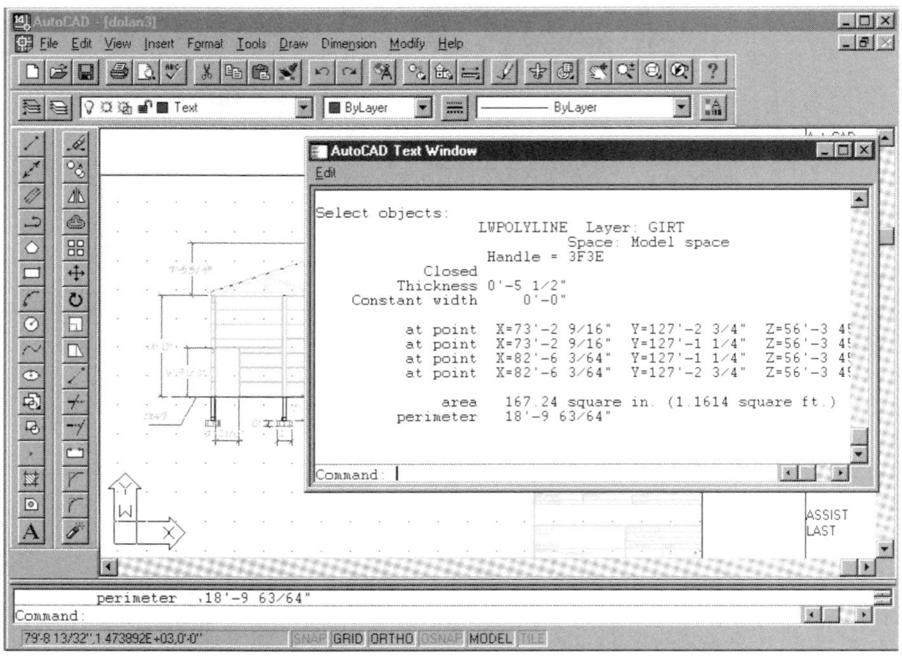

Figure 11–10
List command.

TRY THIS

Use the List command to identify characteristics of an object.

1. Open AutoCAD and select Open a Drawing.
2. Open the Pipes.dwg from the Samples subdirectory of AutoCAD.
3. Type List at the command prompt and select an object.
4. Repeat the command for different objects in the drawing.
5. Exit the drawing without saving it.

Activity 11–1

Practice Using Block Commands

Open drawing ACT8-2 (Flange Bushing). Make the 0 layer the current layer and turn off the text layer. Use the Bmake command to make a block of the right side of the drawing, which will include only the object lines, centerlines, and hidden lines of the object in the block. Name the block Flange. In the Bmake dialog box use the Select Point option to determine the point to which the block will be referenced for insertion into the drawing. Use Osnap int (intersection), and pick the lower left corner of the object as the reference point.

Use the Insert command and insert the block (Flange) into the same drawing. Randomly place the block in the drawing.

Do not save changes when exiting the drawing.

Activity 11–2

Practice Using the Dist Command

Open AutoCAD and select Start from Scratch. Draw horizontal and vertical lines of various lengths. Use the Dist command to measure each of the lines you created. Use Osnap endp (endpoint) to select the ends of the lines.

Do not save changes when exiting the drawing.

Activity 11–3

Practice Using the Area Command

Open AutoCAD and select Start from Scratch. Draw a number of polygons of various sizes. Use the Area command to calculate the area of each polygon.

Do not save changes when exiting the drawing.

ACTIVITY 11–4

Practice Changing Object Properties

Start AutoCAD and open drawing ACT6-4 (Grate). Use the DDchprop or the Chprop command to change the color of the interior squares to red and the linetype to hidden.

Do not save changes when exiting the drawing.

Index

TOOLBARS

STANDARD TOOLBAR

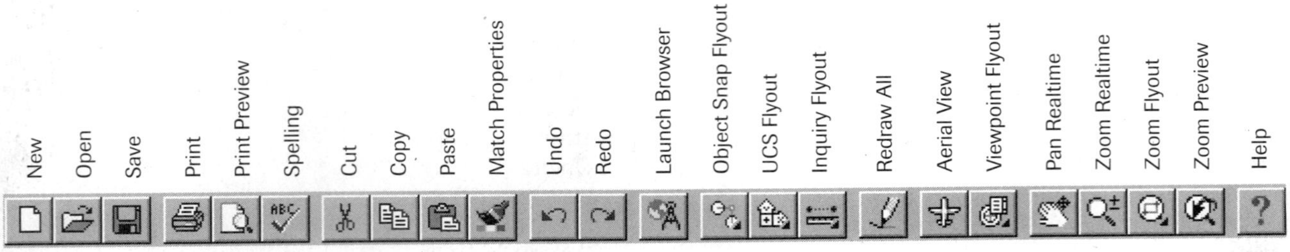

DRAW TOOLBAR

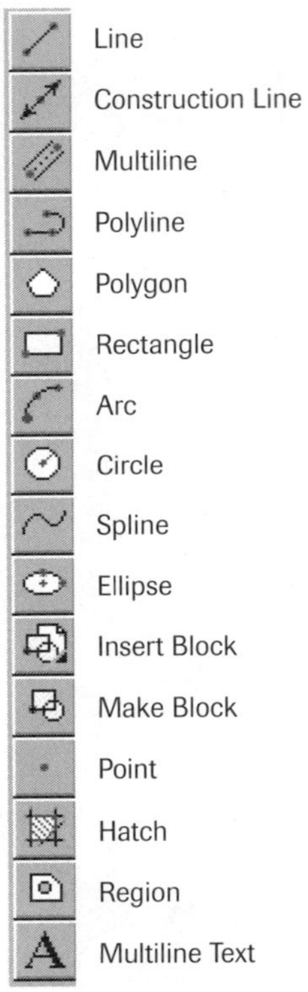

MODIFY TOOLBAR

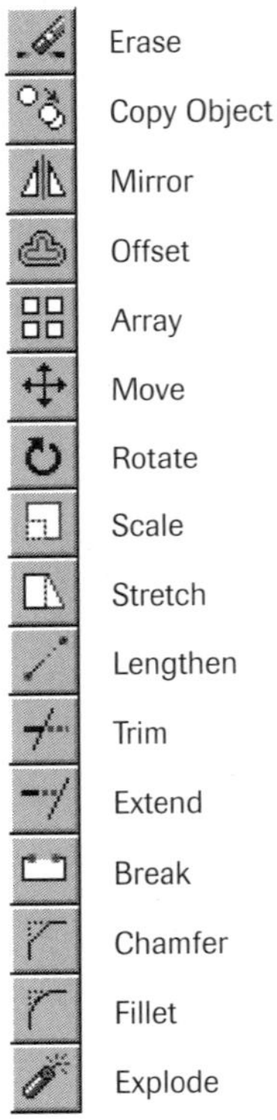

FIGURE 5.18 A FORMATTED AND CUSTOMIZED CHART

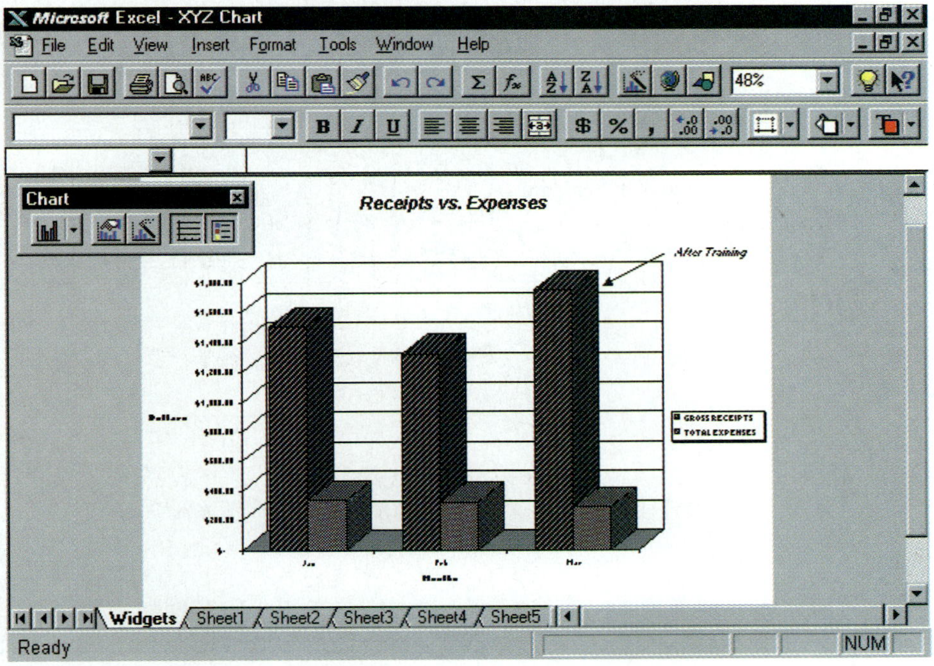

QUICK REFERENCE
Choosing Fonts and Patterns

1. **RIGHT-CLICK: a chart object**
2. **CHOOSE: Format *object***
3. **Complete the dialog box entries.**
4. **PRESS: ENTER or CLICK: OK**

PRINTING A CHART

When a chart is created as a separate chart sheet, you print it directly from the chart sheet using the File, Print command. For the most part, the general print options are identical to printing a worksheet. However, there is one additional set of layout options for scaling the chart to fit on a page. Like a worksheet, you should always preview the chart prior to printing.

Perform the following steps to print the Widgets chart.

1. Ensure that the chart sheet is active.
2. To adjust the page layout options:
   CHOOSE: File, Page Setup
   CLICK: Chart tab
   The Page Setup dialog box appears as shown in Figure 5.19.

FIGURE 5.19 PAGE SETUP DIALOG BOX: CHART TAB

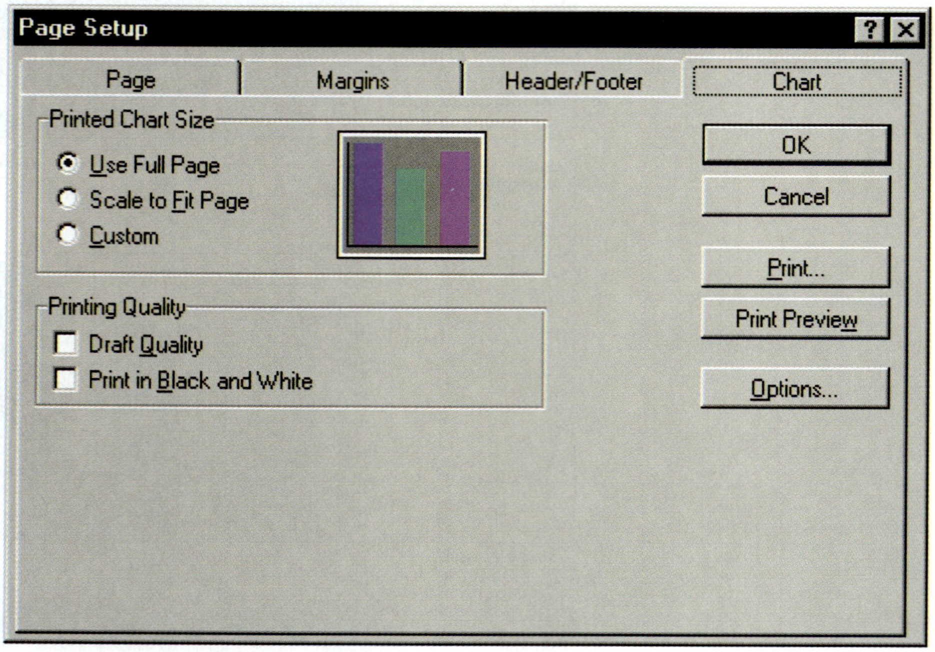

3. In this dialog box, you select the appropriate size option for printing the chart. The *Scale to Fit Page* option prints the chart using the current height to width ratio, and the *Use Full Page* option adjusts the ratio to maximize the print area. Try the following option on your printer:
   SELECT: *Scale to Fit Page* option button
   CLICK: Print Preview
4. When finished viewing the chart, send it to the printer:
   CLICK: Print command button (at the top of the window)
   PRESS: ENTER or CLICK: OK
5. Save the workbook as "XYZ Chart" onto the Advantage Diskette, replacing the existing version.
6. Close the workbook.

QUICK REFERENCE
Printing a Chart

1. **Ensure that the chart sheet is active.**
2. **CHOOSE: File, Page Setup**
3. **CLICK: Chart tab**
4. **SELECT: sizing options for printing the chart**
5. **CLICK: Print Preview command button to view the chart**
6. **CLICK: Print command button**
7. **PRESS: ENTER or CLICK: OK**

EMBEDDING A CHART

This section explains how to embed a chart into a worksheet using the ChartWizard. An embedded chart is placed over—not entered into—a cell range. All of the customizing and formatting for embedded charts is the same as for chart sheets. However, the methods for creating and printing the chart differ from previous sections.

To create an embedded chart, you select the cell range that you want to plot and then choose the Insert, Chart, On This Sheet command or click the ChartWizard button (). Either way, you must click or drag the cross-hair mouse pointer over an area on the worksheet to place the chart. Once the area is chosen, the ChartWizard leads you through a five-step process for formatting and customizing the chart. To remove an embedded chart, you select the chart by clicking on it and then press DELETE. To print worksheet information along with the chart, you select a range that covers both areas of the worksheet and chart, set the desired page layout options, and then choose the File, Print command. To edit an embedded chart, you simply double-click the chart to make it active.

Perform the following steps.

1. Open the "Cruises" workbook located on the Advantage Diskette.
2. SELECT: cell range from A2 to D5
3. To use the ChartWizard:
   CLICK: ChartWizard button ()
   (*Hint:* You should always look in the Status bar for helpful messages. For example, "Drag in document to create a chart" now appears.)
4. To place the embedded chart below the worksheet information, first move the cross-hair mouse pointer to the middle of cell A7.
5. CLICK: cell A7 and hold down the mouse button
   DRAG: cell A7 to D15
   The borderlines extend as you drag the mouse to D15. If you wanted to make a perfect square, you would hold down the SHIFT key as you drag the mouse. If you wanted to align the chart with worksheet cells, you would hold down the ALT key.
6. Release the mouse button.
7. The ChartWizard takes over and displays the first of five dialog boxes for confirming the cell range to plot. Since you selected the cell range before accessing the ChartWizard, the range is correct. To proceed:
   CLICK: Next >

8. In the second dialog box, you specify the type of chart:
   SELECT: Column chart
   CLICK: Next >
   (*Note:* At any time, you can click the < Back command button to return to a previous step.)
9. In the third dialog box, you select the format for the chosen chart type:
   SELECT: option 3 for a stacked column chart
   CLICK: Next >
10. In the fourth dialog box, you confirm the layout of the cell range and the appearance of the Sample Chart. To proceed to the next step:
    CLICK: Next >
11. In the fifth and last dialog box, you specify whether you want a legend and enter the titles for the chart and axes. Do the following:
    SELECT: *Yes* option button for *Add a legend?*
    CLICK: *Chart Title* text box
    TYPE: **Demographics**
    CLICK: *Value (Y)* text box
    TYPE: **Passengers**
    Notice that the information that you typed for the titles is immediately placed into the *Sample Chart* preview window.
12. To finish using the ChartWizard:
    PRESS: ENTER or CLICK: Finish
    The chart appears on the worksheet.
13. To move the chart, first select the chart by clicking in the middle of it and then drag it to a new location:
    CLICK: embedded chart once and hold down the mouse button
    DRAG: chart back and forth to finalize its position
14. To size the chart, first select the chart and then position the mouse pointer over one of the boxes on the embedded chart's borderlines. The mouse pointer should change to a cross hair when you drag the border.
15. CLICK: once and hold down the mouse button
    DRAG: borderline back and forth to finalize the size
    Size the chart to match the worksheet screen in Figure 5.20.

FIGURE 5.20 MANIPULATING AN EMBEDDED CHART

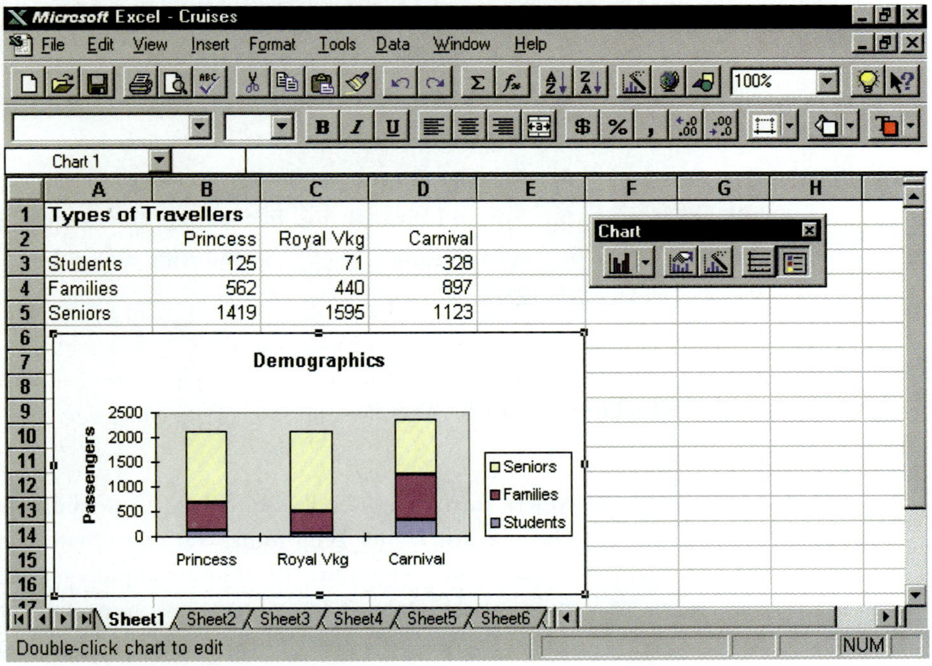

16. To edit or format the chart:
    DOUBLE-CLICK: on any part of the embedded chart
    Notice that it is now surrounded by a hashed border to indicate that you can modify its contents. All of the commands and procedures that you learned in previous sections (for example, adding titles, free-form text, and arrows) are now available for use in formatting the embedded chart.

17. To return the focus to the worksheet cells:
    CLICK: cell A1

18. To print the worksheet along with the embedded chart:
    SELECT: the entire cell range from A1 to the bottom right-hand corner of the embedded chart
    CHOOSE: File, Print Area, Set Print Area
    CHOOSE: File, Print
    PRESS: ENTER or CLICK: OK

19. Save the workbook as "Cruises" onto the Advantage Diskette, replacing the existing version.

20. Close the workbook.

QUICK REFERENCE
Creating an Embedded Chart Using the ChartWizard

1. **Select the cell range or ranges to include in the chart.**
2. **CLICK: ChartWizard button ( ) on the toolbar**
3. **CLICK: cell where you want to place the top-left corner of the chart and hold the left mouse button down**
4. **DRAG: the mouse pointer to the cell where you want to put the bottom-right corner of the chart**
5. **Release the mouse button.**
6. **Proceed through the five dialog boxes making selections for your chart and clicking Next >. In the fifth dialog box, click Finish to finalize the chart.**

USING MICROSOFT DATA MAP

Newly introduced in Excel 7.0 is a specialty charting tool called **Microsoft Data Map.** Using Data Map, you can create a map to analyze your worksheet information geographically. For example, you could plot the number of UFO sightings by state or by country, assuming that you had a worksheet containing this information. Data Map also enables you to quickly analyze trends relative to a region's demographic breakdown. Existing demographic information is provided by Excel and is accessible from a special workbook called "Mapstats" located in the Datamap folder.

CREATING A DATA MAP

To use Data Map with Excel, you need to organize your worksheet data into columns. One column must contain geographic data such as the names of states or countries. This column determines the type of map that will be displayed (for example, a map of the United States, Canada, or the world.) To map your worksheet information, select the cell range that includes the geographic data and then click the Map button ( ) on the Standard toolbar. Similar to embedding a chart, you drag the cross-hair mouse pointer on the worksheet to set the size and location of the map. When you release the mouse button, the selected cell range is analyzed and a map is displayed.

To illustrate, perform the following steps.

1. Open the "Snowboarding" worksheet located on the Advantage Diskette. This worksheet provides a fictitious marketing report for a U.S. snowboarding manufacturer that wants to sell its products in the Canadian market.

2. To create a map showing the relative amount of money spent on snowboarding by each province, do the following:
   SELECT: cell range from A4 to B16
   Notice that you are including the column headings in the selection and that column A contains geographical information.

3. CLICK: Map button ( )
   (*Note:* If you do not see the Map button ( ) on the Standard toolbar, you may not have this feature installed on your computer. If this is the case, you must re-install Microsoft Excel and select the Data Map utility before performing the steps in the remainder of this session.)

4. To place the map to the right of the worksheet information, first move the cross-hair mouse pointer to the middle of cell C4 and then click the left mouse button once. This method for embedding a map provides a "best-fit" size for the map. Scroll the document window so that you can view the entire map and move the Data Map Control dialog box by dragging its Title bar. Notice that the map shows provinces with higher sales using a darker shade of gray. Your screen should now appear similar to Figure 5.21.

FIGURE 5.21 CREATING A MAP FROM WORKSHEET INFORMATION

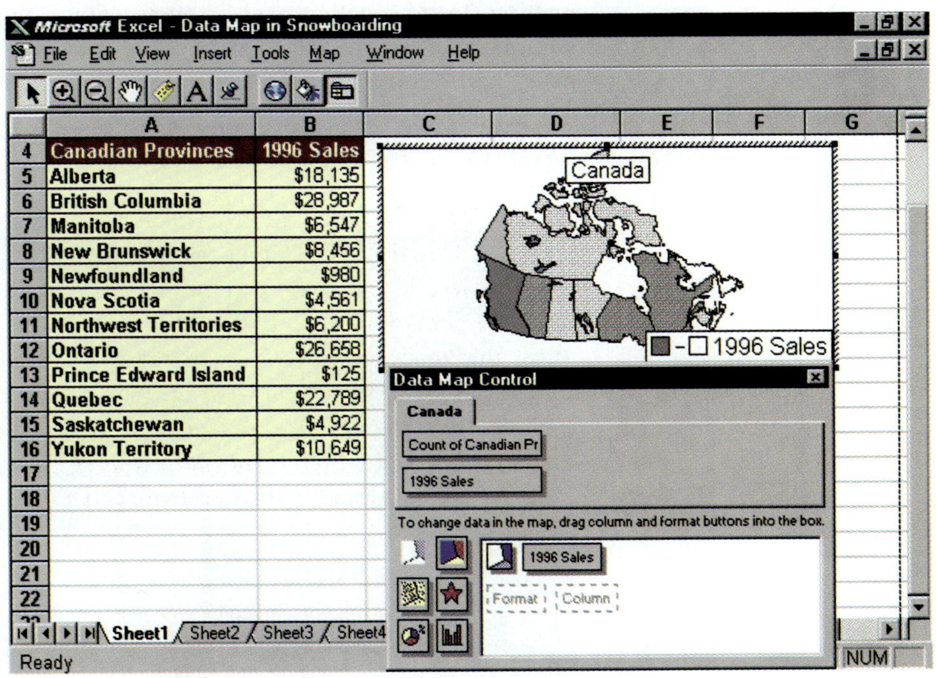

If the selected cell range contains ambiguous data or misspellings of geographic regions (states, provinces, or countries), a dialog box appears asking you for assistance. For the proper spellings and abbreviations of geographic regions, review the "Mapstats" workbook located in the "Program Files\Common

Files\Microsoft Shared\Datamap\Data" folder. If you cannot locate the "Mapstats" workbook, choose the START, Find, Files or Folders command and perform a search of your hard disk.

QUICK REFERENCE
Embedding a Data Map on a Worksheet

1. **Create a worksheet with one column containing geographic data such as names or abbreviations of states, provinces, and countries.**
2. **Select the cell range to include in the data map.**
3. **CLICK: Map button ( ) on the Standard toolbar**
4. **CLICK: cell where you want to place the top-left corner of the map**

FORMATTING A DATA MAP

After embedding a data map on your worksheet, you can customize its appearance using the menu, toolbar, and Data Map Control dialog box (shown in Figure 5.22). For example, you can color-code the geographic regions and change the way data is displayed on the map by simply dragging and double-clicking buttons in the Data Map Control dialog box. However, you should be careful when dragging buttons in the work area of this dialog box. When you drag a new button onto an empty area, you are adding new formatting. When you drag a new button on top of an existing button, you are replacing the current formatting. In this section, you practice using some of the tools available for formatting a data map.

FIGURE 5.22 DATA MAP CONTROL DIALOG BOX

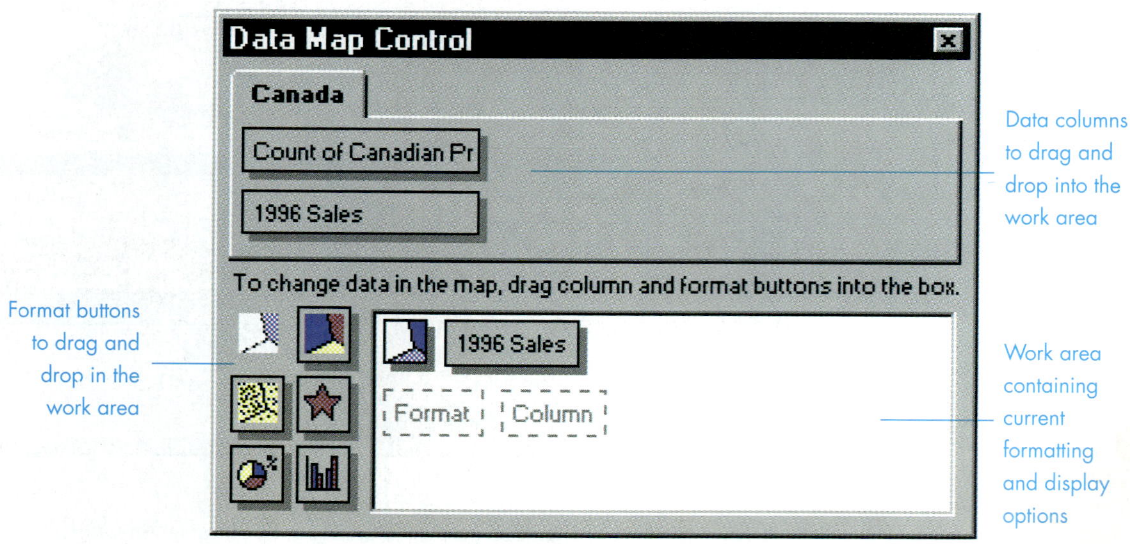

Perform the following steps.

1. Ensure that the data map appears with a hatched border, indicating that it is active and ready for formatting. If no border appears, double-click the data map object. If the data map appears with a hatched border but the Data Map Control dialog box shown in Figure 5.22 does not appear, do the following:
   CLICK: Show/Hide Data Map Control button ( ) on the toolbar
2. To color-code the map of Canada:
   DRAG: Category Shading button ( ) over top of the existing format button in the work area
   (*Note:* You will know that you have positioned the mouse correctly when the row with the 1996 Sales button appears highlighted.)
3. Release the mouse button. Notice that the shades of gray are replaced by a color-coded map.
4. DRAG: Graduated Symbol button ( ) over top of the existing format button in the work area
5. Release the mouse button. Now the map of Canada shows dots of varying sizes for each province, with each dot representing the relative dollar volume of 1996 Sales.
6. DRAG: Value Shading button ( ) over top of the existing format button in the work area
7. Release the mouse button to display the default map format.
8. To hide the Data Map Control dialog box:
   CLICK: Show/Hide Data Map Control button ( )
9. To change the gray-scale shading in the map:
   CHOOSE: Map, Value Shading Options from the menu
   The dialog box in Figure 5.23 appears.

FIGURE 5.23 VALUE SHADING OPTIONS DIALOG BOX

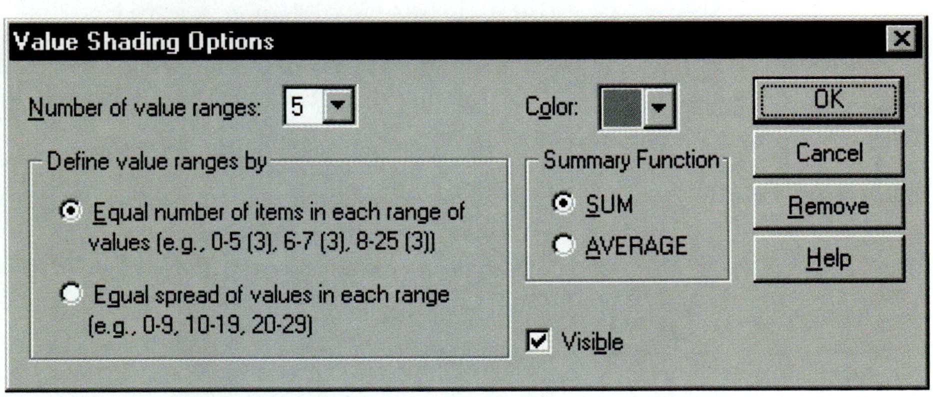

10. SELECT: 2 in the *Number of value ranges* drop-down list box
    PRESS: ENTER or CLICK: OK
    Notice that the map now displays the provinces using only two shading groups.
11. To display four shading categories:
    CHOOSE: Map, Value Shading Options
    SELECT: 4 in the *Number of value ranges* drop-down list box
    PRESS: ENTER or CLICK: OK
12. Let's display some additional features:
    RIGHT-CLICK: on any province in the map
    CHOOSE: Features from the shortcut menu
13. In the Map Features dialog box that appears:
    SELECT: *Canada Major Cities* check box in the *Visible* area
    PRESS: ENTER or CLICK: OK
    Now the map displays the locations of Canada's major cities (for example, Vancouver, Edmonton, Calgary, Toronto, and Montreal).
14. Position the mouse pointer over the black square appearing on the border in the bottom right-hand corner. To resize the map object, drag the border, with the mouse pointer on this black square, to cell G16.
15. Now that you have more room in the data map, let's display a more detailed legend:
    RIGHT-CLICK: on the legend in the bottom right-hand corner
    CHOOSE: Edit from the shortcut menu
    CLICK: *Use Compact Format* check box so that no "✓" appears
    PRESS: ENTER or CLICK: OK
    A new legend appears showing the four value categories used in shading the map of Canada.
16. Unfortunately, the new legend covers part of the map. To move the map to the left side, do the following:
    CLICK: Grabber button () in the toolbar
    CLICK: on any province in the map and hold down the mouse button
    DRAG: the map to appear flush against the left and bottom borders
17. Release the mouse button.
18. DRAG: the legend to the top right-hand corner
    DRAG: the title "CANADA" to the left slightly
19. Ensure that you can see the entire map of Canada and the title.
20. To finish editing the map and return to the worksheet:
    CLICK: any cell in the worksheet
    You are now ready to print the worksheet and data map in the next section.

QUICK REFERENCE
Customizing a Data Map

- **Use the Data Map Control dialog box to change the way data is displayed in the map.**
- **CHOOSE: Map, Value Shading Options to change the number of categories displayed in the map**
- **CHOOSE: Features from the map shortcut menu to add landmarks to the data map such as cities, highways, and lakes**
- **CHOOSE: Edit from the legend shortcut menu to switch the display between a compact and a detailed legend**

PRINTING A DATA MAP

You print a data map as you would print any other embedded chart on your worksheet. Perform the following steps.

1. To print the worksheet with the data map:
   SELECT: the entire cell range from A1 to the bottom right-hand corner of the embedded map, approximately cell H17
   CHOOSE: File, Print Area, Set Print Area

2. Let's print this worksheet with a landscape orientation:
   CHOOSE: File, Page Setup
   CLICK: Page tab
   SELECT: *Landscape* option button in the *Orientation* group
   CLICK: Print Preview command button
   Your screen should now appear similar to Figure 5.24.

FIGURE 5.24 PREVIEWING THE COMPLETED DATA MAP

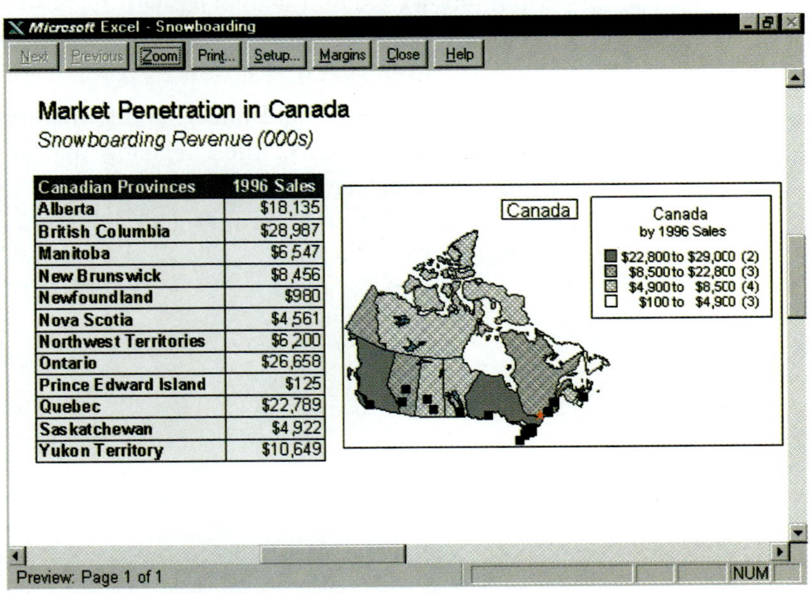

3. To send the worksheet to the printer from the Preview screen:
   CLICK: Print command button (at the top of the window)
4. When the Print dialog box appears:
   PRESS: ENTER or CLICK: OK
   The worksheet and data map are sent to the printer.
5. PRESS: CTRL + ENTER to remove the highlighting from the worksheet cells and return to cell A1
6. Save the workbook as "Snowboarding" onto the Advantage Diskette, replacing the existing file.
7. Close the workbook and then exit Excel.

QUICK REFERENCE
Printing a Data Map with Worksheet Information

1. **Select the cell range containing the worksheet information and the embedded data map.**
2. **CHOOSE: File, Print Area, Set Print Area**
3. **CHOOSE: File, Print**
4. **PRESS: ENTER or CLICK: OK**

SUMMARY

This session discussed the benefits of using graphics to present worksheet information. Besides introducing several types of business graphics, the basic principles of graphing, including simplicity, unity, emphasis, and balance, were explained. In Excel, there are two methods for creating charts from worksheet information. A chart can be created, printed, and saved as a separate sheet in a workbook or embedded into an existing worksheet. In this session, you practiced both methods for creating a chart, including using the ChartWizard's step-by-step approach.

Excel provides several customizing and formatting options for enhancing a chart, including fonts, patterns, titles, legends, and annotations. With approximately 90 different charting formats, it is guaranteed you will find the perfect tool to help you make that winning presentation! Table 5.3 summarizes the commands introduced in this session.

TABLE 5.3

Command Summary

Command	*Description*
Insert, Chart, As New Sheet	Creates a chart in a separate sheet of the current workbook file.
Insert, Chart, On This Sheet	Creates an embedded chart on the current worksheet from the highlighted range.
Format, Chart Type	Selects the type and format of chart to display.
Format, AutoFormat	Selects and applies a predefined style to a chart.
Insert, Titles	Adds titles for the chart and X-axis and Y-axis.
Insert, Legend	Adds a legend to the chart.
Map, Value Shading Options	Changes the number of categories displayed on a data map.

KEY TERMS

ChartWizard
A collection of dialog boxes that leads you through creating an embedded chart on a worksheet.

column chart
A chart that compares one data element with another data element and can show variations over a period of time.

data series
A series of values from the worksheet that are related.

embedded chart
An Excel chart that is placed over worksheet cells and printed and saved along with the worksheet file.

exploding
Refers to a slice in a pie chart that is partially removed from the rest of the pie for emphasis.

graphics
The pictorial representation of words and data.

legend
A key for deciphering the data series appearing in the plot area of a chart.

line chart
A chart that plots trends or shows changes over a period of time.

Microsoft Data Map
A special charting utility that enables you to create an embedded map from geographic data stored in a worksheet.

pie chart

A chart that shows the proportions of individual components compared to the whole.

plot area

The area for plotting values from the worksheet. The plot area contains the axes and data series.

X-axis

The horizontal axis that shows the categories for which the chart is making comparisons.

XY chart

Chart that shows how one or more data elements relate to another data element. Also called *scatter plot diagram.*

Y-axis

The vertical axis that shows the value or measurement unit for making comparisons among the various categories.

EXERCISES

SHORT ANSWER

1. Describe the basic principles of using graphics.
2. Describe the process of creating a chart as a separate sheet.
3. Describe the process of creating an embedded chart.
4. How do you move an embedded chart using the mouse?
5. List the different types of charts found in the Chart Type dialog box.
6. What are some options for moving the legend around the screen?
7. Describe the process of adding a text box to a chart.
8. Describe the process of adding an arrow to a chart.
9. How must you organize a worksheet if you want to create a data map?
10. How do you make an embedded chart or data map active and ready for editing?

HANDS-ON

(*Note:* In the following exercises, save your workbooks onto and retrieve files from the Advantage Diskette.)

1. The objective of this exercise is to create a worksheet and an embedded pie chart that show the breakdown of your total monthly expenses. Perform the following steps.

   a. Ensure that you have an empty workbook.

   b. Enter your name in cell A1.

   c. Create a worksheet that lists the following expense headings on separate rows within a single column: RENT, FOOD, GAS, and FUN.

   d. Enter your monthly expense amounts in the column to the right of the row headings. (You can enter any values, not necessarily your own.)

   e. Select the row headings and values to produce an embedded chart.

   f. CLICK: ChartWizard button ( )

   g. Place the chart to the right of the present worksheet information and size it to cover fifteen rows by five columns.

   h. Following the steps for each dialog box, select a 3-D pie chart that displays the names beside each pie wedge. Add a title to the chart that has the words "Monthly Expenses" on the first line.

   i. Once the chart appears on the worksheet:
   DOUBLE-CLICK: embedded chart to make it active

   j. Select different patterns for the pie wedges for printing on a black-and-white laser or dot matrix printer.

   k. Print the worksheet and chart on the same page.

   l. Save the workbook as "My Expenses" onto the Advantage Diskette.

2. In this exercise you retrieve a workbook and then create a line chart, stacked column chart, and a 3-D column chart.

   a. Close all of the open windows in the document area.

   b. Open the "Charts" workbook located on the Advantage Diskette. This worksheet is a planning tool used by XYZ Company to project sales and production. (Make sure to type your name into cell A3.)

   c. Create one line chart, in a separate chart sheet, showing the number of units sold for each product over the five-year period.

   d. Add an appropriate title to the chart.

   e. Name the sheet's tab LINE.

   f. Print the chart using the *Scale to Fit Page* option.

   g. Create one stacked column chart, in a separate chart sheet, that displays the revenue for each product over the five-year period. A stacked chart displays each product's portion of the total revenue in a single column for each year.

   h. Add an appropriate title to the chart.

i. Name the sheet's tab STACK.

j. Print the chart using the *Use Full Page* option.

k. Create one 3-D column chart, in a separate chart sheet, to compare the Total Revenue versus the Total Costs over the five-year period.

l. Add an appropriate title to the chart.

m. Name the sheet's tab COLUMN.

n. Print the chart using the *Scale to Fit Page* option.

o. Save the workbook as "Charting" onto the Advantage Diskette.

p. Close all of the open windows in the document area.

q. Exit Excel.

CASE PROBLEMS

H2 UNDERSCAPING LTD.

(*Note:* In the following case problems, assume the role of the primary characters and perform the same steps that they identify. You may want to re-read the session opening.)

1. Chip finishes his conversation with Kayla Parker at the local bank and then places the phone gently into its cradle. He glances down at the notes that he scrawled on the borders of the Canadian *Globe and Mail* newspaper. Although thinking to himself, Chip shakes his head and speaks aloud, "So, Kayla wants a financial plan after seven years of doing business." Chip isn't really *that* surprised with Kayla's request; but, perhaps, he's just a little annoyed with his longtime friend and business advisor. Kayla has been there for him since his company's inception and has helped guide him through complicated financing issues, debtor problems, and investment opportunities. But with his latest acquisition of Xeriscaping, Inc., even Kayla must watch Chip and his company's performance with a lot more scrutiny than before.

   Fortunately, Chip just completed entering his past year's results into an Excel worksheet called "H2 Underscaping 1995" stored on the Advantage Diskette. He loads the worksheet and then decides to perform some additional formatting, wanting to ensure that it looks its best for Kayla. After customizing the page setup to a landscape orientation and inserting the current date in the footer, he prints the worksheet to fit on a single page.

   Upon reviewing the printout, Chip decides to impress Kayla even further by embedding a column chart, on the same page, showing comparative sales for the sprinkler installations versus the xeriscaping projects. He adds a title and legend to the chart and then prints the entire worksheet and chart onto a single page. Lastly, Chip saves the workbook as "H2 Underscaping 1995" onto the Advantage Diskette.

2. Impressed with his first printout for Kayla, Chip decides to create a new chart (on a separate sheet in the workbook) and attach it to the first page. Wanting to inform Kayla of the seasonal trend lines for his business, Chip creates a line chart showing the Total Sales, Cost of Sales, and Total Expenses for the entire year. Chip annotates the chart with an arrow and text box pointing out the high and low seasons, in addition to adding titles and a legend to the chart. When finished, Chip prints the chart to fit on a single landscape page and then saves the workbook back to the Advantage Diskette.

3. Arriving quite early the next morning, Chip notices that the answering machine's message indicator light is flashing at the receptionist's desk. Hitting the appropriate button, Chip plays back the following message: "Hi Chip, this is Kayla, down at the bank. I received your financial analysis yesterday and just wanted to commend you on your work. This report is far better than I've seen from most accountants, let alone business owners. I don't see a problem with your seasonal business trends, but I would like you to break down your Total Expenses into a pie diagram for me. That way, I can suggest ways for you to cut your fixed costs during the low period. Thanks again for the report. Bye for now."

   Chip is glad to hear that Kayla approved of his analysis and decides to tackle the expense breakdown right away. After loading the "H2 Underscaping 1995" workbook, Chip enters the following year-to-date expense information into the worksheet:

Administration	25,000
Marketing	60,000
Rent	36,000
Wages	24,000
Total Expenses	**145,000**

   After looking through the available chart formats, Chip decides to create a 3-D pie chart with percentages appearing beside each wedge. He adds a title to the chart and a legend, and then prints the chart to a single landscape page. When finished, he saves the workbook back onto the Advantage Diskette.

Microsoft Excel 7.0 for Windows 95

Toolbar Summary

STANDARD

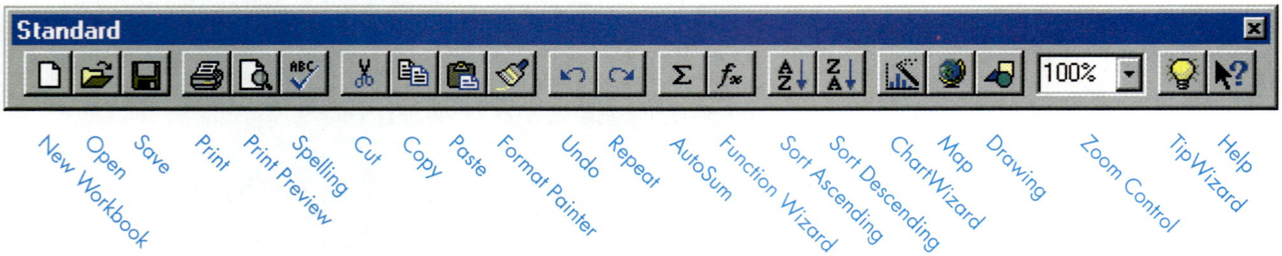

FORMATTING

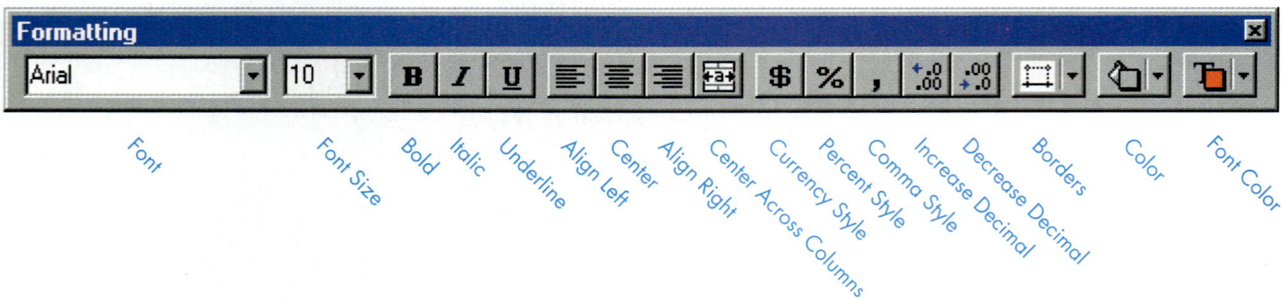

CHART

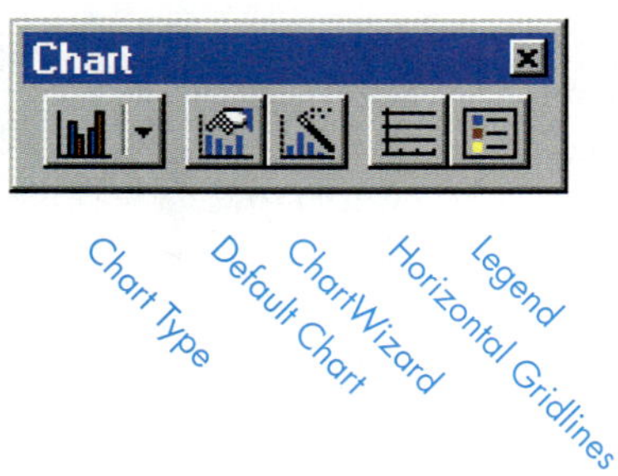

DRAWING

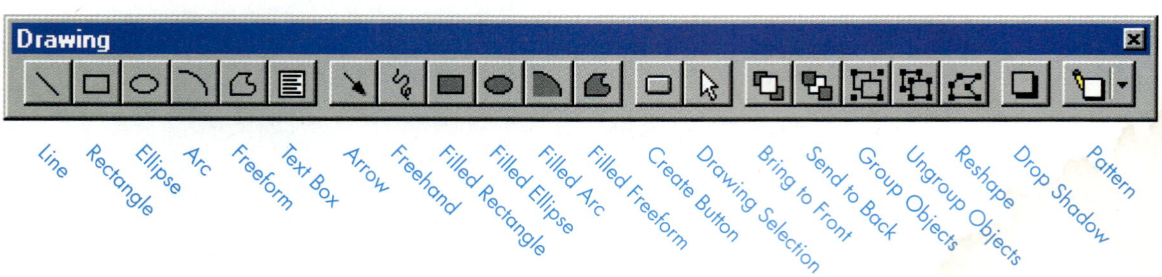

FORMS

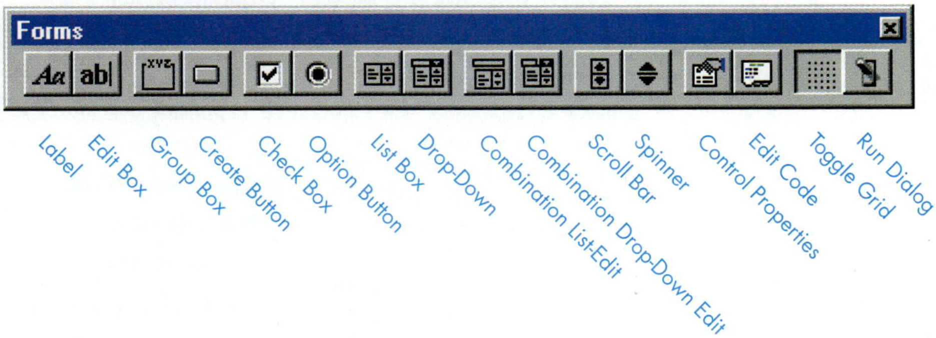

VISUAL BASIC

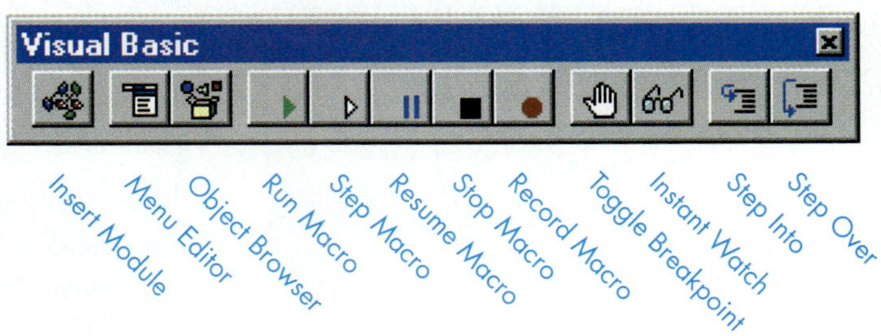

AUDITING

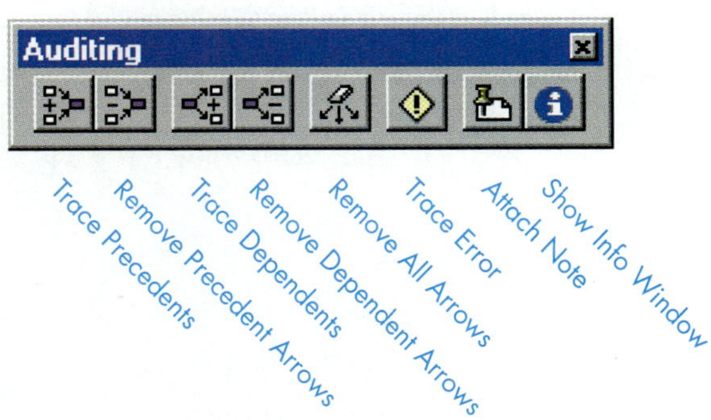

WORKGROUP

Index